Dyslexia, Speech and Language

A Practitioner's Handbook

Margaret Snowling
and
Joy Stackhouse

Whurr Publishers Ltd
London

© 1996 Whurr Publishers Ltd

First published 1996 by Whurr Publishers Ltd,
19b Compton Terrace, London N1 2UN, England

Reprinted 1996, 1997 and 1999

British Library Cataloguing in Publication Data
A catalogue record for this book is available from the
British Library.

ISBN 1-897635-48-6

Printed and bound in the UK by Athenaeum Press Ltd,
Gateshead, Tyne & Wear

Contents

Preface   vii
Contributors   viii

The Nature of Children's Written Language Difficulties

1. Developmental Dyslexia: An Introduction and Theoretical
    Overview   1
    Margaret J. Snowling

2. Speech, Spelling and Reading: Who is at Risk and Why?   12
    Joy Stackhouse

3. Predicting Children's Reading and Spelling Difficulties   31
    Valerie Muter

Assessment

4. Assessing Speech Processing Skills in Children: A Task
    Analysis   45
    Maggie Vance

5. Assessing Language Difficulties in Children and Adolescents   62
    Hanna Klein

6. Assessing Reading and Spelling Skills   77
    Nata K. Goulandris

7. Assessing Reading Comprehension   108
    Susan E. Stothard

Intervention

8. Promoting Phonological Awareness in Preschool Children   129
    Lyn Layton and Karen Deeny

9. Practising Sound Links in Reading Intervention with the
    School-age Child   146
    Peter J. Hatcher

10. Teaching Spelling to Children with Specific Learning
    Difficulties   171
    Claire Cootes and Sarah Simpson

11. Developing Handwriting Skills   192
    Jane Taylor

12. Involving Parents in Helping their Children Overcome
    Reading and Spelling Difficulties   215
    Sybil Hannavy

Epilogue: Current Themes and Future Directions   234
References   243
Index   259

Preface

This book focuses on the relationship between spoken and written language difficulties and represents the culmination of our thinking over some 15 years. The book is aimed at the practitioner in the field of children's language and learning difficulties and aims to forge links between theoretical advances and clinical issues in this field. Our collaborators on this project include former students and professional colleagues who share with us the same theoretical framework and also the desire to improve the educational opportunities of children who have language difficulties.

We are indebted to the many children who have participated in our research, and who have provided us with invaluable insights into the nature and the developmental course of their difficulties. We have enjoyed many valued discussions with too many people to mention by name, but we would particularly like to thank colleagues associated with the Department of Human Communication Science at University College London (formerly the National Hospital's College of Speech Sciences). Most of all, we thank Charles Hulme and Bill Wells for their inspiration, support and encouragement, and our children James, Laura and Christopher for giving us another perspective on speech, language and literacy development!

Maggie Snowling and Joy Stackhouse
January 1996

Contributors

Claire Cootes is Tutor to the RSA Dyslexia Diploma in the Department of Human Communication Science, University College London.

Karen Deeny is a Research Associate in the School of Education, University of Birmingham.

Nata Goulandris is a Lecturer in the Department of Human Communication Science, University College London.

Sybil Hannavy is an Educational Consultant in Cambridgeshire.

Peter Hatcher is Senior Educational Psychologist for Cumbria Education Service and Honorary Research Fellow in the Department of Psychology, University of York.

Hanna Klein is a Lecturer in the Department of Human Communication Science, University College London.

Lyn Layton is a Research Fellow in the School of Education, University of Birmingham.

Valerie Muter is a Chartered Clinical Psychologist and Honorary Research Fellow in the Department of Psychology, University of York.

Sarah Simpson is Tutor to the RSA Dyslexia Diploma in the Department of Human Communication Science, University College London.

Margaret Snowling is Professor of Psychology at the University of York.

Joy Stackhouse is a Senior Lecturer in the Department of Human Communication Science, University College London.

Susan Stothard is a Research Fellow in the Department of Psychology, University of Newcastle-upon-Tyne.

Jane Taylor is an Occupational Therapist and was formerly a Dyslexia Therapist at St. Bartholomew's Hospital, London.

Maggie Vance is a Lecturer in the Department of Human Communication Science, University College London.

Chapter 1
Developmental Dyslexia: An Introduction and Theoretical Overview

Margaret J. Snowling

This book will be published exactly 100 years after the first case of developmental dyslexia was described by Dr. Pringle-Morgan writing in the British Medical Journal in 1896. Pringle-Morgan's report was of an intelligent teenager who had failed to read, and his speculation was that the boy was suffering from congenital 'word-blindness'. For many years following this report, the predominant view was that dyslexic reading difficulties were caused by deficiencies in visual processing and the condition attracted much attention from ophthalmologists such as Hinshelwood (1917).

It was not until some 30 years later that the importance of language factors in the determination of dyslexia became recognized with the publication of Samuel Orton's influential book *Reading, Writing and Speech Problems in Children* (1937). It is interesting that many of the points that Orton made are central to our current concerns. Orton's term for what we now know as *dyslexia* was *strephosymbolia*, literally *a twisting of symbols*. Importantly, he recognized that strephosymbolia tended to run in families, and to be associated with other forms of language disability. He thought that the causes of the difficulty were to be found in incomplete lateralization of the cerebral hemispheres (a theory not of concern here) but that its remediation required specialist teaching.

Although variants of a visual deficit hypothesis are still entertained today, (see Willows, Kruk and Corcos, 1993), the most widely accepted view is that dyslexia can be considered part of the continuum of language disorders and is a verbal processing deficit

1

(Vellutino, 1979). Indeed, there is converging evidence in support of a more specific theory, that dyslexic readers have weaknesses in the domain of phonological, or put more simply, speech processing (Hulme and Snowling, 1992b; Stanovich and Siegel, 1994). Before turning to this theory, we should first consider the strengths and weaknesses of current definitions of dyslexia.

The Definition of Dyslexia

A major difficulty surrounding the diagnosis of dyslexia is that its very definition is contested (Stanovich, 1994). In 1968, the World Federation of Neurology recommended that the term should be applied to children 'who fail to read despite adequate intelligence, conventional instruction and sociocultural opportunity.' However, dissatisfaction with this medical model, coupled with a lack of consensus about the positive signs of dyslexia, means that this view has long since been rejected. In clinical practice, the majority of practitioners have instead adopted what is known as a *discrepancy* definition of dyslexia. The discrepancy definition takes into account that there is a significant correlation between cognitive ability and educational achievement in the normal population. It is therefore reasonable to expect children of above-average ability to be reading above the average for their age group, and children of below-average ability to be below the norm. Children who are reading significantly below the expected level, have unexpected reading difficulties or, as they are often described, Specific Learning Difficulties (dyslexia).

Most practitioners feel comfortable with the discrepancy definition of dyslexia, at least as a starting point for their investigation into the reading and spelling strategies as well as the cognitive processing skills of an affected individual. Possibly as a consequence, little attention has been paid to the important question of whether children with specific reading difficulties differ from children with reading problems in the context of more generally slow learning or indeed, more global language difficulties. The lay view of dyslexia is of a creative person who is good at most things except reading and writing. However, not all dyslexic children are like this. The children we will be concerned about in this book are children who have, or who are at risk of having reading difficulties, irrespective of their talents. We hope to discuss a broad range of difficulties that commonly accompany or predict reading failure, and to consider effective strategies for their remediation. We begin by focusing in on the dyslexic child as a way of articulating our theoretical framework.

Children with specific reading difficulties present us with a sharp illustration of the minimum constellation of problems experienced by children who have difficulty learning to read, for these children tend to bring a range of cognitive strengths to the task. It follows that children who have more extensive difficulties of speech or language have less clear-cut problems. Arguably, such children have fewer resources to allow them to compensate for their difficulties; their reading development is often very slow and sometimes atypical (Stackhouse and Snowling, 1992a).

The Developmental Nature of Dyslexia

By far the most comprehensive picture we have of dyslexia is in the school-age child. Most dyslexic children are referred when they have failed to learn to read, and most research has been done with these children. However, it is important to remember that dyslexia is a life-long difficulty and symptoms that are present at one point in development are not necessarily evident at another. Importantly, it is not uncommon for particular deficits to be compensated for with the passage of time. Reading problems tend to be the key difficulty in the early school years but many dyslexic adults turn out to be fluent readers if poor spellers. Some adult dyslexics have particular difficulty decoding words they have not encountered before and commonly, they have persisting difficulties with phonological awareness, naming at speed and verbal short-term memory tasks (Bruck, 1990, 1992; Pennington, van Orden, Smith, et al., 1990).

Heritability of dyslexia

It has been known for many years that poor reading tends to run in families and there is now conclusive evidence that dyslexia is heritable (DeFries, 1991, for a review). Behaviour geneticists have shown that there is as much as a 50 per cent probability of a boy becoming dyslexic if his father is dyslexic (about 40 per cent if his mother is affected), and a somewhat lower probability of a girl developing dyslexia. What is inherited is not reading disability *per se*, but aspects of language processing. Results of large-scale twin studies suggest there is greater heritability of phonological (phonic) than visual aspects of reading. In turn, phonological reading skills share heritable variance with phonological awareness, the ability to reflect upon the sound structure of spoken words (Olson, Wise, Conners, et al., 1989).

With genetic studies as a backdrop, the earliest age at which dyslexic children have been studied is 2 years (Scarborough, 1990). Scarborough got around the problem of early diagnosis by carrying out a longitudinal study of children who were 'at risk' of dyslexia by virtue of having one dyslexic parent. She compared the development of these children with that of children from non-dyslexic families from the age of 2 to 7 years. When the children were 7 and their reading skills could be assessed, it was possible to look retrospectively at the preschool data and to compare children who went on to become dyslexic with children who did not develop reading difficulties. An important difference between the groups turned out to be in speech production. Although the dyslexic children used as large a range of vocabulary in conversation with their mothers as their non-dyslexic counterparts, they made more speech errors and their use of syntax was more limited. At 5 years, the dyslexic children had more difficulty with object naming and with phonological awareness tasks. Their emerging literacy skills were also poorer; they were less familiar with the letters of the alphabet and worse at matching pictures with print.

A recent study of our own goes some way towards replicating Scarborough's findings. Gallagher, Frith and Snowling (submitted) recruited 73 children from families in which there was a first degree relative with dyslexia, and assessed them on a range of language tasks just prior to their 4th birthday. Although they did not differ in nonverbal ability, the children at risk of dyslexia were generally weaker on tests of speech and language processing than children from control families with no history of dyslexia. In particular, they showed deficits in their understanding of vocabulary and in their naming ability, as well as when repeating novel words (two-syllable nonwords). In terms of preliteracy skills, the at-risk children had poorer knowledge of letters and of nursery rhymes.

These two studies of weaknesses in children at risk of dyslexia well before the traditional time of diagnosis at school-age, suggest that dyslexic children show early language deficits. The data are consistent with the theory that dyslexia is a phonological processing deficit; deficiencies in the speech production system were revealed in both studies, as were problems of emerging phonological awareness. However, these studies also alert us to the possibility of more wide-ranging language difficulties in the case histories of such children. The delays or difficulties in the development of productive syntax and of vocabulary which were revealed are seldom discussed with regard to the school-age dyslexic child. It may be that they are compensated for with development or at the least, they are hidden from the eye (cf. Stackhouse and Wells, 1991).

The evidence from the studies of dyslexia across the life-span is quite consistent with that from group comparisons of dyslexic and normal children. We turn now to examine research that contributes to the generally accepted view that phonological processing deficits are core deficits in dyslexia. In so doing, we remain cognizant of the fact that the behavioural manifestation of the underlying deficits in dyslexia will depend upon the age of the child and the extent to which they have been remediated, either through teaching or other forms of intervention, including speech and language therapy (Frith, 1995; Morton and Frith, 1995).

The Phonological Deficit Hypothesis of Dyslexia

It can reasonably be assumed that throughout speech development, children link the speech they hear with the utterances they produce. Broadly speaking, this is a central aspect of phonological development. As the child's phonological system develops, these links or 'mappings' becoming gradually refined (Nittrouer and Studdert-Kennedy, 1987). It is probable that the refinements bring with them improvements in some of the cognitive skills which underlie reading development, for example, improvements in access to the spoken forms of words, as required in phonological awareness tasks, and increases in verbal short-term memory capacity because this draws upon phonological (speech-based) codes (Snowling and Hulme, 1994).

For the majority of children, the phonological system is fully formed by the time they come to learn to read. It can therefore provide a foundation for the reading system, which can be thought of as parasitic upon it. Indeed, a number of recent theories of reading development propose that children set up direct connections between representations of printed words and representations of spoken words in the child's language system (Ehri, 1992; Goswami, 1994; Rack, Hulme, Snowling, et al., 1994). At a later stage, knowledge embodied in these mappings generalizes to allow novel words to be 'decoded' (cf. Seidenberg and McClelland, 1989). At this point, a more flexible reading system will have been created.

It follows from such theories of reading development, that the status of children's underlying phonological representations determine the ease with which they can learn to read (Hulme and Snowling, 1992b). Performance on a range of phonological processing tasks including tests of phonological awareness, verbal short-term memory or verbal naming also requires access to phonological representations. It is probably for this reason that performance on such tasks tends to be highly correlated with reading performance.

Since 1980, a large number of studies have appeared in the literature pointing to language difficulties in dyslexic children, specifically at the level of phonology (Shankweiler and Crain, 1986). Perhaps the most consistently reported of these difficulties are problems with phonological awareness (Bradley and Bryant, 1978; Manis, Custodio and Szeszulski, 1993) and of verbal short-term memory (Siegel and Linder 1984; Johnston, Rugg and Scott, 1987; Torgeson, Rashotte, Greenstein, et al., 1988). There is also evidence that dyslexic children have trouble with long-term verbal learning, for example, memorizing the months of the year or multiplication tables.

Another task that requires the retrieval of phonological information from long-term memory is naming. Word finding difficulties are often reported in dyslexic children and experimental studies using rapid naming tasks report deficiencies in dyslexics (Denckla and Rudel, 1976). Extending this work to object naming, Katz (1986) found that dyslexic children were less able than controls to label the objects of the *Boston Naming Test*, and had particular difficulty with low-frequency and polysyllabic words. Similarly, Snowling, van Wagtendonk and Stafford (1988) found dyslexics made more naming errors than children of the same age and similar vocabulary skills when required to name objects either following picture presentation or following a spoken definition. Overall, these findings are consistent with the view that dyslexic children experience specific problems in retrieving phonological information from long-term memory, and dovetail with the at-risk studies which point to similar difficulties early in development.

A number of studies have used tests of speech perception and speech production to explore the possible bases of the dyslexic child's difficulty with language processing. Brandt and Rosen (1980) investigated the perception of stop consonants, for example [d] and [p], by dyslexic and normal readers. They found that the dyslexic readers performed like children at an earlier developmental stage, a finding similar to that of Godfrey, Syrdal-Lasky, Millay, et al. (1981). Reed (1989) found that dyslexic children had more difficulty in determining the order in which two consonants or two brief tones were presented than normal readers of the same age. In contrast, temporal order judgements that involved steady state vowels caused no difficulty. The dyslexic children also had more difficulty with a word identification task in which an auditorily presented word had to be matched with one of two pictures, differing by a single phoneme (for example, goal-bowl). They were also less consistent in their phonemic categorization of stimuli.

Taken together, these findings suggest that the dyslexic children have difficulty with the perception of brief auditory cues, a difficulty that could plausibly account for their impaired performance on a range of phonological processing tasks. Such a difficulty has been for many years seen as central to the cause of specific language disorders by Tallal and her colleagues (Tallal and Piercy, 1973; Tallal, Stark, Kallman, et al., 1980)

Dyslexic children have also been reported to have difficulties with speech production (Snowling, 1981, Brady, Shankweiler and Mann, 1983). Snowling, Goulandris, Bowlby, et al. (1986) extended these findings and showed that dyslexic children have specific difficulty with nonword repetition. This difficulty was interpreted as a problem with the segmentation processes that mediate between speech perception and speech production. Arguably, the language deficits observed in these experiments are related to difficulties first in establishing, and later in accessing, adequate phonological representations. These difficulties may ultimately explain more wide-ranging cognitive deficits in dyslexic children.

Written Language Difficulties in Dyslexia

In order to understand the effect of phonological difficulties in the domain of spoken language on the acquisition of written language skills, it is necessary to consider what the development of reading entails. Learning to read in an alphabetic script such as English requires an appreciation of the correspondences between letters and sounds – the alphabetic principle. Even though many young children start out by reading whole words by sight, they need to learn how the letters in printed words map on to the sounds of spoken words if they are to become flexible readers. The first step in this process requires the ability to reflect upon speech, namely 'phonological awareness'. It follows that dyslexic children who have difficulties in the phonological domain are at a disadvantage from the outset. Dyslexic children often continue to rely on a sight vocabulary in reading and thereby make a large number of visual reading errors, for example, GRANDMOTHER → gentleman; FROM → for; ORGAN → orange (see Goulandris, this volume). They are unable to abstract letter-sound correspondences from their experience with printed words and therefore fail to develop phonological (phonic) reading strategies (Manis et al., 1993; Snowling, 1980, 1981). Indeed, there is a great deal of evidence that dyslexic children have nonword reading difficulties that are out of step with their visual reading skills (Rack, Snowling and Olson, 1992).

According to Frith (1985), the classic developmental dyslexic fails to make the transition to the alphabetic phase of literacy development. In addition to their difficulties with reading, these children also tend to have problems spelling words the way they sound. While phonetic spelling errors are common in the writings of young children, for example, PACKET → pakit; YELLOW → yelo, dyslexic children often make non-phonetic attempts, e.g. pagit, yorol. Children who read and spell in this way have sometimes been described as developmental phonological dyslexics (Temple and Marshall, 1983; Seymour, 1986).

However, there are also dyslexic children who appear to have mastered alphabetic skills. According to Frith, these children are failing to make the transition to the orthographic phase of development. Such children are sometimes referred to as developmental dysgraphics or developmental *surface* dyslexics (Coltheart, Masterson, Byng, et al., 1983; Seymour, 1986). In English, spelling alphabetically does not constitute accurate spelling as there are many exceptions to the rules that children have to master (see Cootes and Simpson, this volume). The classic characteristic of these children is that they read fairly well in context but, in single-word reading, they rely heavily upon sounding out. They have particular difficulties with homophones like PEAR-PAIR and LEEK-LEAK which they confuse and their spelling is usually phonetic.

While evidence in favour of distinct subtypes is distinctly lacking (cf. Bryant and Impey, 1986), most systematic studies of individual differences among dyslexics have revealed variations in their reading skills (Castles and Coltheart, 1993). In a recent study, we compared two children who displayed a *phonological dyslexic* style of reading (in reading words significantly better than nonwords), with two children who resembled *surface dyslexics* (in reading irregular words significantly less well than regular words). Assessing these children's development over two years, we found that they differed in the severity of their phonological processing problems (Snowling and Goulandris, in press). The two children who showed a phonological dyslexic profile had more difficulty with phonological processing than the two who showed a surface dyslexic profile, as measured by tests of rhyme, nonword repetition and spelling. However, even the surface dyslexics were worse on the phonological tasks than normal readers of the same age. These findings are in line with the hypothesis that dyslexic reading difficulties stem from phonological processing problems. However, they suggest that the severity of children's phonological difficulties can affect the way in which their reading system becomes set up – and whether they look like phonological or surface dyslexics.

Difficulties Commonly Associated with Dyslexia

The view of dyslexia that we have espoused here is akin to the *phonological core-variable difference* model of dyslexia developed by Stanovich in a series of papers (Stanovich, 1986; Stanovich, 1994; Stanovich and Siegel, 1994). Put simply, the core of dyslexia is a phonological processing deficit, and the closer to the core a particular processing skill is, the more certainty there is that poor readers will differ from normal readers with respect to that skill. Skills close to the core of dyslexia include nonword reading and aspects of phonological awareness, skills at less close proximity include measures of working memory and listening comprehension. It is with regard to these latter skills that we expect differences between dyslexic readers and other types of poor reader, for example, those with general language difficulties.

Children with speech and language difficulties

With the idea of a phonological core in dyslexia in mind, it is useful to return to the issue of children who have speech and language difficulties. Unfortunately, the literature presents a confusing picture that may not help us at the present time. Whereas retrospective studies typically point to a history of speech and language difficulty in children who are dyslexic (Rutter and Yule, 1975), prospective studies of children with speech and language difficulty contradict the assertion. It does not appear to be the case that children who have preschool language impairments go on to have specific reading difficulties (dyslexia); rather they have more general reading problems encompassing difficulties with reading comprehension that are not usually experienced by dyslexic children (Bishop and Adams, 1990; Magnusson and Naucler, 1993; Stothard, Snowling and Bishop, in preparation).

A reasonable resolution to this conundrum is that children with obvious spoken language difficulties have similar phonological problems to those at the core of dyslexia, but are different from dyslexic children in that they have concomitant problems in other language domains. For example, difficulties with grammar and meaning would place such children at risk of reading comprehension difficulty. We will not dwell longer on what are certainly speculative remarks. Suffice it to say, a number of different patterns of reading development can be seen in children with speech and language difficulty, and it is reasonable to assume that the profile of difficulty observed will be dependent upon the precise level of breakdown of their phonological processing skills, in interaction with their other language abilities (Snowling, 1987; Snowling, Stackhouse and Rack, 1986; Stackhouse, this volume)

The role of visual factors in dyslexia

Just as a consideration of subtle language impairments in dyslexic children is important in understanding the precise nature of their reading and spelling difficulties, so their visual processing skills should also be taken into account. As yet, there is no conclusive evidence that visual processing impairments on their own cause dyslexia. But this does not rule out the possibility that such difficulties might compound the reading problem. It is conceivable that visual skills contribute to the development of reading – indeed, they may be particularly important in children who have language difficulties in providing an alternative set of compensatory strategies for them.

There are two main strands to current research on visual factors in dyslexia. Stein and his colleagues (Stein, 1991) have suggested that dyslexic children have deficient ocular motor control. Much of their research has used the *Dunlop Test* as part of an orthoptic assessment and shown that fewer dyslexic children have an established reference eye than normal readers. They recommend monocular occlusion as a means of encouraging binocular control and facilitating learning to read (see Bishop, 1989, for a critique).

Lovegrove and his colleagues have pursued another possibility, that dyslexic children have low-level impairments of the transient visual system (Lovegrove and Williams, 1993). Such difficulties would lead children to experience blurring of print and thus affect their reading. The data that Lovegrove's group present are convincing but, unlike the data on phonological deficits, there is no evidence to suggest that these visual impairments are causally related to reading problems. What is lacking is a longitudinal study examining the role of visual factors in learning to read. It is our view that, until such evidence is forthcoming, it is important for practitioners to be alert to the possibility of perceptual processing impairments and visual memory deficits exacerbating dyslexic difficulties. Where visual perceptual problems exist, then problems of motor control can also be anticipated. Some dyslexic children have difficulties with fine motor skills and these hinder the development of handwriting and related abilities (see Taylor, this volume).

In similar vein, many dyslexic children have problems with concentration particularly in classroom settings. Perhaps the simplest explanation is that the children cannot cope with the written materials presented and so, their minds wander. However, some dyslexic children have more pervasive difficulties with attention control. These require separate investigation as they will, if untreated, exacerbate the dyslexic condition.

Conclusions

Although the use of the term 'dyslexia' remains debated, there is considerable evidence that unexpected reading problems in children are caused by language deficiencies within the phonological domain. Much research in recent years has shown that children who perform well on tests of phonological awareness before they go to school go on to be good readers (see Muter, this volume). The corollary of this is that dyslexics have phonological deficits and that it is these that cause their failure to acquire literacy at the normal rate. The theory gains further support from findings that training phonological skills has a beneficial effect on reading and spelling performance, especially when combined with teaching of letter-sound relationships (see Hatcher, this volume). Practitioners at the interface of dyslexia, speech and language need to be ready to evaluate the extent to which a child's reading difficulty can be attributed to poor phonology, and the extent to which other language and cognitive processing deficits may have a role to play.

Chapter 2
Speech, Spelling and Reading: Who is at Risk and Why?

Joy Stackhouse

Children with dyslexic difficulties often have associated speech and language problems. These include delayed speech and language development, persisting articulatory problems, word-finding problems, immature syntax development, perceptual, memory and sequencing difficulties, and trouble with segmentation and blending skills (Snowling, 1987; Stackhouse, 1990). It is therefore not surprising that young children with speech and language problems are at risk for later literacy difficulties. Children whose speech and language problems are significant enough to result in referral to speech and language therapy may be even more at risk (Dodd, Gillon, Oerlemans, et al., 1995). However, not all children with speech and language problems go on to have serious educational difficulties and many problems resolve or do not interfere with the normal course of literacy development. Early identification of at-risk children is necessary for appropriate intervention to be carried out. However, studies aimed at predicting children's spoken and written language development outcome have had conflicting results. Nevertheless, some vulnerability factors can be identified.

Predicting Reading and Spelling Outcome in Children with Speech and Language Problems

Family history

Speech, language and literacy problems often co-occur and run in families. Children with a family history of speech, language and/or literacy problems are more likely to have problems with their reading and spelling development. Studies of identical and fraternal twins have shown that phonological coding difficulties in particular are highly heritable (Olson, et al., 1989). This is compatible with Crary's (1984) finding that a high percentage of fathers of children with specific speech disorder, or paternal family members, have a history of delayed speech development, articulatory difficulties, stuttering or dyslexia.

Lewis, Ekelman and Aram (1989) compared the performance of 20 children with severe speech disorder and their siblings with normal controls on measures of phonological skill, word repetition, oral motor skills, gross and fine motor skills, language development and reading development. Case history information was also compared. The siblings of the children with speech disorder performed significantly less well than the controls on the measures taken and there was a higher incidence of speech, language and dyslexic difficulties in their families. Similarly, in a longitudinal study examining preschool development and later reading performance, children with a family history of dyslexia (i.e., parents and/or older siblings were diagnosed as having dyslexia) were more likely to develop reading and spelling problems than children where there was no incidence of dyslexia in the family (Scarborough, 1991a). In these studies, there is a predominance of males compared with females in the groups of children with specific speech, language and literacy problems.

Language difficulties as a predictor of literacy performance

In a follow-up study of 83 8-year-old children who had had delayed speech and language development at the age of four, Bishop and Adams (1990) found syntax development (measured by receptive syntax and mean length of utterance expressed) was a particularly sensitive measure of later literacy performance. If the language problems had resolved in the preschool years, literacy development progressed normally. However, if the language problem persisted beyond the age of 5;6 years, then literacy difficulties developed. In contrast, the children's articulatory skill (measured by percentage of consonants correct on picture-naming tasks) was not found to be a strong predictor of later literacy problems.

A similar finding is reported by Magnusson and Naucler (1990). They compared a group of children described as language disordered with a group of normally developing controls on a range of speech, language and phonological awareness tasks at three points in time: preschool, the beginning of school and at the end of their first year at school. Regardless of which group the children were in at the beginning of the study, children with poor literacy development were characterized by poor performance on language comprehension, syntactic production and metaphonological tasks.

In a follow-up study of 56 children with speech and language impairment, Catts (1993) emphasized the importance of defining how reading outcome is being measured. By dividing the reading measures into a) reading comprehension, and b) word recognition, this study showed that receptive and expressive language skills were better predictors of reading comprehension, while phonological awareness and rapid naming skills were better predictors of word recognition. Certainly, there appears to be a close relationship between verbal and reading comprehension (see Stothard, this volume).

Speech difficulties as a predictor of literacy performance

Although there are now a number of studies suggesting that early language problems correlate with later literacy problems, the relationship between early speech difficulties and literacy development has been unclear. None of the above group studies found a strong link between speech problems and literacy development. This should not be surprising given that children with speech problems are such a heterogeneous population. Speech problems can result from faulty input processing (for example, auditory discrimination of sounds or sequences of sounds), representation problems (for example, an imprecise storage of the composition of words) and output problems (for example, assembly of the sounds for speech, timing of the muscles for speech, inability to make precise oral movements). There may be an obvious cause for a child's speech difficulties such as sensory impairment (deafness), structural abnormality (cleft lip and palate) and neurological impairment (cerebral palsy). Many speech problems, however, are of 'no known aetiology' and are often referred to as phonological disability (sometimes delay or disorder is used to denote mild or severe cases). If there is a motor programming difficulty resulting in inconsistent speech output the child may be described as having verbal or articulatory dyspraxia. This is much more than a difficulty with individual sounds. Rather, how sounds are sequenced and stressed is affected.

Interestingly, although Magnusson and Naucler (1990) did not find a strong relationship between speech difficulties and literacy performance in their group results, they did acknowledge at the end of their paper that different types of speech difficulties were included in their sample. The children who were described as having phonological problems in their speech, but who were able to perform the phonological awareness tasks perfectly well, had predominantly segmental speech difficulties, i.e., difficulties with individual sound production (paradigmatic). Those children with speech problems who also had difficulties with the phonological awareness tasks had mainly problems sequencing sounds in words (syntagmatic). This fits well with the description of children with serious speech difficulties of a dyspraxic nature described by Stackhouse and Snowling (1992a, 1992b) and supports the notion that some types of speech difficulty render a child more at risk for literacy problems than others.

In a study designed to examine literacy development in children with different types of speech difficulties, Stackhouse (1982) compared the reading and spelling skills of children in the age range of 7 to 11 years whose speech difficulties were the direct result of a cleft lip and palate, with those who were diagnosed as having verbal dyspraxia. The children with cleft lip and palate were not significantly different from normally developing controls on tests of reading and spelling. When errors were made they followed sounding out strategies, e.g. SABRE was read as ['seɪbri] and CEILING as ['kɛlɪn]. In contrast, the children with verbal dyspraxia were significantly poorer than the normally developing children on reading and spelling tests and their errors suggested guesswork rather than principled sounding out strategies, for example, CANARY was read as *competition*, and DREAM as *under*.

To confirm that the children with verbal dyspraxia were having difficulty decoding via letter-sound rules, a silent reading test was administered (after Coltheart, 1980). The children were asked to sort cards into same and different piles. Each card showed two words which either sounded the same when read (silently) or sounded different, for example, 'fid–phid' compared with 'fid–prid'. The performance of both the normally developing children and those with a cleft lip and palate on this task correlated with reading age. However, in the group of children with verbal dyspraxia, reading age increased without a corresponding increase in performance on this silent reading test. This suggested that children with verbal dyspraxia were relying on a visual reading strategy rather than a phonological one in order to develop their reading skills.

Spelling performance also distinguished the two groups of children with speech difficulties. Again, the children with cleft lip and palate performed similarly to the normally developing children. When errors occurred they reflected intact sound segmentation skills but a lack of conventional spelling rule knowledge, for example:

Target		Spelling
sooner	→	soona
might	→	mit
boat	→	bot

These were in sharp contrast to the errors produced by the children with verbal dyspraxia which appeared much less logical, for example:

Target		Spelling
year	→	andere
health	→	heans
slippery	→	greid

Robinson, Beresford and Dodd (1982) report similar atypical spelling errors in a group of children described as having a phonological disorder; it is noted that in some cases the terms *phonological disorder* and *verbal dyspraxia* are used interchangeably.

It would appear then that children whose speech difficulty comprises an isolated articulatory difficulty arising from a physical abnormality may be no more likely to develop dyslexia than the population with normally developing speech. This finding has been supported by investigations of children with speech problems arising from a physical handicap. In order to evaluate the role of articulation when converting sounds to letters, Bishop (1985) tested seven teenagers with dysarthric speech as a result of cerebral palsy using tasks requiring word and nonword homophone judgement, and word and nonword spelling. She found no difference in performance on these tasks between this group and a matched group of children with cerebral palsy but no speech difficulties. Nevertheless, it is important not to become complacent about such children's literacy development. Any child with hearing and health problems or periods of hospitalization that lead to absenteeism from school, may be at risk for delayed literacy development. However, it is the children with persisting speech difficulties of no obvious medical aetiology who are at risk for related and specific literacy problems.

A study by Bird, Bishop and Freeman (1995) confirms this. They investigated a group of 31 boys in the age range of 5 to 7 years with phonological disability to see if first, the severity of the speech problem, and second, the presence of additional language impairments were significant prognostic factors for literacy development. Their performance on a range of phonological awareness tasks (such as rhyme and word onset matching and segmentation) and reading and spelling tasks (including nonword reading and spelling) was compared with a group of normally developing boys matched on chronological age and nonverbal ability. The boys with phonological disability had particular difficulty with the phonological awareness tasks even when the tasks did not require a spoken response and the majority of them had significant literacy problems when followed up at around 7;6 years of age. The presence of additional language impairments did not significantly affect the child's literacy outcome in this study. However, the severity and persistence of the speech problem did. This supports the *critical age hypothesis* put forward by Bishop and Adams (1990). As long as the child's speech difficulty has resolved by around 5 years of age, then reading and spelling can progress normally.

Spoken to Written Language Disorder: An Unfolding Problem

Just because a child's speech and language development is atypical, it does not mean that it will not change. Changes come about through maturation, intervention and because different demands are made on the child with increasing age. The early manifestations of a speech and language disorder were illustrated in a longitudinal study of 20 children aged 30 months selected from families with a history of dyslexia (Scarborough, 1990). The study aimed to look at the relationship between early language skills and later literacy development. The children who went on to have literacy problems did indeed have early language problems but the nature of these problems appeared to change during the preschool years. At 2;6 years of age the language deficit was most obvious in syntax and pronunciation. Lexical problems became more obvious at 3 years of age through deficits in receptive vocabulary and naming abilites. By 5 years problems with sound awareness and letter-sound knowledge was apparent.

Scarborough's results make sense of the finding by Menyuk, Chesnick, Liebergott, et al., (1991) that although early measures of language awareness are good predictors of later reading performance, different measures of this are good predictors depending on the child's stage of development. They found that by reclassifying their three groups of children who had a) specific language disorder, b) history of language disorder and c) premature birth into three different groups based on language ability: a) low, b) medium and c) high, then different tasks were more strongly predictive of reading performance between the groups. For example, syllable segmentation was a stronger predictor in the low-language ability group while letter-name retrieval was stronger in the middle- and high-language ability groups. This is another perspective on the unfolding nature of the problem – the children in the low-level language group were as yet unable to perform sound segmentation or letter-name tasks whereas these skills were emerging as problematic in the children with more advanced language skills.

Group studies by their nature are limited in revealing details of individual cases. The unfolding nature of speech, language and literacy problems is perhaps best illustrated through longitudinal case studies. One such case of a boy's unfolding speech, language and literacy problems is described by Stackhouse (1992a) at four points in time: preschool, aged 8, 14 and 18 years. Keith was the youngest of three children. Father was employed in a manual occupation, though had periods of unemployment, and mother stayed at home when the children were young. Later she worked as a library assistant. Keith had been referred for speech and language therapy at the age of 2;6 years by his health visitor as she and his mother were worried that he was 'not talking'. His expressive vocabulary comprised a small number of single words: 'no', 'mummy', 'look', and he was not putting words together. However, he was very communicative through gesture, played well and appeared to understand appropriately for his age. Indeed, on formal testing at the age of 2;8 years, his verbal comprehension was 2;3 years, and by 5;5 years, it was at the 6-year level. He had no hearing problems and all milestones apart from speech had been passed appropriately. Although there were no obvious physical disabilities, he was clumsy, had difficulties feeding and was slow establishing handedness. Other members of the family also had delayed laterality and were described as having 'minor speech problems' and 'terrible spelling'.

By 4 years of age Keith talked alot but was very difficult to understand. He used mainly 'b' and 'd' at the beginnings of words. He did not use any fricative sounds ('f, v, s, z, sh') or affricates ('ch, j') and could not produce 'k' or 'g' at all. This means that he would use one word for many, for example, the spoken word *dee* might represent *tea* or *key* or *sea* or *she* and the listener would be reliant on context for meaning. He also left the endings off words which made his speech sound very staccato. It was very difficult to assess his expressive syntax at this stage, but the mean length of utterance he produced was appropriate for his age as was his comprehension of grammatical structures.

At 8 years of age, Keith used 'p, b, t, d, m, n, l, f, v and w' in simple words but rarely 'k, g, th, s, z, sh, ch, j, r, y'. In longer words in particular he had difficulties sequencing sounds in words consistently, for example on different occasions the word BUTTERCUP was pronounced *buttertup, bukertup, butterpuk* and *bukerpup*. At school, teachers commented on his untidy handwriting and disorganized presentation of work. Although he enjoyed looking at books and recognized familiar words he could not read new material. He was not able to apply letter-sound rules and his reading was not developing as quickly as expected for his overall ability. Spelling was difficult to decipher and appeared illogical.

By 14 years of age, Keith was quite intelligible. He no longer had difficulties with individual sounds but would still have speech errors in longer words, for example SYSTEMATIC was pronounced *sinsemakit* and BIBLIOGRAPHY as *biglegrafefi*. Sometimes he would avoid words that he knew he could not say. At other times word finding difficulties prevented him producing a word accurately. Syntax errors were also apparent. The cumulative effect of these difficulties was that he would sound nonfluent. This is demonstrated in the following extract from a tape of Keith reflecting on his difficulties:

> From er the age of two–from er eighteen months – I had er this problem called dyspraxia and since then I had a problem of speaking and pronouncing letters – and er se way of spelling which is dyslexia – and um from a age of two I did not speak for two years – til about four – and um had – I had problem with writing and understanding letters which from a speech therapist which I have managed to learn.

Intelligence testing administered at this time confirmed that Keith was a boy of above average intelligence and yet his reading and spelling skills were still less than age appropriate. Reading had progressed more than spelling and he was now reading for pleasure. Spelling, however, showed signs of specific segmentation difficulties, for example, MYSTERIOUS was spelt as *mistreriles* and CALCULATOR as *catltulater*. Although he usually knew how many syllables were in a word, he had specific difficulty working out which sounds were within the syllables. This segmentation difficulty seemed to be directly related to his inconsistent speech attempts. He was well aware of this and stated quite simply, 'If I can't say it, I can't split it up.'

At 17 years of age Keith was perfectly intelligible though speech errors persisted. Sometimes intrusive sounds occurred, for example SPAGHETTI was pronounced *spleghetti* and the programming of longer words continued to be difficult, for example, HIPPOPOTAMUS → *hitopotanus*, CHRYSANTHEMUM → *chrysanfefum*. His reading comprehension was superior to his reading aloud on which he had a reading age of 12;4 years. Spelling was still difficult particularly of complex words, for example, FAMILIAR was spelt as *ferminiler*, and AMATEUR as *aminayture*. He had a spelling age of 12;6 years. Although he could now perform well on tasks involving rhyme or sound identification at the beginning and ends of words, his segmentation difficulties could still be demonstrated on more complex tasks such as producing spoonerisms on names (Perin 1983), for example, for LED ZEPPELIN he produced *Zed Leppin*. His written work at this age was imaginative, interesting and tidier though it took him longer than his peers to produce a piece of written work—a problem for him in written examinations. He still needed help organizing ideas in sentences and would produce more than one draft in attempting to get it right. The following is an extract from one of his essays:

> Imagine that you are in the fifth year of your secondary school, the end of the school year and perhaps school life is drawing near...So questions rush to your head while you speaking to your careers adviser...Perhaps one of the questions you might of asked in the careers room was 'What about if I want to do just practical you know no written work?'

Although Keith's phonological difficulties persist, his above-average abilities have helped him learn how to compensate for his difficulties. He can use his good verbal comprehension skills to make use of context cues when reading although this will not help him to decode unfamiliar words in isolation. Spelling, however, is more reliant on intact phonological skills and in particular is helped by clear and consistent speech output. Keith's persisting and inconsistent speech difficulties prevent him from using articulation rehearsal to hold a word in memory while he segments it into its bits. This poses particular problems when trying to spell new or difficult words. However, Keith's positive attitude and insight into his difficulties have clearly stood him in good stead. At the age of 24, he has successfully completed a college training in plumbing but works mainly at his first love—sailing, which he took up on a school trip. In spite of some opposition from tutors because of his speech and literacy problems, he is now a qualified sailing instructor.

Keith's case illustrates the unfolding nature of speech and literacy throughout the school years and into adulthood. It suggests inextricable links between spoken and written language. For a number of years spoken and written language were viewed and managed separately—the speech and language therapist 'treated' the speech and spoken language while the teacher 'taught' reading and spelling. It is becoming clear, however, that in some cases the reading and spelling difficulties experienced by a child are an extension of the phonological processing deficit evident in earlier or persisting speech difficulties.

The Same Pattern of Development in Speech and Literacy Skills

To investigate the relationship between speech and literacy development, we carried out detailed investigations of the speech, auditory discrimination, lexical, segmentation, reading and spelling skills of children with verbal dyspraxia over a five-year period (Stackhouse and Snowling, 1992a, 1992b). At the beginning of the study, Michael was aged 10;7 years, and Caroline was 11 years. They attended a comprehensive school where they were integrated into mainstream, but where they received daily remedial teaching and twice-weekly speech and language therapy within a language unit attached to the school. Both were of average intelligence. On the British Ability Scales, Michael gained an estimated IQ of 100 and Caroline an IQ of 111. Their speech had been unintelligible during the preschool years and they had persisting and obvious phonological disorder. In addition they had serious literacy problems. Both children had a history of fluctuating hearing loss but hearing was within normal limits at the time of the study.

Michael and Caroline's speech errors were compared with a group of young normally developing children matched on articulation age (articulation age range: 3 years to 5;6 years, chronological age 3;3 years to 5;6 years). The tasks presented included single-word naming, continuous speech, and word and nonword imitation. The target words increased in syllable length, for example, kite, rocket, caravan, television, and also included words with clusters, such as nest, stamp, spider. Unlike the normally developing children who performed equally well across all conditions, Michael and Caroline's performance was very variable. Surprisingly, Michael and Caroline produced more words perfectly correctly than the younger normally developing controls. However, when they could not produce a word correctly they made multiple speech errors. In contrast, the younger controls made only one or a maximum of two errors per word but in a wider range of words. Although both Michael and Caroline's speech had improved at follow-up, when Michael was 14;5 years, and Caroline was 15;7 years, the same pattern of speech errors persisted. This suggested that Michael and Caroline improved their speech production by developing word-specific articulatory programmes. This lexical approach to acquiring new words is typical of the very young child. The first 50 words or so in a child's vocabulary are learned as individual lexical items (Ingram, 1989). Following this lexical stage of vocabulary development, a more phonologically organized stage follows to deal with the rapid expansion of the child's vocabulary. This finding about Michael and Caroline's speech development is particularly interesting in the context of their literacy development which seemed to be following a similar lexical pattern.

When reading, both Michael and Caroline relied on a visual whole word strategy and confused visually similar words, for example PINT → *paint*, ORGAN → *orange*. They had difficulties decoding words and could not read new material. Spelling of longer words was particularly problematic. Michael attempted (unsuccessfully) to segment words prior to spelling them but then transcribed each of his attempts. The result was rather dramatic, for example:

Target		*Spelling*
umbrella	→	rberherrelrarlsrllles
cigarette	→	satersatarhaelerar.

Caroline adopted a different strategy. Having worked out the syllable structure of the word she produced known words that sounded similar to each beat, for example:

Target		*Spelling*
adventure	→	andbackself
refreshment	→	withfirstmint

Michael and Caroline's pattern of literacy development was similar to that of their speech. Just as they had or had not been able to pronounce words, they could or could not read/spell them. Even though they had letter knowledge, they did not have the phonological processing skills required for segmenting and blending the components of the target words. As with their speech development, Michael and Caroline made progress with their literacy development on a word-by-word basis.

Frith's (1985) account of early literacy development suggests that a child's first attempts at reading are logographic, that is, words are learned as whole units. The normally developing child, however, very quickly breaks through to the alphabetic stage which is characterized by application of letter-sound rules and ability to read and spell new words. Although errors still occur in this stage, children show evidence of intact segmentation skills, such as regularization of irregular words when reading (BROAD read as *brode*) and phonetic spelling (CIGARETTE spelt as *sigaret*). Michael and Caroline's reading and spelling performance indicates that they are still functioning within the logographic phase of literacy development. As in their speech development, they are not able to progress to the next stage of development because of a deficit in utilizing phonological processing skills.

Speech and Spelling

There is no doubt that normal spelling development is mapped in some way onto a speech foundation. Various studies have applied phonological and articulatory analysis skills to spelling and found similarities between speech and spelling development (McCormick, 1995; Treiman, 1993). In general however, it is not the case that children's speech errors will be reproduced in their spelling. In a study investigating the spelling performance of children with speech difficulties described as phonological disorder, Robinson, Beresford and Dodd (1982) found that the children with speech difficulties made as many spelling errors on words they pronounced correctly as they did on words they mispronounced.

This finding was replicated by Snowling and Stackhouse (1983) in their study of a small group of children with verbal dyspraxia in the age range of 8 to 10 years. Each child was asked to imitate, read, spell and copy a series of consonant vowel consonant syllables that varied in their degree of articulatory place change, for example, *mop, bat, peg*. The children with dyspraxia performed as well as normally developing children matched on reading age on reading and copying these words, but significantly less well on imitating and spelling them. Overall there were more spelling than imitation errors and there was no obvious one-to-one correspondence between imitation and spelling responses. During the study, however, it became apparent that the children with dyspraxia had great difficulty in segmenting the target prior to spelling it. For example, PAM was repeated correctly, segmented as *pe-te* and spelt as *potm*, NICK was also repeated correctly, segmented as *ke-ke-ne-i-te* and spelt as *cat*. These errors are not the direct result of the children's usual speech errors, but a manifestation of the inaccurate segmentation process which happens to have been spoken out loud. The first example shows how an intrusive sound was transcribed in spelling, while the second example reveals how the order in which the sounds were segmented determined the triggering of a spelling of a known word.

In summary, the effect of speech on spelling can be manifested in more than one way. First, there may be a direct relationship between what the child says and what is produced in spelling. Second, a speech output difficulty can interfere with the child's rehearsal of the word for segmentation purposes as in the examples above. Third, if the speech output difficulty is related to imprecise representations of words in the lexicon, then this can also result in spelling difficulties.

Lexical Representations and Spelling

The precision of word representations in the child's lexicon is important for efficient naming skills, as well as accurate production in speech and spelling. If a faulty representation has been laid down, then any attempt to generate a word spontaneously will be inaccurate.

A case seen recently with Pam Williams from the Nuffield Speech and Hearing Centre in London and Maggie Vance revealed a very specific relationship between fuzzy sound representations in words and spelling. Thomas had a history of speech and language delay, specific expressive language difficulties and severe verbal dyspraxia. At 7;8 years he had a Performance IQ of 118 and a Verbal IQ of 98 on the WISC. By 8;6 years he had made considerable progress with his reading and language skills. He had an age equivelent score of 8;8 years on the British Picture Vocabulary Scales and performed at the 9;1 years level overall on the *Clinical Evaluation of Language Function – Revised* (Semel, Wiig and Secord, 1987). His reading had improved and was no longer a problem but his spelling was still behind compared with his other skills.

Although Thomas' speech was now intelligible, it still sounded different because of its jerky rhythm and wide pitch changes. In particular, one pattern of errors seemed to be reflected in his spelling. He produced the 'sh', 'ch' and 's' sounds as *th*, and the 'z' sound as *the* so SHADOW was pronounced as *thadow*, and MAGAZINE as *magathine*. However, when the target sound in a word was 'th' or 'the' he pronounced it as 'f' or 'v' respectively, for example, THUMB was pronounced *fum* and WITH was *wiv*. As he could produce the sounds, his errors could not be explained by poor articulatory skills alone.

When spelling, the sound 'sh' was transcribed as *ch* as follows:

Target	Speech	Spelling
shadow	thadow	chadow
membership	memberthip	memberchip

'Sh' and 'ch' were also transcribed as *s* in:

Target		Spelling
refreshment	→	refresment
machinery	→	misnery
politician	→	polltisn
adventure	→	edvenser

These examples show that Thomas had good syllable segmentation skills and was showing signs of developing sound segmentation skills. The specific difficulty with fricative sounds needed further investigation.

A series of spoken words beginning or ending with 'sh', 'ch' and 'j' were presented and Thomas was asked to decide which words began or ended with these sounds. He confused 'ch' and 'sh' on this task. For example, he thought that *cheap* and *chair* began with 'sh' and that *mash* ended with 'ch'. He was then presented with a series of pictures beginning with 'sh', 'ch' and 'j' to sort into piles of the same onsets. There were slightly more confusions on this task where he had to generate the word himself from his own representations compared with the first task where the words were spoken for him by the tester. He classified *chain, chicken* and *jumper* as beginning with 'sh' and *shorts* and *she* as beginning with 'ch'. On an auditory discrimination task, he also had trouble differentiating between vowel sounds, sequences of sounds within clusters (as in *lots/lost*) and within words (as in *ibikus/ikibus*). These input problems are likely to have been more widespread in the past and to have affected the precision of his phonological representations. Therapy aimed at sharpening up the representations paid dividends in both speech and spelling. At the age of 9 years he had no difficulties in producing or transcribing fricative sounds.

It is becoming clear that some spelling errors can be accounted for by speech difficulties. However, speech difficulties themselves can arise at a number of different psycholinguistic levels (Stackhouse and Wells, 1993) and it should not be assumed that the spelling errors which do match speech errors will necessarily be the result of *output* problems. In the case of Thomas both speech and spelling problems of the fricative sounds were stemming from auditory processing problems which resulted in fuzzy lexical representations and not as a direct result of speech output difficulties.

However, persisting speech difficulties do provide a means of identifying the child with specific reading and spelling problems though these may not always be immediately obvious. Children with dyslexia can have subtle speech and language problems that can be missed if not investigated in a particular way (Stackhouse and Wells, forthcoming, and see Vance and Klein, this volume).

The Hidden Speech Problem: What to Look For

Even adults with developmental dyslexia who appear to have normal speech can exhibit speech difficulties on articulatory tests (Lewis and Freebairn, 1992). It is therefore not surprising that children with dyslexia also perform poorly on articulatory tasks (Snowling, 1981). Sometimes children diagnosed as dyslexic in primary school have attended speech and language therapy in the preschool years but were discharged following improved intelligibility. Associated literacy problems are most likely when the earlier speech problem was a specific phonological disorder rather than a more general speech delay or isolated articulatory difficulty (Dodd, et al., 1995). Others have never been referred to speech and language therapy because their problems have not been noticed or considered serious enough to warrant specialist attention.

Sounds

It would be easy to assume that a speech difficulty will be manifested through sound omissions or errors. This is often the case in the preschool years but not necessarily the most obvious feature in the older child. By the time a child starts school he or she should be using a full range of sounds and be intelligible most of the time. By 7 years of age, the child should not have noticeable speech problems, i.e. he or she should not be singled out from their peer group because of speech difficulties. In school-age children, the most common and persisting speech sound errors which can be associated with literacy problems are:

'th' pronounced as 'f', eg THIN → *fin*, THICK → *fick*
'the' pronounced as 'v', eg THEN → *ven*, THATn→ *vat*
'r' pronounced as 'w', eg RUN → *wun*, RED → *wed*

Of course, in some local accents 'f' → *th* and 'the' → *v* are the *norm* and should not be labelled as a *speech error*. However, the accent may still mask an underlying problem. If there is concern about this, it should be checked if the child can a) hear and see the difference between 'f/th' and 'the/v' and b) differentiates 'f', 'th', 'v', 'the' in spelling as well as his peer group with the same accent. There is also wide variation on how 'r' is pronounced in the English language within and between countries. Again, the child's production should be compared with the peer group at school as well as with other members of the family.

Words which contain 'wrly' sounds may be problematic for children with subtle speech difficulties, for example, gorilla, lorry, wellies. Such sound combinations makes these words particularly difficult to segment for spelling, for example, LIBRARY spelt as *libili*, and SLIPPERY as *sliply*.

Another speech problem that can persist into the school years is one with clusters such as CLEAN produced as *telean*, STREAM as *tweam*, or WASP as *waps*. If the child is unable to produce the clusters or has trouble sequencing the sounds in the cluster he will be disadvantaged when trying to spell them. Assessment needs to establish if this is due to auditory processing or speech output skills.

Robert aged 9 years had 'unclear' speech and was diagnosed as having specific reading and spelling problems. His persisting speech error of *f* for 'th' and *v* for 'the' (which was not typical of his accent or of his family's speech) was manifested in his spelling but reversed – the digraph *th* was used to represent the sound 'f', for example:

Target		*Spelling*
traffic	→	trathic
finger	→	thinger
nerve	→	nerth

This confusion should alert us to the likelihood of further difficulties. Indeed, when spelling multisyllabic words with clusters, more serious sound segmentation skills were evident when his imprecise speech did not allow an effective rehearsal of target words prior to spelling them, as in:

Target		*Spelling*
discovery	→	dicoary
umbrella	→	upbla

Words

The speech errors typically associated with dyslexia in the older child, however, are more evident at the word rather the sound level. For example, Christian was referred for speech and language therapy for the first time at the age of 16;5 years. He could produce all speech sounds in isolation but had difficulties sequencing these in words. For example he produced MELANIE as *Menelie* and SYSTEMATIC as *synstemacit*. His difficulty was at the level of programming his speech output.

Another warning sign to look out for is when the child appears to be groping for the word or trying to improve pronunciation through repeated attempts. Katie aged 7;7 years did just this. She pronounced SCREWDRIVER as *screw griver, stru griver*, and MICROSCOPE as *micostope, mi micto spoke*. Assessment revealed that she had difficulties with auditory discrimination, word storage and naming. When trying to name pictures she clearly had difficulties naming words that she knew, for example for BINOCULARS she said,

'kind of glasses. You put them on your eyes. You can put them round your hand and you can see really close',

and for SADDLE she said,

'kind of seat when you go on a horsie. and you put your feet through there.'

These word-finding difficulties are often associated with speech and phonological processing problems and need careful investigation (Constable, Stackhouse and Wells, 1994).

Continuous speech

It is important to note that just because a child can pronounce sounds individually it does not mean that he or she can combine them in words. A word has to be *stored, accessed* and *programmed* for pronunciation. Children with dyslexia can have problems at any or all of these levels. Their task is complicated further by the fact that spoken communication is rarely in the form of isolated words. The following are common descriptions of the continuous speech from children with dyslexia:

- unclear
- mumbly
- muffled
- jerky
- hesitant
- nonfluent

If the speech assessment includes only tests of sounds and words, important information about a child's speech difficulties will be missed. In particular, a continuous speech assessment should be included and attention given to what happens at the junction between words and between sentences (Wells, 1994).

Richard is a good example of how a speech and language disorder can remain hidden unless investigated in this way. He was referred for a speech and language therapy assessment for the first time at the age of 11;8 years, following a diagnosis of dyslexia. He was a boy of at least average intelligence but with a reading age of 8;9 years and a spelling age of 7;2 years. Parents described him as 'a mumbler' and wondered if he had a speech problem but they had not been able to identify any particular sound difficulties. Although quiet, Richard was a good communicator and was particulary knowledgeable about marine life. The following extract of his spontaneous speech reveals why his speech was unclear – he missed off the ends of words and deleted unstressed syllables (everything in brackets was omitted):

> whe(n) I we(nt) dow(n) for my hol(i)day in Poole
> they('ve) got a(n a)quarium
> they('ve) got (to) turn over on the(ir) stoma(ch)

A psycholinguistic assessment revealed that Richard had intact input processing skills but a specific output difficulty. He had word-finding difficulties, spoken segmentation problems and subtle speech difficulties. In contrast, he had good verbal comprehension and could use complex grammatical structures. In fact, these strengths had masked the speech difficulties associated with his reading and in particular, his spelling problems (Stackhouse and Wells 1991).

Conclusions

Although some visual deficits may affect reading performance, there remains an overwhelming consensus that verbal skills are most influential in literacy development (Catts, Hu, Larrivee, et al., 1994). Written language clearly is dependent on spoken language skills but the relationship between these skills is a complex one. Language problems affect comprehension and semantic development and are likely to restrict the use the child can make of contextual cues to develop reading skills. Speech difficulties affect spelling development in particular but for a number of reasons. In the same way that speech and language problems arise from a variety of sources, so do reading and spelling problems.

It is clear that phonological processing skills play a major role in the development of reading and spelling. Without intact input phonology a child cannot discriminate and sequence what he or she hears. This auditory processing problem will have a knock-on effect to how words are stored in the child's lexicon. Fuzzy lexical representations will be problematic when the child needs to name or spell. Output phonology is particularly important for rehearsing verbal material in memory and for reflecting on the structure in preparation for speech and spelling. Problems with rehearsal affect the child's ability to develop phonological awareness – a necessary skill for literacy to develop satisfactorily. Literacy success is dependent on coupling these phonological processing skills at the input, representation and output levels with alphabetic knowledge gained through orthographic experience.

Children with speech and language difficulties have a faulty foundation on which to base their literacy development. However, they do not form a homogeneous group but present with a range of different psycholinguistic profiles. The precise nature of an individual child's literacy problems will be determined by the balance of strengths and weaknesses in their speech and language processing skills and the his/her ability to compensate for the associated written language difficulties.

Chapter 3
Predicting Children's Reading and Spelling Difficulties

Valerie Muter

The importance of early identification of reading failure, including dyslexia, has attracted increasing attention from teachers, psychologists, speech and language therapists and indeed the media over the last 10 years. The impetus to develop screening and intervention instruments has constituted a significant step forward in the systematic early identification and management of children at risk for reading problems.

The Importance and Advantages of Early Identification

The severe costs in terms of human and financial resources when children suffer persistent reading failure is an issue with which many parents, teachers and students can identify. The reasons for promoting early identification are not difficult to enumerate. In general terms, early identification permits the setting up of a communication and support network within which the child's needs can be both accurately met and sensitively handled.

Children whose at-risk status has been recognized at ages 5 or 6 will have far less educational ground to make up than those children identified later in their schooling. Bridging an underachievement gap of only 12 months at age 6–7 is a far easier and quicker accomplished task than making up for five years of lost reading progress in a child shortly due to face the demands of a secondary school curriculum.

From a practising psychologist's perspective, assessing a child of only 5, 6 or 7 results in a test profile that is 'purer' and therefore easier to interpret than one obtained from an older child, whose pattern of scoring may have become distorted or obscured through experiential factors, for example, different teaching methods or compensatory strategies the child has developed.

Most teachers acknowledge the greater ease of working with younger children who have not yet experienced excessive frustration and feelings of failure that can adversely affect their motivation and responsivity. Praise and other reinforcers can be more readily implemented with small children and can have powerful effects in initiating and sustaining children's cooperation and motivation. Also, teachers often find it easier to work with young early identified children who have not had the opportunity to establish too many bad habits which then have to be unlearned before they can be replaced by new and more effective strategies.

There may be negative behavioural consequences of untreated persisting reading problems. Many failed readers who have effectively given up are significantly at risk of becoming increasingly behaviourally disruptive or even disturbed. Recent research has demonstrated a substantial link between early reading failure and later social adjustment problems and delinquent behaviour, at least into the adolescent years and in some instances beyond (see Maughan, 1994 and 1995 for reviews).

Finally, and most powerful politically, is the economic advantage of early identification. Implementing a 2–3 times weekly teaching programme over a one year period for a 6-year-old is clearly many times cheaper than having to provide long-term daily help (or even special schooling) to a late-diagnosed 10-year-old whose behaviour is becoming increasingly anti-social.

Predictors of Early Reading Success and Failure

It is clear that the early identification of reading failure is a desirable goal with many advantages. One approach to the screening and assessment of reading failure begins with the specification of skills and abilities which might have a bearing on early reading development. If we know which particular abilities contribute to early reading progress, we have in effect a set of predictors which are definable, measurable in individual children and potentially capable of modification through teaching. These predictors are then able to form the basis, either for the screening of preschool or Year 1 school populations or, more conservatively, for initial diagnostic assessments of young children whose histories are suggestive of an at-risk predisposition, for example, other family members with literacy problems, early developmental delay or unevenness.

There are a number of potential candidates for predictors of reading success and failure: these might be general intelligence (IQ), speech and language abilities, attention span, memory processes, motor skills and so on. Several large scale studies of beginning readers in the United States in the 1960s concentrated on measuring abilities such as these (Bond and Dykstra, 1967; Chall, 1967). Typically, large numbers of preschool children underwent testing on a wide range of possible predictor skills and abilities. The children were then followed up one or two years later, after they had started school, and their early reading skills were assessed. These studies showed that IQ was not, as we might expect, the best predictor of beginning reading. In fact, it came in a modest third after the children's knowledge of letter-names, and their phonological awareness (in these studies, the ability to discriminate phonemes auditorially).

Extensive research into individual differences in phonological skills has resulted in the conclusion that these are causally related to the normal acquisition of beginning reading skill. Phonological abilities have been measured in a variety of ways. Adams (1990) divides tasks that successfully predict reading skill into four main types:

1. Syllable and Phoneme Segmentation Tasks in which the child taps, counts out or identifies the constituent syllable and/or phonemes within words (see Liberman, Shankweiler, Fischer and Carter, 1974).
2. Phoneme Manipulation Tasks which require the child to delete, add or transpose phonemes within words (see Bruce, 1964; Share, Jorm, Maclean, et al., 1984).
3. Sound Blending Tasks in which the examiner provides the phonemes of a word and the child is asked to put them together (see Perfetti, Bell, Beck and Hughes, 1987).
4. Rhyming Tasks that include knowledge of nursery rhymes (MacLean, Bryant and Bradley, 1987), and the identification of the 'odd word out' (non-rhyming word) in a sequence of 3 or 4 words as in the sound categorization test of Bradley and Bryant (1983).

It is evident that phonological processing skills, tapped by the above tasks, are significantly related to reading success or failure, although the direction of these causal relations remains a source of controversy. While phonological skills clearly exert a substantial influence over subsequent reading development, there is good evidence that learning to read may affect the further development of phonological skills (Alegria, Pignot and Morais, 1982). Liberman et al. (1974) demonstrated that, although the majority of preschoolers can segment words into syllables, very few can readily segment them into phonemes. The more sophisticated stage of phoneme segmentation is not reached until the child has received formal instruction in letter-sound knowledge. The available evidence would seem to suggest that there is a two-way interactive process between phonological skills and learning to read.

Prediction studies such as those described above tell us a great deal about the knowledge and skills young children bring to bear on the task of learning to read. They might also, if generated from sufficiently large samples of children, provide norms for the purposes of screening of whole populations of young children. However, whether such studies can suggest a strategy for reliably identifying children who go on to have dyslexic problems that necessitate special needs intervention is a rather more complex issue. When considering individual children, it is not always possible to confidently conclude that a child who obtains a low score on a measure of phonological awareness will necessarily go on to have significant and persisting reading problems. In Bradley and Bryant's (1985) longitudinal study of early readers, only 30 per cent of those children who initially produced good sound categorization scores became exceptionally good readers. Of greater relevance to the early identification issue is the finding that just 28 per cent of those who initially produced poor sound categorization scores became exceptionally poor readers. These authors suggest that a phonological awareness test on its own might not be a particularly effective way of predicting persisting reading problems.

That said, studies of dyslexic children have consistently pointed to their having specific deficiencies in phonological skill (see Snowling, Stackhouse and Rack, 1986). Furthermore, the main reading problem experienced by dyslexic children is often in the use of phonological strategies to read and spell words. This problem is usually manifest in the processing of novel words, but can also be seen in difficulties with long polysyllabic words (Rack, Snowling and Olson, 1992).

To complement the work on predictors of reading success and failure in normal populations, we need longitudinal prospective studies of children who exhibit early at-risk features of dyslexia. However, such studies are as yet a rarity, and the results of the few that have been conducted indicate that we should be cautious about predictor research with normal children as the sole basis for reliable early identification. To illustrate, one early predictor of later dyslexia is thought to be specific developmental language delay. Retrospective studies find an unusually high proportion of children with specific reading disability were late in starting to talk (Rutter, Tizard and Whitmore, 1970). However, a follow-up study of children identified as having a specific language impairment at age 4 found that these children rarely had problems of reading accuracy when followed up at age 8;6 years (Bishop and Adams, 1990). Those children whose language impairment had resolved by age 5;6 years were as proficient as other 8-year-olds in single word reading, nonword reading and use of phonics. Those children who still had language deficits at 5;6 years were poor at reading at age 8. However, this was not an isolated impairment, but occurred in the context of widespread verbal deficits and rather poor nonverbal skills.

A rather different approach, though still within a longitudinal prospective framework, was taken by Hollis Scarborough (1990, 1991b) who focused on the language and phonological development of children who eventually went on to have reading problems. She compared the performance of reading disabled children from dyslexic families on language, phonological and preliteracy measures at several different ages with that of normal reading children from non-dyslexic families, all of whom had been recruited for the study at age 2. The children in the reading disabled group were significantly poorer than those in the control group on tests of expressive syntax and sentence comprehension at 30–48 months, and on tests of phonological awareness, letter-sound knowledge, letter identification and object naming at 60 months. Scarborough has suggested that dyslexic children have a broader language disorder that is not simply reflected in reading failure. This disorder is expressed as different observable weaknesses at different ages: first, syntax problems; then weaknesses in phonological awareness, naming and other preliteracy skills; and finally, difficulties with reading and spelling during the school years. The extent to which the language disorder affects the child's educational progress and eventual outcome may be modified by factors like quality of teaching and the child's motivation. The fact that different cognitive skills have differing predictive power according to the age at which they are assessed is an important consideration when devising predictor instruments; a series of tests relevant for 3-year-olds may have a very different content to that devised for 5-year-olds.

Assessing the Predictors

It will be evident from the foregoing that phonological awareness is a major determiner of beginning reading success when assessed in children aged 3–6 years. It does, therefore, become a prime candidate for inclusion in any early identification protocol. However, there are many different types of tasks that might be employed to assess phonological skill. Which leads to the question: are there different types of phonological skill, and if so, which play the most important role in early reading?

Early studies by Stanovich, Cunningham and Cramer (1984) and by Wagner and Torgesen (1987) reported that the intercorrelations between different measures of phonology could be accounted for by one factor i.e., that the different tasks were tapping essentially the same latent ability. However, Yopp (1988) uncovered two factors in her analysis of 10 phonological awareness tests. These were highly correlated and appeared to reflect two levels of difficulty rather than two qualitatively different kinds of skill. The first factor, simple phoneme awareness, required only one cognitive operation – the segmentation, blending or isolation of a given sound followed by a response. The second factor, compound phoneme awareness, involved two operations, and placed a heavier burden on memory; the child had to perform an operation such as isolating a given sound and then hold the resulting sound in memory while performing a further operation (phoneme manipulation tasks). Rhyming ability was only minimally involved in these two factors, leading Yopp to conclude 'rhyme tasks may tap a different underlying ability than other tasks of phonemic awareness' (p. 172).

This latter observation is consistent with the theoretical position taken by Goswami and Bryant (1990). They propose that there are different levels of segmental analysis of words, that these develop at different rates, and that they exert different influences over early reading development. They have argued that segmentation, deletion and similar tasks are measures of phonemic awareness, whereas rhyming tests are sensitive, not to individual phonemes within words, but to onset-rime units within words. Within an English syllable the onset refers to the initial consonant or consonant cluster, while the rime comprises the vowel and final consonant/s. So, tests of phonemic awareness tap the phonemic structure of the word, for example, c-a-t whereas tests of rhyming access its onset-rime boundary for example, c-at. According to Goswami and Bryant (1990), rhyming and segmentation skills should exert different influences over reading and spelling development. They have argued that onset-rime awareness forms a basis for children's ability to make use of analogical strategies in reading and spelling. Analogy in reading involves using the spelling-sound relationship of one word to predict the pronunciation of an unknown word which shares a similar spelling pattern. Goswami has demonstrated that children as young as 6 can use a clue word like *beak* to help them read new words such as *weak* and *peak* which share the clue word's rime (see Goswami and Bryant, 1992, for a review). In this model, tests of phoneme segmentation and deletion reflect children's awareness of the smaller phonemic units within words which they use, not so much in early reading, but certainly in 'sounding out' words they are asked to spell.

Sara Taylor and I (Muter, 1994) had the opportunity to test out the Goswami and Bryant model of phonological awareness in a longitudinal study of 38 normal children who were given five tests of phonological awareness at ages 4, 5 and 6. There were two tests of rhyming, one of rhyme detection and one of rhyme production. In the detection test, the children had to say which of three words rhymed with the stimulus word. In the rhyme production test, the children were give 10 seconds to produce words that rhymed with each of two stimulus words. The third test was one of phoneme identification in which the subjects had to finish off the final phoneme of a single syllable word for which the examiner supplied the initial part. The fourth test was an initial consonant deletion test. The final test was the sound blending test from the *Illinois Test of Psycholinguistic Ability* (Kirk, McCarthy and Kirk, 1968).

The children's scores on each of the tests were entered into a series of statistical analyses, separately for each year of the study. Two independent factors emerged. The first of these was a *segmentation* factor that accounted well for performance on the phoneme identification, blending and deletion tests. The second was a *rhyming* factor accounting for performance on the rhyme detection and production tests. These findings provide empirical support for Goswami and Bryant's model of phonological awareness in which two independent subskills, tapping different levels of subsyllabic segmentation are proposed, i.e., onset-rime and phonemic awareness.

Goswami and Bryant (1990) have suggested that rhyming exerts an important early influence over reading development, while segmentation plays a later role and has a greater influence over spelling than reading. Sara Taylor and I explored these issues in our longitudinal study using path analysis, a technique that permits the charting of causal relationships between reading-related measures. We were first interested in asking the question: What are the relative contributions of rhyming and segmentation to reading and spelling during the first year at primary school? In addition to the phonological awareness tests, we gave the children an IQ test (Wechsler Preschool and Primary Scale of Intelligence, 1967) when they were 4, and tests of reading and spelling when they were 5 and 6 (*British Abilities Scale Reading Test*, *Neale Analysis of Reading Ability* and *Schonell Spelling Test*). We found that segmentation made a highly significant contribution to both early reading and spelling, but rhyming did not. IQ had an effect on early literacy but it was indirect; it exerted its influence through segmentation ability, i.e., brighter children found segmenting words into phonemes easier than less bright children, but it was the skill in segmentation that directly drove literacy acquisition.

Our results were in accord with the view of Goswami and Bryant that rhyming and segmentation are independent phonological subskills and that they differentially affect early literacy development. However, we clearly showed that it is segmentation, reflecting phonemic awareness, that promotes beginning literacy development, not rhyming which reflects onset-rime awareness. Thus, in developing instruments for identifying children at risk for reading problems, at least from age 4 onwards, our findings suggest that segmentation tasks should take precedence over rhyming tasks.

It would be misleading, however, to give the impression that rhyming has no contribution to make to early reading and spelling. Indeed, when the children in our study were aged 6 and in the second year at primary school, we found that rhyming influenced two aspects of their literacy performance. First, it significantly contributed, along with segmentation, to spelling; perhaps rhyming skill, in promoting children's awareness of onset-rime boundaries, influences their use of analogy in spelling. Second, in an experimental study of analogy in reading, we were able to demonstrate a significant concurrent relationship between the ability to rhyme and to use analogies at age 6 (Muter, Snowling and Taylor, 1994).

Alongside phonological awareness, the major predictor of beginning reading for children aged 4–6 years is thought to be their letter knowledge. In the study conducted by Sara Taylor and me, we found that children's knowledge of letter names proved a powerful contributor to reading and spelling processes during the first year at school. We were also interested in the contribution to reading and spelling of the *interaction* of segmentation skill and letter knowledge. We suspected that for children to progress in reading, they need to explicitly connect their ability to segment words into sounds with their knowledge of letters. This linkage process was captured in a calculated product term, i.e., Letter Knowledge x Segmentation. The product term made a separate and additional contribution to reading, and in particular spelling, beyond the simple additive effects of letter knowledge and segmentation. Putting letter knowledge, segmentation and the product term together explained a total of 60 per cent of the variance in first year reading and 70 per cent of the variance in spelling. This finding supports the Phonological Linkage Hypothesis proposed by Hatcher, Hulme and Ellis (1994) (see Hatcher, this volume); children make optimal progress in reading when explicit links are formed between their underlying phonological awareness and their experiences in learning to read.

Wagner, Torgesen and Rashotte (1994) have considered other reading-related phonological processing abilities, including naming skill and phonological memory, in their longitudinal study of 244 children from kindergarten through second grade. They included several measures for each of the following five variables: phonological analysis, phonological synthesis, phonological coding in working memory, isolated naming and serial naming. All five, when considered individually, appeared to have a causal influence over subsequent reading decoding skill in each year of the study. However, when viewed simultaneously within a single model analysis, the relations between the individual processing abilities proved redundant. In the simultaneous analyses, only phonological analysis (essentially segmentation) causally influenced first grade reading, while only phonological synthesis (blending) influenced second grade reading (though analysis and synthesis were highly correlated). The findings from this and an earlier study (Wagner, Torgesen, Laughon, et al., 1993) led these authors to conclude that the various phonological processing tasks are tapping the quality of underlying phonological representations, and it is the quality of these representations which in turn affects children's ability to learn to read.

This is a similar view to that held by Hulme and Roodenrys (1995) in their review of impairments of memory span in dyslexic children. These authors review evidence that has clearly shown that dyslexic children do poorly on digit span tests and on other measures of short-term memory. However, these memory problems are not

necessarily causal. Hulme and Roodenrys consider the more relevant issue to be: How do the short-term memory problems of poor
readers relate to their other phonological difficulties, and which
phonological problems are causally related to difficulties in learning
to read? They agree with the view of Wagner, et al., that memory and
phonological awareness tasks are indices of the integrity of the child's
phonological representations, and that dyslexic children, in having
coarsened or degraded phonological representations, fail to progress
as they should in reading. Further support for this position comes
from McDougall, Hulme, Ellis, et al. (1994) who studied the relationship between memory span, speech rate and phonological awareness
in good, average and poor readers. They were able to demonstrate
that differences in reading ability are associated with differences in
the efficiency of the speech-based rehearsal component of short-
term memory span. Children's scores on a test of speech rate (repeating words as quickly as possible) made a significant contribution to
reading skill independent of that made by two measures of phonological awareness (a rhyme recognition and a phoneme deletion test).
Furthermore, after accounting for speech rate, memory span made
no contribution to reading skill. Conversely, however, speech rate did
predict reading skill even after controlling for the effects of memory
span. Hulme and Roodenrys propose that short-term memory problems are an index of other phonological deficits that are actually
tapped more effectively by simply having children repeat words as
quickly as they can. In speech rate, we may have another easy to
implement and quick measurement technique that will supplement
and complement the more extensively documented measures of
phonological awareness and letter knowledge.

The foregoing discussion has highlighted the importance of
measures of phonological processing ability and letter knowledge, in
predicting beginning literacy success. Instruments that purport to
identify children at risk for reading failure should include measures
of these skills. However, there may be other tasks that could usefully
predict literacy success. Tunmer (1989) has emphasized the importance of syntactic awareness as an important contributor to early
reading. In a one-year longitudinal study of normal 6–7-year-old
children, he demonstrated that both phonological awareness and
syntactic awareness made independent and significant contributions
to reading skill. Scarborough (1990, 1991b) has suggested that early
syntactic and language comprehension skills are deficient in children
who later prove to be dyslexic. However, one caution to be borne in
mind from Scarborough's work is that the syntactic tests she

employed were only predictive of later reading failure when administered between the ages of 30–48 months. Syntactic abilities, though obviously of relevance to early reading development, may not prove as robust nor as durable indicators of eventual reading success or failure as perhaps phonological measures.

Predicting Reading in the Longer Term

Much of the research that has been carried out on predictors of reading success, has followed children during the first two or three years of schooling. The longitudinal research conducted by Sara Taylor and me was of this type and had pointed to likely powerful predictors of reading achievement. We have recently followed up the children in our study some three years later and our preliminary results provide striking confirmation of the efficacy of the early screening we did (Muter and Snowling, in preparation); a combination of phonological awareness and letter knowledge measures obtained at 4–6 years predicted longer-term reading success or failure. Thirty-four children from the original sample of 38 were available at follow-up; the children's ages ranging from 9;3 years to 10;2 years, with a mean age of 9;9 years. Sixteen children met a criterion of being above the 25th centile for reading (*Neale Analysis of Reading Ability*) and/or spelling (*BAS Spelling Test*); these were termed the good readers/spellers. Eight children met the criterion of being below the 25th centile for reading and/or spelling; these were termed the poor readers/spellers. A composite score based on the sum of the children's phoneme identification and phoneme deletion test scores at age 5 was calculated (out of a possible 18). Note was also taken of the children's letter-name knowledge at age 5.

Table 3.1: Scores obtained by good and poor 9-year-old readers on tests of phonological analysis and letter knowledge when they were 5-years-old

	Status at Age 9	
	Good readers/spellers	Poor readers/spellers
Scores at Age 5		
Phonological analysis (max = 18)	9.6	3.5
Letter knowledge (max = 26)	16.8	7.6

Inspection of Table 3.1 shows that the poor readers/spellers were substantially worse than the good readers/spellers on the measures of phonological analysis and letter knowledge given four years earlier. While these figures are little more than a preliminary flavour of the findings of this follow-up study, they nonetheless add weight to the argument that short and simple tests of phonological processing allied to a measure of letter knowledge, could prove highly successful in isolating at-risk children before their problems have amounted to very real educational failure.

It is worth illustrating the above preliminary findings in a concrete way by looking in detail at the two children in the follow-up sample who were having the greatest difficulty in reading and spelling at 9 –10 years. Nicholas was originally assessed as having a WPPSI IQ of 109 at age 4. At that time, he scored zero on both the phoneme segmentation and phoneme deletion tests, and he identified only one letter correctly. When seen one year later, he scored zero on the segmentation test and one on the deletion test, and he was able to identify only 5 letters of the alphabet by name. At that time, he read just 4 words correctly from the *BAS Reading Test* and was unable to write any of the Schonell spelling words. Matters had improved very little by the time Nicholas was seen in the following year, age 6. His phoneme segmentation score had risen to 5 (out of a possible 8), but his phoneme deletion score was zero and he read a mere 5 of the letters of the alphabet correctly. He was able to read just 5 words from the *BAS Reading Test* and to spell only one word from the spelling test. That said, his oral and written arithmetic at age 6 were well up to the standard of the rest of the sample.

Nicholas problems were thus specific to the development of literacy skill and could not be regarded as representative of general educational failure. Now aged 10;2 years, Nicholas reading and spelling attainments fall at the third and eighth centiles respectively, although his written arithmetic (*BAS Basic Number Skills*) is of a higher standard, i.e., 39th centile. He read only 2 words correctly from the *Graded Nonword Reading Test* (Snowling, Stothard and McLean, in press) in contrast to the mean score for the follow up sample of 14.56. Nicholas continues to have substantial problems of phonological awareness; on a phoneme deletion test developed by McDougall, et al., (1994), he scored only 4 out of 24, while the mean for the sample as a whole was 17.24. His speech rate score was 3.39 words per second, nearly two standard deviations below the sample mean of 4.82. Nicholas frustration over his severe and persisting reading failure is now beginning to affect his behavioural adjustment. His scores on the 'anxious/depressed' and 'attention problem' scales of the *Achenbach Child Behaviour Checklist* (Achenbach, 1991) fall within the clinical problem range.

A similarly consistent pattern emerged for child Robert. At age 4, he registered a WPPSI IQ of 106. Throughout the first three years of the study, he recorded zero scores on the *BAS Reading* and *Schonell Spelling Tests*, i.e., he was effectively a non-reader at age 6, although his scores on tests of oral and written arithmetic by that age were within normal limits. Robert never scored above zero on the phoneme deletion test given from ages 4 to 6 years, though he did progress on phoneme segmentation, achieving the ceiling score of 8 by age 6. He was unable to name any of the letters of the alphabet at ages 4 and 5, but managed to read 11 correctly by the time he was 6 years of age. Now aged 10 years, Robert's reading and spelling scores are at the first and sixth centiles respectively, while his arithmetic achievement is a little higher, i.e., 13th centile. His ability to read nonwords is extremely limited (only 3 read correctly), and his phoneme deletion skill is, with a score of 9, well below the mean for the follow up sample. His speech rate score (3.38) is, as with Nicholas, almost two standard deviations below the mean for the sample as a whole. Robert's teachers and parents are concerned about his disruptive behaviour, and he is in the process of being considered for 'statementing' for his special educational needs.

These clinical vignettes suggest that measures of phonological awareness, letter knowledge and perhaps also speech rate might serve as potentially powerful early indicators and diagnostic tools to assess children who are likely to display persisting reading failure. The pattern of deficit appears to be consistent throughout the middle childhood years which is very much in agreement with the view of Wagner, Torgesen and Rashotte (1994) who have shown that individual differences in phonological processing abilities are remarkably stable from age 4–7 years (and as our follow-up study shows, perhaps even well beyond). Thus, phonological abilities should be viewed as coherent individual difference variables rather like other cognitive abilities, as opposed to being transitory indices of reading-related knowledge. As these authors point out 'the stability of individual differences in young children's phonological processing abilities reinforces the value of early screening of phonological processing abilities to identify children who are at risk for reading failure' (pp. 84).

Conclusions

It is evident from the foregoing that tasks that tap children's phonological processing abilities are the prime candidates for inclusion in screening or early diagnostic reading batteries (see Chapters 8 and 9, this volume). The evidence tends to favour segmentation over rhyming tasks in predicting beginning literacy achievement, though inclusion of some rhyming tests as measures sensitive to onset-rime awareness may be important for predicting the use of analogy in reading and spelling. Letter knowledge as an indicator of the thoroughness and possibly ease with which the letter identities have been learned is also seen to be an important element in early identification screening. Finally, one might wish to include a measure of children's phonological memory processes through the adoption of a span test, or as recent research suggests, more economically a test of speech rate. The practical applicability of such batteries for use by psychologists, speech and language therapists, special needs teachers and classroom teachers is enormous.

Acknowledgement

This chapter was prepared with the support of a grant from the Nuffield Foundation.

Chapter 4

Assessing Speech Processing Skills in Children: A Task Analysis

Maggie Vance

There is now a great deal of research showing that learning to read is dependent upon adequate speech processing skills. To the lay person this may seem strange. Why should learning what might be regarded as a visible language require speech processing capabilities? The answer lies in the alphabetic system of languages such as English. These systems are not arbitrary but embody systematic mappings between the segments of spoken words and the letters (or graphemes) of printed words. In order to learn to read, a child has to become aware of these relationships and in turn, this depends upon having proficient speech processing skills.

It is useful to think of speech processing as a chain of steps, involving:

1. Auditory discrimination of incoming verbal information;
2. Accessing phonological (sound), semantic (meaning) and orthographic (written) representations of words stored in the lexicon;
3. Producing spoken responses.

Figure 4.1 encapsulates the essence of this speech processing chain.

A first aim when assessing a child with speech and literacy difficulties is to identify at what level or levels the processing system is breaking down. The second aim is to draw up a child's profile of strengths and weaknesses by comparing a child's performance on a range of tasks designed to tap from peripheral to central levels (bottom to top on Figure 4.1) and input/output channels of process-

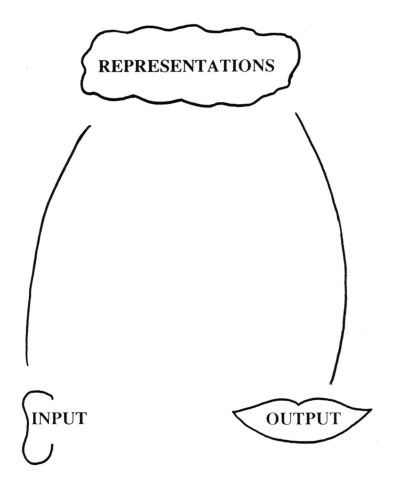

Figure 4.1: The speech processing chain (from Stackhouse and Wells, forthcoming)

ing (left and right on Figure 4.1). As a result, more accurate remediation can be targeted. For example, a different approach is
needed with a child who has difficulties with input processing
compared with another who has difficulties with output processing.
Children with severe and persisting difficulties may have problems
with both input and output skills (Stackhouse and Wells, 1993, and
forthcoming).

This assessment approach has been used to uncover the hidden
spoken language problems in children with dyslexia as well as to
investigate the relationship between more obvious spoken language
and literacy difficulties (Stackhouse and Wells, 1991). Children

with difficulties in speech processing are at risk for literacy problems (Snowling, Goulandris and Stackhouse, 1994). In fact, the nature of the speech processing difficulty is reflected in the child's reading and spelling performance (Snowling, Stackhouse and Rack, 1986).

This chapter will consider the processing demands of tasks of auditory discrimination, rhyming skills and speech production, and how children's performance on such tasks might be interpreted within a psycholinguistic assessment framework that distinguishes between input and output processing and phonological representations. In assessing children with speech and/or literacy difficulties it is important to compare findings with the pattern of normal development. For example, a child under investigation may perform less well on a task of nonword repetition than word repetition. This may or may not be a problem depending on the age of the child (Vance, Stackhouse and Wells, 1995). Without evidence of how normally developing children perform across such tasks, the significance of such a finding is difficult to interpret. It is often the *degree* of the difference in performance on two tasks compared with normal controls that indicates a significant processing difficulty.

It is also particularly important to carefully assess the processing skills of children with reading and spelling difficulties who are not showing any obvious speech difficulties. Such children may perform reasonably well on some tasks requiring speech processing skills because they have developed strategies to compensate for inefficiencies in processing, but deficits within the speech processing system might still remain and affect literacy development. Tasks of speech processing will need to be sufficiently taxing to signal these more subtle deficits.

Auditory Skills

Research findings have indicated a link between difficulties with some aspects of auditory perception and discrimination and the presence of dyslexia (Masterson, Hazan and Wijayatilake, 1995; Tallal, 1980). Clinical evidence is that many children with literacy difficulties misperceive words said to them. An example comes from Patrick, a 10-year-old dyslexic child, while playing on his computer. The screen message 'The Zulus seek friendship with the Russians' was read out to him by an adult, and he asked, 'What have the French got to do with it?' (Vance, 1994). It is, therefore, important to assess input processing in children with literacy difficulties.

Input processing skills play a vital role in the development of phonological representations. The first information that a child receives about the speech sounds contained within a word is through hearing and perceiving the word. Where input processing difficulties exist, inaccurate or fuzzy phonological representations will have knock-on effects to speech and to spelling.

Thomas, described by Joy Stackhouse in Chapter 2, is a good example of a child with input difficulties. He was 8;6 years, had a history of mild hearing difficulties and still made errors on some tasks of auditory discrimination. Speech errors included incorrect pronunciations of the sounds 'sh' and 'ch', and there was evidence that his representations of words containing these sounds were inaccurate. Thomas also made frequent errors in spelling words containing these sounds. Since Thomas had to rely on the same faulty lexical representations to say words and to segment them for spelling, both speech and spelling were impaired. The integrity of the phonological representations is also important in reading unfamiliar words as a child will sound out the words he encounters either vocally, or sub-vocally, and then attempt to map the sound of the word onto his existing memory of word forms. Although other factors such as context may help the child 'see' a match, inaccurate or incomplete representations arising from poor auditory perception can contribute to difficulties.

Auditory discrimination tasks using the same/different paradigm

Tasks of auditory discrimination often involve the use of pairs of words that differ by only one speech sound, such as *bat/pat* and *fork/fort*. Such pairs of words are referred to as minimal pairs. Word pairs that contain the same sounds but in a different order can also be used, such as *tap/pat*. There are a number of published tests of auditory discrimination skills, such as the *Auditory Discrimination Test* (Wepman and Reynolds, 1987) and the *Sound Discrimination Test* in *The Aston Index* (Newton and Thomson, 1976). In these tests the examiner says the same word twice (*chap/chap*) or says two different words (*tub/tug*), and the child reports whether he has heard the same word or different words. The child's success with such a task will depend on his ability to use the concept of same/different in this way.

Tasks such as these allow examination of a child's ability to detect similarities and differences between words spoken to him. However, the word pairs used in some existing published material do not allow more subtle input processing difficulties to be revealed in that only simple single-syllable words are used. The word pairs selected do not always differ by two sounds that are similar enough for children to have difficulty in discriminating between them. For example *gear/deer* are more similar than *gear/beer* (used in the Wepman Auditory Discrimination Test). Whereas some children experience difficulties in learning the difference between 'g' and 'd' and using these sounds appropriately, children less often confuse 'g' and 'b'. Children with input processing difficulties might perform quite well on same/different tasks if the words used are not demanding enough to highlight their difficulty. More subtle measures of auditory discrimination should include the use of minimal pairs that are more similar in sound, and of longer and more complex words.

Auditory discrimination using nonsense words

Input processing difficulties can be revealed by using nonword pairs in addition to word pairs for auditory discrimination tasks. When words are presented, a child can use stored knowledge of a word (semantic, phonological and orthographic) to help complete the task. However, when nonwords are presented, the child does not have any existing knowledge to help complete the task. (It is important to remember that if the child is not familiar with a word that has been presented, i.e., there is no phonological representation for that word, then it will be processed in the same way as a nonword.)

Contrasting performance on word and nonword tasks highlights the levels involved in speech processing. In order to process nonwords bottom-up processing is required. All information about the sounds contained in the stimuli must be derived from an analysis of the speech signal. On the other hand, when words familiar to the child are presented, top-down processing can occur, involving the use of prior linguistic knowledge (i.e., semantic, phonological and orthographic). As soon as the word presented has been recognized, the child no longer needs to rely solely on the analysis of the speech signal to do the task. Speech processing normally involves an interaction between bottom-up and top-down processing. Children often perform better on auditory discrimination tasks in which words are presented. However, children whose phonological representations are inaccurate and interfere with their judgement may not show this word superiority effect.

Stimuli used in a same/different task can be made more taxing by incorporating subtle sequencing differences. An example of how different types of stimuli can reveal input processing difficulties was provided by Bridgeman and Snowling (1988). In this study pairs of words were presented to 12 children with persistent speech difficulties, aged between 7 and 11 years, for judgement as same or different. The stimuli included minimal pairs in which a) one segment was changed, *loss/lot*; b) the sequence of speech sounds was changed, *lost/lots*; and c) sets of nonwords that mirrored these two types of changes, *vos/vot* and *vost/vots*. The children with speech disorders had more difficulties than the control group (matched on reading age) in discriminating differences in the nonwords that had sequence changes, i.e., *vost/vots*. However, they were as good as the control children in discriminating differences between the other types of word pairs. This finding highlights the importance of using a range of stimuli when testing for input processing difficulties. If only simple consonant/vowel/consonant words and nonword pairs had been used, the conclusion would have been that the children with speech disorders had normal auditory discrimination skills. This was not the case.

ABX tasks

An alternative to the same/different paradigm used in auditory discrimination tasks is an ABX presentation. This might involve words or nonwords. For example, in a recent study children aged between 5 and 7 years were presented with two puppets who each said a nonword (Vance, Stackhouse and Wells, in progress). One of the nonwords was then repeated and the child had to select which puppet had said the repeated nonword. For example:

> This puppet says brish
> This puppet says bris
> Which puppet said bris?

Many of the 5-year-old children performed at chance level on this task. Some of the children did not understand what they were required to do, even after some training items, demonstration and feedback. However, the 7-year-old children were able to complete the task successfully. Clearly, this task involves a greater short-term memory component than the same/different task discussed above. For the same/different judgement the child briefly retains the two items for immediate comparison whereas the ABX paradigm requires the child to hold and compare three items. In both tasks the level of processing required depends on whether words or nonwords are presented.

These findings indicate the importance of a developmental perspective when choosing assessment materials. For younger children a same/different task is preferred to the ABX paradigm. The ABX task, however, is more challenging for older children and reveals subtle input processing difficulties.

Auditory discrimination tasks using pictures

Another task commonly used in the assessment of auditory discrimination skills is a picture pointing task, such as the *Auditory Discrimination and Attention Test* (ADAT) (Morgan-Barry, 1988) and the *Diagnostic Auditory Discrimination Tests* of the *Goldman-Fristoe-Woodcock Auditory Skills Test Battery* (Goldman, Fristoe and Woodcock, 1976). The child is shown two pictures illustrating two minimal pair words, *pear/bear* (see Figure 4.2). The examiner says one of the words and the child indicates (usually by pointing or placing a counter) which picture corresponds to the word that has been spoken.

Figure 4.2: Minimal pair pictures: bear/pear

This paradigm assesses another level of input processing. In order to decide which picture has been named, the child needs to compare the word heard with his or her own phonological representations of the words accessed via the picture stimuli. If the child's representations for these words are inaccurate or incomplete, then the response to this task will be wrong or inconsistent. This type of task can be used with quite young children, as many 3-year-olds are able to understand what they are required to do. However, it is limited in its range of possible test items since there are only a small number of minimal pairs that can be drawn which are also familiar to young children. Further, most of these pairs are single-syllable words.

As an alternative, Locke (1980) described a useful procedure in which the child is presented with a picture portraying a single word that is named either correctly or incorrectly by the examiner. For example, the child is presented with a picture of a *cat*, and is asked 'Is it a tat?'/'Is it a cat?' The child responds *yes* or *no* after each question. The examiner then goes on to name the picture as 'tat' or 'cat' (at random) for the child to judge whether the correct or incorrect form was used for the given picture. Correct and incorrect presentations of the word must be compared with the child's stored knowledge of the word, in order to decide whether the word perceived matches the representation or not.

This task therefore also reveals the precision of the child's own phonological representations. However, compared with the minimal pair picture task above, it allows auditory discrimination of a wider range of items since only one picture is required and nonwords can be used for the incorrect presentation.

Within this procedure, it is also possible to feed back the child's own production errors to establish the origin of the speech problem. For example, if the child says *tat* instead of *cat* but knows that *tat* is incorrect when produced by the examiner, it suggests that the phonological representation is correct and the child's speech difficulties are arising at the output level. However, if the child accepts *tat* as being the correct pronunciation, it suggests that the child's phonological representation is incorrect and auditory processing skills should be investigated further.

Comparisons between different auditory discrimination tasks

It is useful to compare a child's performance on several different tasks of auditory discrimination involving different types of matched material, i.e., words and nonwords. If possible different modes of presentation of the same stimuli (i.e., verbal or visual), should also be contrasted to discover where the child's difficulties in input processing are occurring.

This principle is illustrated in the case of Amy, a child of 7;7 years, who had persisting speech difficulties. Amy was assessed by Juliette Corrin at the Nuffield Hearing and Speech Centre, London. She was given an auditory discrimination picture task, in which pictures were either named correctly or incorrectly (after Locke, 1980 as described above), and an ABX task using nonwords, matched with the words used for the picture task. For example, the picture auditory discrimination task included a picture of a ladder. The pronunciations *ladder* and *yadder* were produced by the examiner for Amy to judge correct/incorrect. The ABX task included the stimuli *leddy* and *yeddy*, for Amy to decide which puppet said *yeddy*.

Amy performed as well as normally developing 7-year-olds when single-syllable words and nonwords were presented. However, she was significantly poorer at discriminating multisyllabic words and nonwords than the 7-year-olds. When performance across the two tasks was analysed, it was found that she had significantly more difficulties than the normally developing children on the picture task compared to the ABX nonword task. These findings suggested that, although Amy has some degree of auditory discrimination deficit, her main difficulty is with the accuracy of her phonological representations.

Rhyme Skills

A number of tasks tap children's rhyming abilities, such as judging whether two words rhyme, spotting the odd one out, producing rhyming words. Analysis of the processing requirements of the different types of tasks will allow us to make more useful interpretations of children's rhyme performance. The same principles of psycholinguistic assessment apply to the design of rhyme tasks, as to the auditory tasks discussed above. If classified in a particular way, rhyme tasks can be used to tap the integrity of a child's speech processing system (Marion, Sussman and Marquardt, 1993; Vance, Stackhouse and Wells, 1994).

Rhyme judgement and detection tasks

Tasks that require a child to decide whether two words rhyme in a judgement task (example, 'Do cat and hat rhyme?'), or a detection task (example, 'Does cat rhyme with cup or hat?') are dependent on input processing skills. If the words for rhyme judgement and detection tasks are spoken by the examiner, then the child has the examiner's production of the stimuli on which to base a decision. Similar skills to those required for a same/different auditory discrimination task might be involved in that the child is listening and judging similarities and differences between words heard. However, if the words are presented visually through pictures, then the child must access his/her own phonological representations of the words in order to decide whether the words rhyme or not.

Nonwords can also be used in these rhyme tasks. Comparing a child's performance across real and nonword tasks indicates the level of difficulty experienced by the child. Normally developing children show no significant difference on word vs nonword rhyme judgement and detection tasks. Thus, if a child's performance is superior on real word tasks, it suggests that existing representations are being used to compensate for a lower level processing difficulty. Further, children can do better on real word tasks because of previous practice on the items. This cannot be the case when unfamiliar items are introduced. Tasks comprising nonwords are therefore an important measure of the child's bottom-up speech processing skills.

Rhyme production

In a rhyme production task, a child is asked to produce a string of rhyming words, example, 'Tell me some words that rhyme with cat.' Thus, rhyme production tasks require output processing skills. However, different strategies can be used to produce rhyme. For example, the child may carry out a lexical search for items that have the same rime unit as the target, example, *mat, hat, sat, fat*. Alternately, the rime unit *at* could be segmented from the stimulus and different onsets attached to this to create rhyming responses, example, *bat, dat, fat, gat*. This strategy results in a string of responses that includes nonwords as well as words. By definition, however, a lexical search strategy can only result in word responses. Research findings have shown that normally developing children produce a mixture of words and nonwords on rhyme production tasks. This suggests that they are not totally reliant on a lexical search strategy (Wells, Stackhouse and Vance, 1996).

Comparisons between rhyme tasks

Normally developing children perform at a similar level across a range of input rhyme detection tasks regardless of whether these tasks comprise words or nonwords or are presented verbally or through pictures (Vance, Stackhouse and Wells, 1994). In contrast, children with speech and/or literacy difficulties have performed differently across tasks depending on the type of word stimuli or mode of presentation used.

In analysing the normal profile of performance on rhyme tasks in a group of children aged 3–7 years, it was found that some of the younger children were able to produce some rhyming responses on a rhyme production task. However, they were unable to judge whether two words rhymed or to detect which two of three words rhymed. These results suggest that rhyme production is more automatic than rhyme judgement or detection. The input rhyme tasks require a more conscious level of metaphonological awareness which these younger children did not have. Indeed, the reverse profile of judging/detecting rhyme without being able to produce rhyming words was not typical of the normally developing children in this group. All the 7-year-old children were proficient at rhyme production, with only occasional non-rhyming responses being given.

This is in marked contrast to data collected from children with speech and literacy difficulties who often show persisting difficulties with rhyme production even though they perform at ceiling on tasks of rhyme judgement and detection. The following examples illustrate the rhyme production skills of three children with speech and literacy difficulties. Their responses illustrate that although some rhyme production skill was present, it was limited in both range of response and strategies utilized.

Case 1

Richard was a dyslexic boy aged 11;8 years, with associated speech and language problems (see Stackhouse and Wells 1991 for a full account of his difficulties). When asked to produce a rhyme string to target words he gave the following responses:

Target	Response
hat	mat
key	me
draw	more
shell	mell

Although he could produce some rhyming responses these were limited to one per target with the use of only one onset: 'm'. The strategy of using a limited number of onsets is not uncommon in younger normally developing children, but it is atypical of a child of Richard's age. Therefore, although Richard demonstrated some rhyme skill, speech processing difficulties were militating against fluent and flexible rhyme production.

His case highlights the need to go beyond right/wrong scoring of children's responses when assessing older children with literacy problems. Qualitative comparisons with responses from normally developing children can also be very helpful when planning remediation programmes.

Case 2

Mark, aged 7;8 years, had received speech and language therapy when younger but no longer had any obvious speech and language difficulties. However, his responses on a rhyme production task were as follows:

Target	*Response*
coat	coat peg
	coat lot
purse	purse money
	purse bag
sock	sock ve lock
	sock leet
	sock lack
	sock back

Evidently Mark relied on a semantic strategy to produce his responses. These findings suggest that Mark's earlier speech and language difficulties had only resolved superficially. He still had underlying speech processing difficulties that would be detrimental to his literacy development.

Case 3

Zoe was 9;8 years, and although her speech was intelligible, there were still traces of an earlier severe speech disorder. She had marked difficulties with spelling. Her responses to a rhyme production task were as follows:

Stimulus	*Response*
coat	coat
	coat a loat a putty tot
	coat the pot the wotty totty
sock	sock pock silly old tock
	sock tock pack too
	sock loo goolie goo
cat	cat valpy tat
	cat pat vallie voo
	cat vat vallie voo
	cat boo diddly voo

Zoe was using a frame in which to fit her rhyme responses. This strategy was found in younger normally developing children, but it reduced the accuracy of the rhyme production response and was clearly inappropriate for a 9-year-old (Wells, Stackhouse and Vance, 1996).

The children's range of rhyme production errors shown above suggests that rhyme production is a persisting difficulty in children with speech and literacy problems. Rhyme production tasks have proved most useful when trying to identify underlying speech processing problems.

Speech Production

Speech problems in children can result from a number of different speech processing deficits. Measures of speech production provide information about the nature of the child's spoken and written difficulties. Sometimes a child's speech production skills can indicate specific sources of spelling errors. For example, inaccurate or imprecise phonological representations may be the source of both speech and spelling errors (as in the case of Thomas, described earlier). Other spelling errors may be the result of difficulties with speech rehearsal. This is particularly evident in children with developmental verbal dyspraxia who have inconsistent speech output (see Stackhouse, this volume). Comparing a child's performance across tasks of speech production within a psycholinguistic framework allows the underlying speech processing deficits to be identified.

Children with speech processing difficulties may be able to supply fairly accurate productions of short and simple words provided these contain a limited number of speech sounds to be sequenced. However, increasing word length can expose the child with less efficient skills who has developed strategies for coping with short words. Thus, suitably taxing stimuli must be used to assess speech production adequately, particularly as the child gets older and becomes more intelligible.

Naming

Children are often asked to name pictures in order to collect information about their speech production. Such assessment may use standardized procedures, such as the *Edinburgh Articulation Test* (Anthony, Bogle, Ingram, et al., 1971), or informal sets of pictures. In order to name pictures, the child must access his or her own phonological representation and motor programme (the blueprint of the syllable structure of the word and the order in which sounds occur) for the target since the examiner does not produce the word first. Errors on a naming test may therefore arise at the level of the representations or somewhere along the output side of the model presented in Figure 4.1. By following Locke's (1980) procedure outlined above (see pp. 51–2, 'auditory discrimination tasks using pictures'), the examiner can establish the precise level of deficit. If the child consistently rejects his or her own naming error as being an incorrect pronunciation of the word, then it can be assumed that the phonological representation is intact but that the source of the speech production difficulty is occurring at some level of speech output processing. If the child accepts his or her naming error as being the correct pronunciation of the word when it is spoken back to him, this indicates that the child's phonological representation is not accurate and may be directly related to the mispronunciations.

Repetition tasks

Ability to repeat words also provides useful information about the proficiency of a child's speech processing skills. In contrast to the naming task above, the child is less reliant on his own phonological representations since the examiner provides the target to be repeated. In the most basic repetition task the child is asked to repeat familiar words. If the target word is recognized as a known word then the child can utilize an already assembled motor programme to produce that word.

In order to examine the child's ability to assemble a new motor programme, nonwords can be presented for repetition. If the nonword contains the same consonants as a word, example, *brish/brush*, or if the consonants are closely matched with those of a word in terms of phonetic similarity and difficulty, example, *gloguz/crocus* (Ryder, 1991), then the child's performance on nonword repetition can be directly compared with his or her performance on word repetition. This allows the different processing demands of the two tasks to be used to establish if the child has specific output difficulties at the motor programming level.

Clinical evidence suggests that a number of children with speech and/or literacy problems have particular difficulty with nonword repetition that is not evident in their production of words. It has been argued that nonword repetition is a task requiring well-developed working memory (Gathercole and Baddeley, 1993). Indeed, the child needs to remember the structural sequence of the nonword in order to repeat it. However, there are other speech processing demands to consider. The child must be able to perceive and discriminate the components of the nonword. This input information is then used to establish a new motor programme on which the speech output will be based. Snowling and Hulme (1994) summarize this process as follows: 'children's skill in repeating nonwords might usefully be considered as an index of their language learning skill since it requires mapping speech inputs onto outputs.'

Nonword repetition therefore taps a range of skills involved in new word learning. As with rhyme production, nonword repetition is a persisting difficulty for children with speech and/or literacy problems. Poor performance on nonword repetition is indicative of speech processing difficulty. It is a particularly useful assessment for older children who do not have obvious speech production difficulties.

Comparisons between speech production tasks

These three speech production tasks, naming, word repetition, and nonword repetition, have been used to investigate children with speech disorders (Bryan and Howard, 1992; Stackhouse and Snowling, 1992b; Williams and Chiat, 1993). To make sense of the findings from these procedures it is important to understand how normally developing children perform across these tasks.

One hundred normally developing children, in the age range of 3–7 years, were given tasks of naming, word and nonword repetition (Vance, Stackhouse and Wells, 1995). Matched stimuli were used to allow direct comparison across performance on the tasks. The same words were used for naming and for word repetition and the nonwords were matched with the words by keeping the consonants the same and changing the vowels, for example, *brush/brish, toilet/tailet, caterpillar/kiterpallor*. Words of increasing length were used to allow more subtle output processing difficulties to be revealed. There was a clear developmental progression. Performance increased with age and there was a significant effect of word-length, with more errors being made on the longer words. The normally developing children made significantly fewer errors when repeating words compared with naming pictures. Any repetition task relies on how well the child hears the word or nonword. Occasionally a normally developing child mistook a word he heard for another word, such as *jelly* repeated as *jenny*. This illustrates how, if input processing is a major difficulty for a child, performance on naming may be better than on word repetition.

The normally developing children made significantly more errors in repeating nonwords than words. This suggests that it is not diagnostically significant if a child has more difficulty repeating nonwords. Rather, it is the size of the discrepancy between word and nonword repetition that is critical (the normally developing children involved in this study were about 10 per cent better at word than nonword repetition). This illustrates an important principle of testing within the psycholinguistic framework: no test should be carried out in isolation since an accurate diagnosis can only be made by comparing performance across tasks.

Zoe's responses on a rhyme production task were shown in the rhyme skills section (Case 3). Although her speech was intelligible and she was in a mainstream primary school, she was showing marked literacy difficulties. When given speech tasks comprising matched words and nonwords (Ryder, 1991), Zoe produced 17/24 correct repetitions on the word task but only 8/24 correct on the nonword task. This showed that although Zoe could produce well practised words correctly, she still had marked difficulty assembling motor programmes for new words. This not only had an effect on her speech output but also prevented Zoe from using speech rehearsal effectively for practising the segmentation of words for reading and spelling.

Profiles of Phonological Processing

The discussion of different levels of speech processing in this chapter makes clear that it is useful to include a range of different tasks of auditory discrimination, rhyme and speech production when assessing children suspected of having literacy difficulties. The ways in which the demands of different tasks rely on different levels of processing have been described. The importance of using both word and nonword stimuli, of presenting stimuli visually and verbally, and of always comparing performance on one task with performance on another has been emphasized. The presentation of pictures requires the child to use his or her own phonological representations in processing. In contrast, when stimuli comprise spoken words, the child can use the adult's model to complete the task. Use of words in discrimination and repetition tasks allows the child to use existing semantic, phonological and orthographic representations for support. This support is not available when nonwords are used. The use of complex stimuli has been advocated, particularly for older children and those with less marked speech processing difficulties who may have developed strategies to process short and simple words competently.

The psycholinguistic assessment framework outlined by Stackhouse and Wells (1993, and forthcoming) provides a structure in which findings can be interpreted in order to build up a profile of an individual child's phonological processing skills. Different patterns of speech processing deficits are possible between children. Identification of the level of processing deficit and breakdown allows therapy and teaching to be targeted specifically at the child's difficulty. The psycholinguistic approach to assessment also has the advantage of allowing a child's relative strengths in the speech processing chain to be identified and utilized within a remediation programme.

Chapter 5
Assessing Language Difficulties in Children and Adolescents

Hanna Klein

Some children and adolescents fail to reach their potential at school. Their ability to use language creatively and to understand abstract concepts to solve problems is limited. They may be able to use visual cues to make sense of classroom material, but when faced with new topics and challenging ideas they begin to falter. Suddenly their good practical skills are not enough to mask an inability to cope when concrete cues are reduced or removed.

As such children get older, the ability to decode spoken and written language at a higher level is necessary if they are to manage in different environments. Speed and accuracy in making inferences and solving problems becomes paramount for achieving a measure of academic competence and social success. They need to listen to, absorb, and use different forms of language in the classroom, at the dinner table, while playing computer games, when they watch television, and when they visit museums and the cinema. School texts often contain abstract data written in complex sentences, with unfamiliar technical vocabulary or idiomatic language (Noordman and Vonk, 1992; Oakhill and Garman, 1988). Many of these children have learned to read late, and have reading comprehension difficulties (see Stothard, this volume). This chapter focuses on the language problems encountered by the school-age child and examines how these might be assessed.

Information Gathering

When assessing a child with a language difficulty it is important to gather information from a variety of sources including parents or carers, teachers and other professionals.

Family history

It is often noted that there is a family history of speech and language delay or difficulty in children who present with language problems. Frequently a member of the family may have a specific language impairment (Bishop, North and Donlan, 1995), have fluency difficulties (Gopnick and Crago, 1991; Wolk, Conture and Edwards, 1990) or be dyslexic (Galaburda, 1993; Snowling, 1987).

Consider Martin who at the age of 10 years presented with severe behaviour problems. Martin had been seen by clinical psychologists since the age of 2 for temper tantrums and very poor attention. He had always been difficult to manage at school, and at the initial meeting was 'on review' for sniffing petrol. His parents attended the assessment with him to find out whether his problems could be attributed to an underlying language disorder. Martin's mother chatted fluently with his sister Amy, aged 6, while Martin's father sat very quietly. Martin's mother usually answered for Martin's father, and spoke openly about his 'poor talking'. Martin's father's school history was described as 'dodgy' and he had left school without qualifications. His sister had been 'dyslexic', and had 'never got very far'. There was a family history of language and learning difficulties, and the mother's nephew, who was 5 years old, was in a special language unit.

An in-depth knowledge of the degree of severity of the different types of associated linguistic disorders present in any one family can reveal the nature of the difficulties a child is experiencing and also the environment to which the child is exposed.

Liaison with teachers and other professionals.

Where possible, it is helpful to see the child at school. It is also advisable to read school reports in advance in order to be aware of the specific academic and social difficulties faced by the child. Collaboration between the speech and language therapist and teacher is crucial throughout the referral and management process (Wright, 1992). It can also be informative to consult with other members of the educational and health-care teams. In practice key members tend to be educational psychologists, occupational therapists (especially where the child has associated motor problems), paediatricians and ENT surgeons. Often children with language difficulties have suffered from recurrent bouts of otitis media. Parents are often reassured that an intermittent conductive hearing loss caused by disease of the middle ear does not in itself cause the language impairment, nor the specific learning difficulties which may subsequently ensue

(Bishop and Edmundson, 1986; Grievink, Peters, Van Bon, et al., 1993; Paul, Lynn and Lohr-Flanders, 1993). A family history of speech or language problems, dyslexia or non-fluency is a more important predictor of poor language skills than intermittent hearing loss alone (Bishop, North and Donlan, 1995).

A Protocol for Assessing Language Development in Children in Mainstream School

There are numerous standardized language assessments available for school-age children, some British but the majority American. Standardized tests are important to establish objective measures of the child's language skills (Gillon and Dodd, 1994; Klein, 1985; Webster, 1994). However, structured observations can also be very helpful when investigating language functioning in the school-age child.

Take Daniel who was referred at 10 years of age with no significant medical history. There was no known family history of a written or spoken language disorder. Daniel was good at sport, loved building with Lego and clay, but had a long history of expressive language delay and reading and spelling problems. His school reports constantly noted that he lacked concentration, was poor at mathematics, had limited ability to work with abstract concepts, his written work was slow and inconsistent, reading was laboured, and he often showed signs of aggressive behaviour. On the WISC-III (Wechsler, 1992) his Verbal IQ was 85 and his Performance IQ 103.

Daniel was asked why he had been asked to see the speech and language therapist. He said, 'Cos I'm stupid at school and forget things.' Daniel's parents were concerned that he did not remember material learned for school tests, and that he did not seem to 'cotton on' like other children. He was morose and sullen and his mother described his speech as 'monosyllabic, if we're lucky!'. The speech and language therapist hoped that the group meeting would enable each parent to obtain a useful overview of the current status of Daniel's ability to understand and use language effectively in the classroom and the playground.

At the first meeting it is difficult to know just what linguistic difficulties will be found. The following sequence of tests are useful as a preliminary guide in determining where the child's linguistic strengths and weaknesses might lie. The speech and language therapist can use the data from these tests to decide what linguistic deficits require further investigation and how they may be remediated.

Knowledge of automatic sequences

Even though Daniel was 10-years-old, he did not know his address, his telephone number, nor the date of his birthday. He could not say the months of the year, nor recite the more common arithmetic tables.

Telling a story from a sequence of pictures

Daniel was asked to sort a series of seven picture-story cards into a meaningful sequence. When placed in the correct order these depicted: *Going to the Dentist.* He was able to sort the cards rapidly, but the story he told was pedestrian, punctuated by fillers, showed no evidence of inference and ended rather abruptly:

D: at the, the, ton–dentist. He sits wif his mum.
They come to get him. (Long silence).

SLT: Who?

D: The lady in the white, uh, er, the white coat. He sits on the high seat. They open, er, his mouth. (Long silence).

SLT: Why?

D: They look. Its OK. They go home.

Daniel was unable to say what might have happened before or after the events shown and found it difficult to infer the reason for regular visits to the dentist. Mother reported that Daniel had only recently completed a similar topic in class! When Daniel wrote down his story, the speech and language therapist noted that his written language also showed evidence of poor grammar and syntax and limited vocabulary:

> The tentos
>
> One day there was a man Boy and a lady they are sitting in a dentos and they are reading. then a lady came in and said are you ready and then his mum gets and she says yes he is ready and then she say come here.

Receptive vocabulary

Vocabulary acquisition is one of the best indicators of school success and one of the most important contributors to measures of intelligence. The *British Picture Vocabulary Scales* (Dunn, Dunn, Whetton, et al., 1982) is a test designed to measure receptive vocabulary by means of single words graded in difficulty. The child is shown a page with four pictures on it and is asked to point to the picture that best shows the meaning of a given word. For example, the picture items for the word STEAM are: *lightning, smoke, steam* and *fire*. The test is discontinued when 6 out of 8 consecutive words are mis-identified. When Daniel started to falter he pointed to: *smoke* for STEAM; *cactus* for SEED; *horn* for TUSK and *beehive* for BLOOM.

Children, like Daniel, whose vocabulary age on the *British Picture Vocabulary Scales* is two years lower or more than their chronological age, may experience great difficulty understanding much of what is spoken or written about in the classroom.

Word retrieval

It is important to investigate expressive as well as receptive vocabulary. The *Test of Word Finding* (German, 1989) is a test standardized in America on normally developing children (age range: 6;6 years to 12;11 years). It measures accuracy in naming and is divided into five sections:

Picture naming for nouns

The child is shown a picture (such as an electric drill) and asked to name it. Accuracy and latency of response are measured. Each correct response is credited by one point and each incorrect is fully transcribed. The tester also counts silently the response time taken by the child, and notes whether it is more or less than the four-second cut-off time allowed. Daniel named DRILL as *screwdriver;* PATCH as *stitch*; and BINOCULARS as *microscope.*

In addition to these semantic errors Daniel also made speech errors. For example he stumbled over the word: DOMINOES pronouncing it as *don-dom-donimoes*. Other speech errors included: OCTATUS for *octopus; calv* for CALF; *arkologist* for ARCHAEOLO-GIST; and *vocabablry* for VOCABULARY.

Sentence completion naming

In this section the child listens to a sentence and is asked to supply the missing word. For example: 'The yellow part of an egg is the ————.' To which Daniel responded *chicken*. Overall, he needed more time than was allowed to complete some of the sentences.

Description naming

The description naming subtest requires the child to supply a single word in response to a description of an object. For example, the tester asks: 'What floats in the sky, may be full of rain, and is grey or white?' Answer: *clouds*. Daniel found this very difficult, and either responded with one of the stimuli words, for example, *rain* or an associated word, for example, *weather*.

Picture naming for verbs

In picture naming for verbs the child is shown, for example, a picture of a person pouring, and is asked, 'What is she doing?' Daniel completed this section with no errors.

Category naming

In the category naming subtest, the child is shown three pictures, for example: APPLES, PEARS, BANANAS, and is asked to give one word that could be used for all three, i.e., *fruit*. Daniel found this section difficult and for the more complex items he named one of the stimulus words rather than supplying a collective word. For example, he responded *pills* instead of *medicine* for the picture sequence: PILLS; PILL CONTAINER; COUGH MIXTURE.

A comprehension assessment is also included in the *Test of Word Finding* to check the child's knowledge of the target word. This enables the clinician to differentiate between a comprehension and/or expressive difficulty. Daniel showed no comprehension errors for the stimuli on this test. However, by the end of the test it was clear that Daniel had significant naming difficulties.

Receptive and expressive semantics

The *Test of Word Knowledge* is designed to:

> assess a student's skill in the reception and expression of an important component of language – semantics, or the meaning system... students who evidence difficulty with semantic development will be severely hampered in both communication and learning. (Wiig and Secord, 1992)

Daniel had particular difficulty with the following subtests:

Word opposites

This subtest is used to test a child's knowledge of how words may be related. A stimulus word, for example: AFTER, is given. The child then chooses the most appropriate word from three or four further words which are printed on the stimulus card, for example: *during, before, earlier, next.*

This subtest has an 8-year start level and Daniel had problems with it right from the beginning. He was unable to choose which was the opposite of FRONT from: *back, middle, over*; and of TOGETHER from: *along, inside, apart, here.*

Word definitions

In this subtest the child has to define target words. Daniel was asked to tell the speech and language therapist all he could about the following:

Target	Response
apple	to eat with
bird	aminal (sic) that flies around in the sky
aquarium	where you see all the fishes in the water
nephew	a relative, someone you know
atlas	a Europe – countries–in all different colours

Multiple contexts

In this subtest the child must show the ability to describe two different contexts for a single word by producing the target word in two different sentences. Items include: POUND, BARK, HURDLE, MANUAL. Although Daniel appeared to understand the demonstration items, he was unable to express how one word may mean two things. For example, for BAT he responded with one sentence only: *What you hit.*

Figurative usage

To demonstrate understanding of figurative usage, the child needs to give a simple explanation of proverbs or idioms. Daniel's use of figurative language was very poor. He was unable to answer any of the questions posed, even though four possible choices were given for the response, for example:

'Which one tells about someone not being noisy?':

a) busy as a bee   b) quiet as a mouse
c) sly as a fox   d) eats like a bird

Daniel's classteacher had reported that inflexibility, or concreteness in his comprehension and use of language seriously hampered Daniel's ability to deal with subjects that were becoming more abstract and inferential. This was particularly apparent in mathematical problems and topics that required an understanding of how different areas of study could come together, say, in the form of a project.

Naming – categorization and classification

To investigate Daniel's difficulties further, the speech and language therapist gave Daniel colour photographs of familiar high frequency objects to sort into appropriate semantic categories. Daniel named some of the pictures incorrectly, although he had pointed to the appropriate pictures when they were named by the speech and language therapist:

Target	Response
tomato	onion
salt	sugar
a glass of beer	cup of beer
broom	a sweeper
radiator	an oven
barrel	a round water can
headphones	music for your ears

Daniel's approach to this task revealed that he seemed to have a visual rather than a semantic rationale for sorting the cards. He stated that HEADPHONES and RADIATOR go together *because they are both in the living room* and that APPLES, SAUSAGES and CHICKEN go together *cause my Mum packs them in the fridge together.*

In later sessions, using school texts as a source of specific vocabulary, Daniel's serious expressive naming difficulties were confirmed. His error rate increased as he was asked to respond quickly or to novel material.

Naming difficulties in discourse

The standardized tests discussed above provide a useful screening device for detecting word-finding problems at the single word level. However, it is also necessary to assess if there are any specific retrieval or word-finding difficulties in spoken discourse, this being a less constrained situation than a single-word response paradigm. German (1991) has designed such a test which samples ongoing language behaviour in a variety of contexts. The language samples are recorded and scored for three different linguistic situations.

Daniel's responses correlated closely with responses made on single word tests, and also confirmed reports from his parents and teacher that he failed to use language to manipulate his environment successfully. In fact, he had few friends and played with children who were younger than him. He could not use language to negotiate effectively with his parents, teachers or peer group. Daniel had begun to be excluded, perhaps unwittingly, from ongoing social action. These difficulties which often co-occur with behavioural disorders may be a consequence of linguistic exclusion (Hummel and Prizant, 1993; Williams and McGee, 1994).

Classroom observations

Each child presents with an individual profile of language difficulties. A programme was therefore designed for Daniel which took account of his strengths and weaknesses. The programme relied on linguistic material found in the classroom. Textbooks, videos and classroom objects formed the primary materials for planning ongoing therapy for individual sessions as well as for supporting Daniel in the classroom.

The Ladybird book: *Living Things* (Showell, 1975) was one resource being used in the classroom. Daniel brought this to his session with his speech and language therapist. A passage was read to Daniel, while he studied the print and the very clear colour drawings on the relevant pages. He was told to think carefully about the beginning and end of the story and how and why certain things might be happening. A framework was given to Daniel to try to help his comprehension and recall. The topic on the page was discussed, and then Daniel was asked to tell the speech and language therapist in his own words what he had remembered. This is what he said:

> Nature.Wildlife – protecting it. Pond life – all fish go – come in.
> Flowers, snails, somefings what come from a different paf – like butterflies, birds, penguins.

Daniel's output was slow and laboured, and bore almost no resemblance to the text that had been read to him or to the ensuing discussion. However, it indicated that he was very responsive to the visual details on the page. Unfortunately, these were often unconnected to the overall meaning conveyed by the written text. Many children with language disorders seem unable to link visual detail and verbal flow. For example, Daniel looked at the drawings of the pond, the snails, the plants, but failed to make the inferential leap from the plants to their role in providing oxygen for the fishes, even though these constructions were implicit in the written text. He responded to what he saw; inference had not yet developed. Continuous collaboration between the class teacher and the speech and language therapist enabled Daniel to begin to access the curriculum more meaningfully, and to become a more effective member of his peer group (Wiig and Semel, 1990; Wright, 1992).

Summary of Daniel's difficulties

The assessment protocol outlined here comprised standardized as well as less formal procedures. Data were collected from a variety of sources. The overall findings of the assessment showed that Daniel had a number of difficulties. The programme offered took into account the following areas with particular reference to Daniel's classroom needs:

- comprehension of spoken vocabulary
- word-finding
- comprehension of syntax
- conversation skills
- quick and accurate problem solving
- making inferences
- self-esteem

Working With Older Children

Increasingly, adolescents with language difficulties are coming to the attention of special needs departments in mainstream school (Wiig, 1995). Their language problems may not be so apparent in everyday conversation but can be a serious handicap to their educational progress.

John was a 14-year-old boy who had difficulties comprehending spoken language. His ability to keep up in class was seriously compromised by his poor attention and lack of interest. Consistently poor academic results had previously been ascribed to a problematic home life. As school work became more demanding, John's teachers and parents became concerned that he was rapidly losing interest in classroom activities. He had stopped reading for pleasure; project work was disorganized and brief; his essays were simplistic; he was finding it difficult to keep up with mathematics and to master French.

John scored four-and-a-half years below age level on the *British Picture Vocabulary Scales*. His reading was also four years behind. On the *Auditory Synthesis* subtest of the *The Fullerton Language Test for Adolescent* (Thorum, 1986), he was unable to blend phonemes and syllables into their constituent words. He also had great difficulty explaining idioms, for example:

Idiom	*Explanation*
take a joke	you give it to someone
see eye to eye	see them close up
runs in the family	like your family can have a disease

John's poor language skills and in particular his inability to maintain a topic in conversation, meant that he could not tune into the levels of language used by his family, teachers and friends. He missed a great deal of important spoken information about what was, and was not, acceptable behaviour. In fact John was getting into trouble at school, and on the streets. Structured conversations, using videos and tape recordings about specific situations were used to help John begin to understand the nuances, the unspoken rules of discourse, which young people of his age use, for example, topics such as drink/drive, AIDS and bullying. In addition, the speech and language therapist paired John with a volunteer from his class, and together they discussed issues such as truancy, special friendships, acting out (after Rustin and Purser, 1984). The therapist acted as a moderator in this discussion. In addition there was close collaboration among all the professionals working with John. Enhancing his level of literacy was a major aim, not only to improve his ability to access classroom texts and public notices, but also to bolster his feelings of self-worth (Williams and McGee, 1994).

Adolescents who stammer

Some adolescents who stammer also have language problems (Nippold, 1990; Wolk, et al., 1990). Linguistic assessments of the spoken and written language of older stammerers often reveal disordered development of language form and content (Boberg, 1993; Rustin and Klein, 1991). It is essential that any child who stammers has a full language and literacy assessment even if the nonfluency is only mild.

Adolescents with language difficulties who need support for vocational training

Keith was an adolescent who had many complex social and educational needs. When he was 16-years-old, Keith's secondary school felt he could only proceed to specialized vocational training if he received continued support from a speech and language therapist. Primary schooling had been in a local school, but with no special input. From the age of 12, Keith attended a language unit for older children, based on a statement of need, where 'satisfactory progress' had been recorded.

Some adolescents and young adults who have a language disorder show aptitude for creative, practical and/or spatial skills. Many are good at sport, computing, art, construction, car engines, drama or commerce. None of these were reported as strengths in Keith's case. However, he did enjoy football, swimming and playing games on the computer.

Both parents were present throughout the assessment session. Keith settled well, was co-operative, but had difficulty following the conversation between his parents and the speech and language therapist. His performance on the *British Picture Vocabulary Scales* was extremely low (centile:1, standard score:62). There was therefore cause for concern about the amount of new information which Keith would be able to listen to, store and integrate when training for a vocation. Further subtests from the *Fullerton Language Test for Adolescents* (Thorum, 1986), *Test of Word Knowledge* (Wiig and Secord, et al., 1992) and the *Test of Adolescent Language* (Hammill, Brown and Larsen, 1987) confirmed the above observations of Keith's difficulty with understanding complex linguistic structures.

The Fullerton Language Test for Adolescents (Thorum, 1986)

The subtest Divergent Production assesses the ability to name at speed items belonging to five specific categories, for example: sports, subjects offered in school. Keith started off with one or two appropriate items per category but could proceed no further.

The Test of Word Knowledge (Wiig and Secord, 1992)

The supplementary subtest of conjunctions (for ages 8–17 years) was given. Keith was asked to read a short paragraph and to choose from a list the missing word which would tell 'about the relationship between the ideas' in the paragraph. For example:

The sun rises every morning.
It happens (_____) you are there to see it.

Choose from: whether or not
              so that
              now that
              as long as

Keith could read the paragraph, but chose *so that* as the correct response.

The Test of Adolescent Language – 2 (Hammill, et al., 1987)

Keith was given Subtest II which assesses Listening/Grammar. He had to listen to three sentences, decide which two were the closest in meaning to each other, and then mark the two items on his response form with a X. For example:

A. If you work slowly, you make fewer mistakes
B. Slow work may mean fewer mistakes
C. Fewer mistakes make you work slowly.

Although he was shown exactly what was required, Keith was unable to complete more than two out of 35 items. He could read the sentences but not detect the differences. He said that the sentences all meant the same thing.

In addition to these tests of understanding a number of tests of expressive language were administered.

Expressive language

Keith was unable to tell the speech and language therapist why he had come to see her, and had little expressive language to discuss issues like the options of future training and employment, and how he might like to spend any money he earned. He felt it might be rather nice to work in a shop, a supermarket, or the local garden centre, but seemed to have no strong interests at all.

To assess any word-finding difficulties the *Test of Adolescent Word Finding* (German, 1990) and the *Graded Naming Test* (McKenna and Warrington, 1983) were used. Keith found these tests very difficult to complete. He made both speech (SUBMARINE → *sumbarine,* PROPELLOR → *popeller*) and lexical (UNICORN → *capricorn*) errors.

The following word definitions he produced illustrate his restricted output:

Word	*Definition*
steam	watery – (gesture) – it boils itself – and the water starts bubbling and all the steam comes up and turns into water
seed	something to plant with and the root comes up out of the shell
swamp	all-um-all grass, trees, dirty
pyramid	got three sides, where Pharaohs are kept in the pyramid

Keith obviously had many levels of difficulty both with the comprehension and expression of language. To get a clearer picture of the extent of his difficulties, parts of the CELF-R (Semel, Wiig and Secord, 1987) were presented. This test assesses receptive and expressive language function in a population aged 5;00 –16;11 years of age. The normative data were collected in the United States but the test has been adapted for use in the UK (Klein, Constable, Goulandris, Stackhouse and Tarplee, 1994).

The following subtests of the CELF-R (UK) were presented to Keith:

Linguistic concepts

This assesses the ability to interpret oral directions. Keith was required to follow various commands which assessed coordination (point to the blue line and the red line); temporal sequencing (after you point to a yellow line, point to a red line); conditional (instead of pointing to a blue line, point to the red line) and quantitative categories (point to all the red lines, and all but one of the yellow lines). He managed well until the complexity and the length of the utterance increased when he began to fail; scoring only 10/20 correct.

Formulated sentences

Keith was asked to listen to a word and to use it in a suitable sentence. Where possible he was to use an accompanying picture as an aid. Here are some of his responses:

Word	Response
Either	They either choose what's on the menu.
Neither	Neither the shoes don't fit.
And/Because	The man stopped because...stops the traffic coming past and the men are working on the building site.
Whatever/Until	The car must be fixed until tomorrow whatever is wrong with it.

Sentence assembly

In this subtest, printed words that make up a sentence are presented in the wrong order, for example: *the girl; the boy; a letter; send; did*. The sentences increase in complexity. Although Keith could read all the words by themselves, he had difficulty arranging them into meaningful sentences. He responded correctly to only 12 out of the 22 sentences.

Keith scored three to four years below age level on all of the standardized tests given him. It was concluded that Keith would need further in-depth assessments of his specific comprehension and expressive difficulties, and in particular, how these deficits might prevent him from accessing a chosen vocation. Close collaboration with professionals would be essential to achieve any success for

Keith. Adolescents with language difficulties often benefit from the joint advice of the educational psychologist, the classteacher and the speech and language therapist on which school subjects would be best for them. For example, many adolescents with a language difficulty are able to do well at GCSE if they take art, sciences (as long as there are good laboratories for practical demonstrations), geography, design and technology, and computing. Study skills training (Mitchell, 1994), sensitive career counselling, and continued linguistic support are essential if these adolescents are to achieve their maximum potential. The continued support of the speech and language therapist is often crucial for the adolescent and young adult so that they can continue to access the specialist language of their chosen field.

Conclusions

The case descriptions presented here are not meant to be single case studies or to explain different levels of psycholinguistic breakdown. Rather, they have evolved as a means of illustrating the range of assessments available for older children. These tests provide a strategy for drawing up a language profile as a basis for a management programme which takes into account a child's strengths and weaknesses. Even subtle language difficulties can affect performance in mainstream school. Comprehensive assessments of a child's language needs can be carried out effectively by the speech and language therapist working in collaboration with the classroom teacher. Treatment programmes will emerge from specific assessment results, but the process is circular:

'for diagnosis ends when therapy ends' (Frederic Darley, 1964).

Chapter 6
Assessing Reading and Spelling Skills

Nata K. Goulandris

Learning to read and spell is relatively effortless for most children in a classroom. However, the underlying linguistic and cognitive skills which are needed before learning can take place are numerous and complex. It is, therefore, not surprising that a number of children are unable to learn these skills in the normal way. A child whose progress in reading and spelling is slow by comparison to the others in the class, or even when compared with the child's ability in other areas of the curriculum, needs to be assessed.

Assessment is *not* simply a process of identification but is a vital prerequisite of effective teaching, enabling the teacher to pinpoint precise strengths and weaknesses and so provide appropriate learning experiences and instruction for that individual. By taking the time to assess a number of different reading and spelling skills and analysing the results with care, the learning process can be facilitated as effectively as possible. The purpose of assessment is:

1.   To determine whether an individual has reading and/or spelling difficulties. Are this child's literacy skills significantly behind other children of the same age? Standardized tests help us to decide whether a child is only somewhat poorer (as a rule of thumb, 9 months below the mean) or significantly below its peers (more than 18 months if the child is less than 8-years-old or 24 months or more from 8 years onwards).

2.   To undertake a detailed analysis of the individual's current literacy skills in order to construct a profile of the child's strengths and weaknesses;

3.   To establish a baseline for continuous monitoring;

4.   To determine the most effective type of remediation so that teaching and learning can be coordinated, with teaching firmly based on an individual's cognitive and literacy profile.

However, in order to assess literacy skills competently, we need to consider two sorts of question. First, how do children who are *not* having difficulties learn to read and spell? It is important to adopt a developmental model of reading and spelling so that we can compare the performance of this child with that of normally developing readers. The more explicit and detailed the models, the easier it will be for us to pinpoint this child's difficulties in relation to children who are progressing along normal lines. Second, what is the relationship between this individual's cognitive skills and performance on reading and spelling tests? Does the learner have cognitive skills which are not being used? What cognitive skills need to be developed in order to improve literacy in both the short and the long term?

The Development of Reading and Spelling

The two different models of literacy discussed in this chapter provide alternative perspectives on the development of reading and spelling, giving insights into the way children's strategies shift with the passage of time and improving skills.

Frith (1985) has proposed three phases of literacy development: *logographic, alphabetic* and *orthographic*. During the *logographic phase* the child's word recognition is based on partial cues, often simple first letter cues, and reading is consequently inaccurate because so little letter information is taken into account. Picture and contextual cues provide additional information and for many beginners this may be the primary source of information about words. Spelling ability is rudimentary at this stage, consisting primarily of words learned by heart and recalled as a collection of arbitrary shapes.

The logographic phase is gradually superseded by the appearance of alphabetic strategies for spelling. The child who does not yet know the correct spelling, relies on knowledge of the word's pronunciation to construct a spelling (Read, 1986; Treiman, 1993) and the *alphabetic stage* is marked by the realization that a particular speech sound can be represented by a specific letter, for example, the initial sound in the words *snake, sit, sand* and *some* will be spelled with the letter *s*. Once this alphabetic principle has been grasped, the learner can begin to extrapolate information about the basic sound-letter mappings which form the basis of an alphabetic language, for example, the sound of [b] is represented by the letter *b*, the sound of [m] by the letter *m*, the sound of [ks] by the letter *x*. The use of sound-letter correspondences is gradually extended to reading and propels beginners into a more independent reading style, by enabling them to decode unfamiliar words.

However, alphabetic readers are restricted by their dependence on letter-by-letter decoding and are not yet aware that letter-sound rules may also be influenced by the position of the letter within a word. Their errors may include CITY → *kitty*, CENTRE → *kenter* [kentə], GEM → *guem* [gɛm] and GYM → *guim* [gɪm]. It is not until the commencement of the *orthographic phase*, that the reader becomes conscious of other equally important linguistic features which are represented by the English spelling system. At this point the reader recognizes that words can be subdivided into larger units such as common letter strings, -ing, -tion, -ture, prefixes such as auto-, hydro-, pseudo- and suffixes such as -graph and -phobia. Orthographic spelling is the final step of development and is characterized by precise knowledge of word spellings.

Alternative interactive theories of learning to read (Ehri, 1985; Hulme, Snowling and Quinlan, 1991; Seidenberg and McClelland, 1989) throw some doubt on the rigid sequence of stage models, suggesting instead that learning whole word spellings, sound-letter rules and spelling patterns may take place concurrently, with each type of information facilitating and promoting the development of the others. According to such models, learners generalize information about spelling-sound mappings continuously as they encounter new words. Since English is notorious for the unreliability of its spelling system, a beginner's initial attempts to understand such patterns are bound to be somewhat inaccurate and many previous conclusions about letter-sound mappings will require adaptation.

To take a hypothetical example, Harry aged 7, has read several early readers and has learned to recognize a number of words which are repeated frequently within these texts. Without realizing it, he has managed to detect some common patterns amongst the words he has already learned. For example, he perceives that *mum, mouse,* and *milk* all begin with the same sound and has linked this information successfully with the letter-sound [m]. He is therefore able to predict quite reliably that other unfamiliar words which start with *m* will begin with the same sound [m]. He has arrived at a similar conclusion for the letter *c* based on his encounters with the words *cat, caterpillar, can, cop* and *cup* but is bemused when he realises that in words such as *city, ice* or *bicycle* the letter *c* represents an altogether different sound, [s]. However, repeated exposure to the alternative sounds which the letter *c* represents, enables him to reformulate his understanding about the behaviour of the letter *c*, and the sounds which it can map. He will have to reconsider these conclusions later when he realizes that in some cases such as in the word *efficient*, the letters *ci* represent a different speech sound altogether *sh* [ʃ].

Interactive models suggest that the beginner reader may not just learn isolated letter-sound patterns but learns letter-sound mappings in the context of other letters. When Harry has come across more words containing *ci* or *ce* or *cy*, his experience of written language will enable him to incorporate additional information about the importance of letter position in phonological mapping, the possible influence of neighbouring letters, and how often these alternatives occur. This implicit, but nonetheless, extensive knowledge of more complex letter-sound mappings will enable him to differentiate words which contain *ce* and those which contain *ca*. In this kind of model there is therefore no distinction between the learning of whole words and the learning of spelling-sound rules. On the contrary, understanding of letter-sound mappings is a consequence of the child's familiarity with words. In turn, grasp of common sound-letter mappings enables the reader to recognize unfamiliar words more easily.

Both kinds of model have one fundamental similarity. They emphasize the importance of letter-sound mappings in the acquisition of literacy and stress that these serve as the framework upon which the more difficult and complex orthographic rules are based. According to the Frith model, a reader and speller needs to have alphabetic knowledge before the more complex orthographic knowledge can be learned. Frith's model of literacy development also highlights the fact that reading and spelling develop at different rates with each skill contributing to the evolution of the other; children first learn about sound-letter mappings through trying to figure out how to spell new words. Spelling therefore plays a particularly important role in literacy development by helping children to uncover the fundamental relationship between the individual speech sounds in words and the letters used to represent them.

Requisites of reading and spelling

Stage models of literacy development make explicit that the learning of reading and spelling requires different sets of cognitive abilities at different points of the acquisition process. If the requisite cognitive resources are not available, literacy skills will not be able to proceed along normal lines. Early logographic reading can be achieved using the visual recognition skills normally needed for ordinary object recognition tasks. Consequently, few children fail to achieve rudimentary word recognition although they may mistake words which resemble each other. Linguistic and cognitive skills also play an important role in this early learning period as they permit an inexperienced reader to determine the approximate meaning conveyed by a particular text.

In contrast, attaining alphabetic skills requires an array of specialized phonological skills. Initially, *phonological awareness*, the ability to detect similar speech sounds in words enables children to map sound segments onto written language. However, learning to read in turn engenders more advanced types of phonological awareness, as children become aware of and learn to manipulate different types of phonological units namely, syllables, onsets, rimes and phonemes. Awareness of phonemes, the smallest units of speech sounds which can change the meaning of a word (for example, [p] and [b] sounds in the words *pin* and *bin*) develops as a result of repeated attempts to map speech units to written words when trying to spell. Moreover, learning to delete a phoneme from the initial, middle or final segments of words allows children to manipulate word segments and identify words by analogy to familiar words, as for example, when reading *dread* by analogy to *bread*.

Children whose phonological skills are weak will not realize that some words begin with the same phoneme and will consequently be unable to understand the 'alphabetic principle' which underlies written language. These readers will therefore have great difficulty learning about sound-letter mappings because they fail to appreciate the phonological characteristics of words. Both models concur that children who do not learn letter-sounds mappings will have severe difficulties with some aspects of reading and spelling. This conclusion is supported by substantial research evidence demonstrating that individuals who have difficulty perceiving, comparing and identifying speech sounds in words, commonly referred to as phonological processing difficulties, are likely to have reading difficulties and extensive spelling problems (see Snowling, this volume).

Reading and Spelling Deficits in Children with Developmental Dyslexia

There are two basic profiles of developmental dyslexia with many gradations of severity: individuals with both reading and spelling problems and those whose difficulty lies primarily with spelling. The first and easiest to identify, is the learner with obvious reading and spelling difficulties. During the early school years reading tends to be slow and inaccurate, and unfamiliar words cannot be decoded but must be guessed. Phonological processing difficulties are usually at the root of these problems. Children with phonological problems have little sensitivity to the sound properties of language, do not learn letter-sound mappings as easily as phonologically competent children and therefore do not acquire decoding skills normally (see also Stackhouse, this volume). Writing in the early years of schooling is frequently indecipherable as the illustration in Figure 6.1 shows.

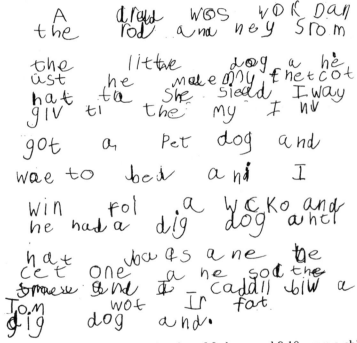

Figure 6.1: Example of handwriting from Mathew aged 9:10 years a child with specific learning difficulties

However, with exposure to print and specialist tuition, these children can often learn to read quite proficiently, especially if they have good visual memory to help them recognize words they have encountered frequently. The underlying problems with phonological processing may remain, although more difficult tasks are required to uncover them. Reading new words, decoding longer orthographically complex words and spelling remain problematic for the majority (Snowling, Goulandris and Defty, submitted).

The second group of dyslexic children, sometimes referred to as dysgraphics, appear to be competent readers but have inordinate difficulty with spelling. The underlying cognitive difficulties of this group are still not resolved. Many researchers have reported that dysgraphics continue to have underlying phonological deficits into adulthood although these difficulties are only evident in more demanding phonological tasks such as spoonerisms or repetition of polysyllabic, difficult to pronounce words and nonwords (Bruck, 1990; Perin, 1983). Problems with decoding persist although these are often masked by good compensatory strategies.

The third group whose difficulties do not appear to be accompanied by phonological deficits have been referred to as 'good readers/ poor spellers' (Frith, 1980) or Type B spellers (Frith,1985). These individuals seem to have achieved reasonably good alphabetic skills when reading but are unable to recall the letter-by-letter sequences of words that do not conform to regular spelling patterns. When assessing these individuals it is important to determine whether the individual's difficulties encompass both reading and spelling, or whether they are restricted to spelling.

Assessing Reading Skills

Reading consists of three quite different components or subskills: word recognition, decoding and comprehension. Individuals with reading problems may have difficulties in only one or in several of these components. In this chapter I will only discuss reading comprehension when it contributes to word recognition and decoding since detailed discussion of comprehension difficulties can be found in Stothard (this volume).

A comprehensive assessment of reading can be undertaken using the following tests:

1. A standardized single-word reading test.
2. A standardized text reading test.
3. A test of nonword reading.
4. A test of alphabet knowledge.

This battery of reading tests would take approximately half an hour to administer and could be undertaken in a single session or in several shorter ones, provided they are all administered within a month of each other.

Assessing word recognition

The ability to recognize words quickly and accurately, also referred to as lexical processing, is a hallmark of skilled reading. It has been suggested that familiar words or lexical items, are stored in a lexicon or mental word store. New words can be added to the lexicon if a skilled reader supplies the word or when the learner identifies it using contextual cues. Alternatively, the reader can use phonological reading strategies to sound out the word and identify it – a strategy which enables the child to become a more independent learner.

Although some influential educators have argued that reading is primarily a psycholinguistic process in which words are recognized through context (Goodman, 1967; Smith, 1971), there is convincing evidence that competent readers identify words at such a fast rate that they do not require the assistance of context to aid recognition. In contrast, many poor readers have difficulty establishing a reliable word recognition system. These children need to use context to supply more information about the word they are trying to recognize.

The best way to assess word recognition is by using a single-word reading test which precludes the use of psycholinguistic, pictorial and contextual cues. Children will normally attempt to use all possible cues when trying to read, particularly if reading does not come easily to them. Hence, a number of children appear to read proficiently but are unable to recognize the same words if they are presented out of context. Although it is customary to encourage beginners to read by guessing the content of books in the early years, such a strategy is self-defeating when it remains the primary strategy beyond the early stages.

A standardized single-word reading test will provide information about the child's performance in relation to its peers. (See Appendix 6.1 for a list of some currently available standardized single-word reading tests.) Obtaining a reading age is certainly an important component of the identification procedure but does not reveal the exact nature of the child's problems. The child's reading approach should be observed and all the incorrect responses recorded so that these can be examined and classified according to error type at a later stage.

Whilst administering a single-word reading test, consideration should be given to the following questions. How does the child approach the task of reading single words? Are the words read easily and relatively quickly or is each word identified slowly and laboriously? The response to this question will indicate whether the word

Table 6.1: Examples of reading error classifications

Visually similar— few shared letters	Visually similar— many shared letters	Regularizations	Unsuccessful sound attempts	Partial phonological access
SAID → she	CHAIN → chin	PINT → pinnt	CURIOSITY → si ris ty	CONSCIENCE → con consequence
JUMP → jack	BEARD → bread	COLONEL → kol o nell	ABODES → ad bodeas	COMPEL → com complete
COAT → cut	USELESS → unless	CHAOS → tcha oss		GENERALLY → gen generate
SHIP → shout	THROUGH → though	DOUGH → doug		TRANSPARENT → trans transport

the word recognition system is functioning adequately or whether the reader is having excessive difficulties identifying words out of context.

Word attack skill should also be considered. For example, how does the reader attempt to identify unfamiliar words? Are there any observable attempts to sound out unfamiliar words? If yes, is the child generally successful? If the reader is generally unsuccessful, at what stage in the process is the child having difficulty?

- identifying the correct letter;
- grouping the letters correctly, i.e. reading the word *then* as [t] [h] [e] [n];
- blending the sounds.

Error analysis can provide further valuable information about the learner's reading strategies. Errors may be classified according to the following categories: visually similar, regularizations, unsuccessful sound attempts and refusals. See Table 6.1 for examples of each type of error.

Visually similar errors

Visually similar word errors indicate that the child is identifying the target as a word which resembles it but is unable to perceive the difference between the two spellings. Beginning readers often make visual errors in which the target and the response share few letters, often only the initial letter, for example, STOPPED read as *sat*, AND read as *as*, HORSE read as *his*. More advanced readers make visual errors in which the response resembles the target more closely, for example, CHOIR read as *chair* or as *chore*. The number of letters shared by the target and the response is a good measure of the amount of letter information used by the reader for word recognition (Stuart and Coltheart, 1988) See Table 6.2.

Table 6.2: Examples of visual reading errors according to number of letter cues taken into account

First letter cue only	More than one letter cue	Minus one letter cue only
SIEGE → *spring*	GLOVE → *gave*	MATCH → *march*
GLOBE → *jug*	POLICE → *place*	FLOOD → *food*
SWORD → *shower*	HATCH → *hut*	PLAN → *plane*
THIMBLE → *tapping*	SIGN → *song*	FELL → *felt*
LEVER → *life*	RUBBER → *robin*	CEASED → *cased*

Sound-based errors

There are two quite different types of sound-based errors, the one type resulting from unsuccessful decoding and other from the inappropriate use of decoding strategies on irregular words, such as *island* or *colonel*, whose pronunciation cannot be correctly arrived at using correspondence rules.

Unsuccessful sound attempts

These errors occur when the reader tries to use letter-sound mappings, letter strings or other units to sound-out words which could not be recognized automatically. Failure may occur because:

* parsing is inaccurate, i.e. THE read as *t-h-e*; LAUGH read as *l-a-u-g-h*, with each letter sounded out as a separate speech sound
* incomplete or inaccurate knowledge of letter-sound rules
* poor blending skills

(A more detailed discussion of the subskills involved when using phonological processing is available in the section on nonword reading).

Sometimes words are identified using a *partial decoding strategy* in which a segment (usually the beginning) of a word is sounded out, and provides sufficient information for the retrieval of a word which shares a phonemic segment with the target but is in fact a different word, for example, COLLECT → *col; collar*, SPORT → *sp; Spain*. This type of error indicates that the reader has developed some decoding skills but is prone to guess without taking meaning and the letter content of the rest of the word into account.

Regularization errors

These errors occur when irregular words are sounded out and pronounced as if they were regular words, for example, FLOOD read as if it rhymes with *food*, HALF read as *hallf* [hælf], with the [l] sound included.

No response

Beginners who have limited sight vocabulary and insufficient phonic skills to decode unfamiliar words frequently refuse to respond.

Other errors

Some errors do not fit into any of the previous categories because it is difficult to determine conclusively why a child has made a particular error. A certain amount of detective work may be needed and is occasions in order to identify a common strategy. For example, if most words containing final *e* are read as if the vowels were short (for example, HOPE read as *hop*, TUBE read as *tub*) the reader may need to be taught that a final *e* lengthens the preceding vowel. On the other hand, the errors may be simply caused by a tendency to process words superficially and make visual errors. It is helpful to clear up this ambiguity. Table 6.3 contains some guidelines for assessing word recognition.

Table 6.3: Checklist to determine a reading profile

Reading Profile

Name:.....................................   Date:...
School:...................................   Chronological Age:.......................
Class:......................................

I. Word Recognition
1. Is word recognition   good....... average........poor........
2. Is there a predominance of refusals suggesting that the child has limited sight vocabulary and immature word attack skills?
          yes......... no.........
3. Is there a predominance of visual errors indicating a tendency to identify words using partial cues?   yes......... no.........
          (insert examples of errors and target...
4. Are most words recognized on sight or is the child sounding out the majority of words?
          sight.....
          sounding out: often.....   never...... excessive......
          (insert examples of errors and target...
....

5. Is there a predominance of sounding out errors suggesting:
          a. excessive reliance on decoding   yes......... no......... example ....
          b. unreliable decoding skills   yes......... no......... example ....
          c. inappropriate use of decoding on irregular words?
                    yes......... no......... example ....
(insert examples of errors and target)..
6. Is speed of word recognition
                    fast..... acceptable..... slow..... extremely slow.....

II. Decoding
1. Letter knowledge   good..... moderate..... poor.....
          Letters to teach:...

2. Letter-sounds good..... moderate..... poor.....
Sounds to teach:...

3. Application of letter-sound rules
                    good..... moderate..... poor.....
          Types of errors:..

Table 6.3: (Contd)

4. Blending   good..... moderate.....   poor.....
   Types of errors:..

5. Accessing correct word   after blending
           good.........moderate........... poor..........
   Errors:...

III. Comprehension:
1. Use of context good..... average.....   poor.....
2. Reading for meaning using semantically appropriate guesses
   good.....   average.....   poor.....
3. Use of phonic word attack skills
   good.....   average.....   poor.....
4. Self correction
   frequently.....sometimes.....not at all.....
5. Phrasing meaningful or disjointed and meaningless
   meaningful..... meaningless.....
6. Intonation
   good.....   average.....   poor.....
7. Has the reader understood the text when asked pertinent questions?
           yes.....   no.....
8. Can the reader make sensible inferences about the behaviour of the characters in
   the story or predict their future behaviour?   yes.....   no.....

Assessing decoding skills

As already mentioned decoding consists of a number of subskills:

1. The ability to divide a word into its component speech sounds, for example, HIM → [h] [ɪ] [m]
2. Use of letter-sound conversion to translate each letter to the appropriate speech sound, for example, $h →$ [h], etc
3. Blending the speech sounds to form a word;
4. Identifying the correct word and its meaning.

Because of time constraints it is rarely possible to test all these components separately but by evaluating knowledge of letter-names, letter-sounds and administering a nonword reading test, it is possible to identify the locus of difficulties.

Letter naming

Letter-name knowledge has proven to be a remarkably good predictor of eventual reading and spelling attainment (see Muter, this volume). There are numerous reasons for this. First, children who learn letter-names easily are more likely to have good phonological skills. Second, early readers can often use letter-names to deduce which sound a letter represents. (Treiman, Weatherston and Berch, 1994). The use of letter-name strategies is not always easy to detect but is evident when readers report that the sound of Y is [w] and the sounds of F, M and N is [e], an assumption arrived at by identifying the first phoneme of the letter name. Although the letter-name strategy is sometimes unreliable, as indicated above, it gives children a good basis from which to derive sound-letter correspondences.

Two related tests can be used to assess letter knowledge. First, print each letter on a blank card. After shuffling the cards, ask the child to tell you the name of each letter. After shuffling the pack again, ask the child to tell you the sound of each letter. Children who know few letter-names will need instruction, as will children whose letter-name knowledge is quite good but who have not been able to extrapolate sounds from the letter-names.

Nonword reading

Nonword reading tests are used to determine how well readers can decode words they have never seen before. If we try to assess decoding ability using real words, it is not always possible to distinguish conclusively between word recognition and decoding strategies. When we use nonwords, on the other hand, there is no likelihood that the items will be familiar. These tests have proved extremely useful diagnostically despite some people's instinctive aversion to meaningless material.

Nonwords are letter strings which resemble English words, conforming to the sound and spelling structure of English, but do not make sense, e.g., SLINT, CRIDGE, DELINKERATOR. For most purposes, nonwords can be derived from real words by changing one or more letters e.g., PUMPKIN can be changed to LUMPKIN or LUMPGIT. Nonwords can also be derived from irregular words with unusual spellings e.g., ISLAND and COLONEL. These irregular nonwords can either be sounded out, grapheme by grapheme i.e. read as *f-o-l-o-n-e-l* ['fɒ'lɒ'nɛl] or pronounced by analogy, in the same way as the irregular word COLONEL → *fernul* [fɜn̩ˌl]. The use of nonwords derived from irregular words enables us to monitor a reader's strategies with greater accuracy.

Practitioners may wish to use a standardized test of nonword reading, e.g., *The Graded Nonword Reading Test* (Snowling, Stothard and McLean, in press). Alternatively, they may wish to compile their own: the nonwords listed below (see Table 6.4) were used originally by Snowling, Stackhouse and Rack (1986). Each nonword should be printed on an index card. The first set should be presented first in random order (shuffling the cards will do), followed by the remaining set also in random order. The test should be discontinued if the child is not able to read at least five of the nonwords in the first set. The following instructions should be given before presenting the test.

> I am going to ask you to read some make-believe words. These make-believe words sound like words but they do not make sense. Even though they don't make sense it is possible to read them. See how many of them you can read.

Record the child's pronunciation of each item so that error analysis can be undertaken later. Pronunciations arrived at either through the use of sound-letter rules or through lexical analogy with an irregular word are correct. For example CHOVE can be pronounced so it rhymes with *clove* (regular) or with *love* (irregular) and PETTUCE can be pronounced as *petyoos* ['petˌjus] (regular) or so it rhymes with *lettuce, i.e., petis* ['peˌtɪs] (irregular). Comparison of the incidence of the two types of responses (decoding or analogy) will give useful information about the strategies used when reading new words. Lexicalization errors in which the reader pronounces the nonword as if it were a real word also occur frequently, for example, ISLANK read as *island*, KISCUIT read as *biscuit*. Excessive use of lexicalization indicates reliance on a holistic visual strategy when reading nonwords.

The number of nonwords read correctly should be calculated first and the score compared with the mean for children in the comparable age group. See cut off points for the *Nonword Reading Test* in Table 6.4 which indicate if scores are unduly low. In addition, it is often useful to count the number of phonemes correctly represented and to make a tally of the sounds which the child has found most difficult.

In order to identify the origin of the child's decoding difficulties, it is useful to examine their reading errors, looking for evidence of difficulty with one or more of the following processes: parsing, sound-letter knowledge or blending. Parsing refers to the process by which the letters in a word are separated into units corresponding to speech sounds, so that sound-letter rules can be applied. Whereas one letter usually represents one speech sound or phoneme, some phonemes are represented by a grapheme consisting of two letters, i.e. *th* in the word *with*, *sh* and *ou* in *should*, or *gh* and *ou* in *cough*. When a reader reads the *oo* in *plood* as two separate units, for example, *o-o* or pronounces the *ea* grapheme in *cread* as *e-a*, they need to be taught that some letter strings function as units and must be decoded as a unit.

Table 6.4: A test for assessing nonword reading

Nonword Reading Test

Have the child read the following nonwords. Each nonword should be written on a separate card. Record reading responses in detail.
Either a regular or an irregular pronunciation is acceptable.
i.e. If FONGUE is pronounced as *fongew* [fɒŋgu] it is regular whereas if is pronounced so that it rhymes with *tongue*, an analogy strategy has been used. ISLANK pronounced as *izlank* [ˈɪzˌlæŋk] is regular but pronounced as *ilank* [ˈaɪˌlæŋk] with no [z] sound is irregular.

One syllable	Two syllable
plood	louble
aund	hausage
wolt	soser
jint	pettuce
hign	kolice
pove	skeady
wamp	dever
cread	bitre
slove	islank
fongue	polonel
nowl	narine
swad	kiscuit
chove	
duede	
sworf	
jase	
freath	
warg	
choiy	

Control data : (Snowling, Stackhouse and Rack, 1986)

Nonwords read correctly

Reading age		One syllable	Two syllable
7 years*	Mean	9.5	3.6
	SD	3.6	2.9
	range	3–16	0–9
10 years**	Mean	17.3	10.7
	SD	1.4	1.8
	range	15–16	6–12

* A score below 3 on one-syllable words falls significantly below the norm.
**A score below 13 on one-syllable and 7 on two-syllable words falls significantly below the norm.

Knowledge of sound-letter mappings can be very limited in children with reading difficulties. In severe cases, the child is unable to identify any new words or read any nonwords. Others can produce the sound of the initial letter but can decode no further. As skill improves, the child may remain uncertain of some letter-sound mappings, especially the short vowel sounds, consonant and vowel digraphs (*sh, gh, ou, aw, ei*) blends (*bl, sw, shr,*) and infrequent letters (*x* and *q*).

Blending presents a particular problem to children with severe short-term memory problems. Such children are unable to recall the sounds they have just identified long enough to blend them together correctly. Other children may have articulatory problems which impede correct blending (see Stackhouse, this volume). Blending errors may result from omissions (PED blended as *pe* [pɛ]), insertions (PED blended as *pedder*), substitutions often due to change of voicing or place of articulation (*peg*) and lexicalization (PED blended as *bed* or *pet*), vowel changes (PED blended as *pud*) or a combination of the above errors as AUND sounded out correctly but blended as *anud* [ˈæˌnʌd].

Reading text

A comparison of reading accuracy and comprehension is of diagnostic significance because it enables us to determine whether a child has competent comprehension skills, despite poor word recognition, or whether comprehension deficits are the main cause of reading backwardness. A pupil whose word recognition is excellent but comprehension limited will require very different remediation from a child who makes numerous reading errors but can nevertheless answer searching questions about the text, if the unfamiliar words are supplied.

There are a large number of different reading comprehension tests (see Stothard, this volume). *The Neale Analysis of Reading Ability – Revised* (1989) is particularly useful because it provides three reading ages: a reading accuracy age, a reading comprehension age and a reading rate age. The individual is asked to read a prose passage aloud and is told that questions about the passage will follow. The examiner supplies any word which cannot be recognized and makes corrections if the reader identifies a word incorrectly.

Once again the tester should record every error for subsequent analysis and identification of strategies in use. To facilitate error analysis, a list of important behaviours is included which should be monitored when assessing reading comprehension. These are listed in Table 6.5.

Table 6.5: Guidelines for the analysis of errors made in reading text

1. *Word recognition errors* (tick as applicable)
......a. Confuses visually similar words (*scheme* and *school*;)
......b. Substitutes phonologically similar words (*compare* for *compassion*)
......c. Omission of short words especially function words (i.e., to, of)
2. *Use of context and linguistic prediction*
Type of substitutions (insert examples of errors and target, for example, *is* read as WERE)
a. Meaningful ....
Meaningless..
b. Grammatically correct..
Grammatically incorrect..
3. *Reading rate:* (tick as applicable)
..........Too slow (Difficult to integrate the meaning of the text at this rate)
..........Average (Reasonable speed enabling adequate comprehension and recall)
..........Too fast (Text read at a speed which precludes adequate comprehension and recall)
4. *Type of word attack used for identifying unfamiliar words* (tick as applicable)
............a. Use of letter sound correspondences
............b. Use of analogy
............c. Use of context
............d. Use of pictorial clues
5. *Monitoring Skills and self-correction* (tick as applicable)
Immediate.......... Delayed........... Does not occur...........
6. *Ability to apply alternative reading strategies as needed and appropriate*
................a. Word recognition
................b. Reading for Meaning and use of context
With letter cues.......... Without letter cues............
................c. Decoding
7. *Intonation*
good..... average poor.....
8. *Has the reader understood the text when asked pertinent questions?* Yes..... No.....
9. *Can the reader make sensible inferences about the behaviour of the characters in the story or predict their future behaviour?* Yes..... No.....

The importance of assessing the different types of reading strategies in tandem and evaluating the ease with which a reader can shift from one strategy to another as necessary cannot be overemphasized. However, skilled reading necessitates more than just knowing and being able to use different reading strategies, it also requires amalgamating these strategies so that 'reading for meaning' does not consist of guess-work alone but is guided by graphemic information. Even readers whose phonological skills remain poor into adulthood can be taught to read effectively and with comprehension if they are instructed to attend to sufficient graphemic information to ensure reasonable accuracy. Second, it is essential to identify any discrepancies between reading accuracy and comprehension so an accurate assessment can be made of the true nature of the reader's problems.

Dan, for example, had severe reading and spelling difficulties during early and middle childhood. At 14 his reading scores was still several years below his chronological age but his reading comprehension of text, as measured by the *Neale Analysis of Reading Ability – Revised* was excellent. He was able to answer almost all the comprehension questions on the two most difficult passages of Form 1. Nonetheless, Dan's word recognition remained inaccurate despite the availability of context. He misread SUSPICIOUS as *surprises*, PURSUED as *pressured*, THROUGH as *though* and NEGLECTED as *negligent*. All these errors showed a tendency to identify words as other visually similar words which began with similar sounds. Monitoring skills were also surprisingly weak since he did not notice his errors or self-correct them except on one occasion. Word attack skills were still poor and seriously impeded identification of new words. As Dan was about to begin GCSE studies that year, his ability to cope with these exams was of concern. Although he was certainly bright enough to understand the content of his courses, he would have great difficulty identifying the many unfamiliar words he would encounter in his reading. Weekly support was therefore recommended consisting of teaching Dan:

1. To monitor his reading more successfully.
2. To make use of his excellent comprehension skills to aid word identification while paying attention to graphemic information.
3. To subdivide words into syllables and morphemes to help him decode words more accurately.

Assessing Spelling

Spelling can be assessed using a standardized spelling test (see Appendix 6.1 for some suggestions), a test in which the person to be assessed spells words of different syllable length (see Table 6.7) and a sample of free writing. The standardized spelling test will furnish a spelling age and indicate the level of a child's attainment compared with other children of the same age. However, as our aim is to understand the strategies used, further error analysis will be needed.

Spelling errors should be evaluated at two levels. First, the *phonological* level: does the spelling sound like the word intended? Second, the *orthographic* level: are the correct letters used? To examine phonological ability, errors can be classified as either *phonetic, semi-phonetic* or *nonphonetic* according to how accurately the speech sounds are represented (Snowling, 1987).

Phonetic errors

Phonetic errors are spellings which contain all the speech sounds in the target word but are spelled incorrectly, for example, KNOWL-EDGE → *nolej*; CROWDED → *croudid*; SUITABLE → *sootibol*.

Semi-phonetic errors

In semi-phonetic spellings all or almost all of the consonant sounds are represented, for example, DOG → *dg*, ISLAND → *ild*. The spelling is usually reasonably easy to identify in context although of course not all the component speech sounds are included. Most normally developing children make these errors in the early stages of spelling acquisition. Consequently semi-phonetic errors have been referred to as 'normal immaturities' by Snowling (1985). However, children with spelling difficulties are likely to continue making them well beyond the age when normal spellers have discontinued them.

Spellings should be assigned to this category if one or more of the following types of errors are present:

1. Vowel sounds are sometimes omitted, for example, CUT → *ct* , BALL → *bl*, or are incorrect, for example, CUT → *cat*, BALL → *bul*.
2. Nasals (n, m, ng) which alter the sound of the vowel but are not a distinct phoneme are omitted for example, TENT → *tet*, BUMP → *bup*, CONTENTED → *coteted*.
3. Omission of one of the letters in a consonant cluster usually the second, for example, TRAIN → *tane*, DRESS → *des*.
4. Omission of unaccented syllables in longer polysyllabic words, for example, AUTOGRAPH → *orgraf*, UMBRELLA → *umbrel*.

Nonphonetic spelling errors

Nonphonetic spellings, more commonly referred to as dysphonetic errors, do not sound like the target words and a reader would be unable to identify such a spelling unless he or she knew which word the writer was attempting to spell. See Table 6.6 for examples of these error types.

It is possible to examine dysphonetic spellings in more detail by counting the number of phonemes correctly represented in each attempt. This is a very objective and reliable technique of error analysis which enables the tester to decide whether the speller consistently uses an appropriate letter for each phoneme or whether only a few phonemes are accurately represented, for example, CALCULA-TOR → *cala*, CATALOGUE → *cang*. The fewer speech sounds represented in the written version, the more severe the spelling difficulty.

By sorting errors according to these categories it is easier to establish whether a speller is having difficulties with the phonological or the orthographic component of spelling or both. See Table 6.6 for examples of each type of spelling error.

Table 6.6: Sample of spelling errors according to error categories

Phonetic		Semi-phonetic		Nonphonetic	
croudid	(crowded)	complet	(complete)	msnrey	(machinery)
trafick	(traffic)	polsh	(polish)	aferch	(adventure)
koler	(collar)	rowt	(route)	insind	(understand)
citon	(kitten)	tap	(trap)	cepint	(contented)
tuch	(touch)	seet	(street)	pepr	(bump)
blud	(blood)	sad	(sand)	sgrk	(cigarette)
coam	(comb)	bup	(bump)	goegagh	(geography)
ort	(ought)	back	(bank)	muore	(mother)
cigeret	(cigarette)	radater	(radiator)	calutur	(calculator)
shuvel	(shovel)	content	(contented)	prany	(people)

Spelling error analysis in practice

Daniel, aged 9 years, was asked to spell the words on the *Spelling by Syllable Length Spelling Test* shown in Table 6.7.

He spelled 4/10 of the one-syllable words correctly, making mainly semi-phonetic errors on these words, FISH → *fis*, TRAP → *trp*, BUMP → *bup*, and NEST → *net*. He misspelled all the two-syllable words. Three of his errors were phonetic (*appll, pakit, citn*), one was semi-phonetic (POLISH → *polis*) and the remainder were non-phonetic (TRUMPET → *tupt*; TRAFFIC → *tapt*; COLLAR → *cll*, TULIP → *tllrnp*, FINGER → *frgn*).

Although Daniel's spelling of *trumpet* was easily explainable in terms of normal immaturities, i.e., he omitted the vowels and the second letter in the cluster *tr*, his other nonphonetic spellings were more bizarre. A phoneme count showed that approximately half of the phonemes were represented correctly, but he inserted a number of extraneous letters in several words (*frgn* and *tllrnp*) which contributed to making all the nonphonetic spellings impossible to identify. Three conclusions can be arrived at from this analysis.

Table 6.7: Diagnostic spelling test (after Snowling, 1985)

Test of Spelling by Syllable Length

Instructions Dictate the word, dictate the sentence or phrase containing the word, then dictate the word again.

pet	A dog is a *pet*. Spell the word *pet*.
lip	He bit his *lip*. Spell the word *lip*.
cap	The little boy wore a *cap*. Spell the word *cap*.
fish	She caught a *fish* in the pond. Spell the word *fish*.
sack	A *sack* of potatoes. Spell the word *sack*.
tent	Indians used to sleep in a *tent*. Spell the word *tent*.
trap	The rabbit was caught in a *trap*. Spell the word *trap*.
bump	Do not *bump* your head. Spell the word *bump*.
nest	The were chicks in the *nest*. Spell the word *nest*.
bank	The robbers robbed the *bank*. Spell the word *bank*.
apple	An *apple* is a type of fruit. Spell the word *apple*.
puppy	A *puppy* is a baby dog. Spell the word *puppy*.
packet	A *packet* of crisps. Spell the word *packet*.
trumpet	To play the *trumpet*. Spell the word *trumpet*.
kitten	A *kitten* is a baby cat. Spell the word *kitten*.
traffic	There is a lot of *traffic* in the street. Spell the word *traffic*.
collar	The *collar* of your shirt is dirty. Spell the word *collar*.
tulip	A *tulip* is a type of flower. Spell the word *tulip*.
polish	*Polish* your shoes. Spell the word *polish*.
finger	He cut his *finger*. Spell the word *finger*.
membership	*Membership* to a club. Spell the word *membership*.
cigarette	To smoke a *cigarette*. Spell the word *cigarette*.
catalogue	A *catalogue* from a toy shop. Spell the word *catalogue*.
September	My birthday is in *September*. Spell the word *September*.
adventure	An exciting *adventure*. Spell the word *adventure*.
understand	Do you *understand*? Spell the word *understand*.
contented	To be *contented* is to be happy. Spell the word *contented*.
refreshment	A drink is a type of *refreshment*. Spell the word *refreshment*.
instructed	The teacher *instructed* the children to behave. Spell the word *instructed*.
umbrella	It is raining. You need an *umbrella*. Spell the word *umbrella*.
mysterious	The haunted house was *mysterious*. Spell the word *mysterious*.
machinery	The factory uses *machinery*. Spell the word *machinery*.
politician	A *politician* works in politics. Spell the word *politician*.
congratulate	I *congratulate* you on your fine work. Spell the word *congratulate*.
geography	In *geography* we study other countries. Spell the word *geography* .
magnificent	You have done a *magnificent* job. Spell the word *magnificent*.
calculator	You need a *calculator* to do that sum. Spell the word *calculator*.
discovery	The *discovery* of America. Spell the word *discovery*.
radiator	It is cold. Turn the *radiator* on. Spell the word *radiator*.
automatic	Do you have an *automatic* car? Spell the word *automatic*.

1. Daniel has attained reasonable competence in representing basic sound-letter mapping of consonants in one-syllable words, but is unsure of sounds which require two letters, for example, *sh*.

2. He is making many semi-phonetic errors and should be given some structured help with vowels, consonant clusters and nasals to enable him to pass through this stage. Although he knows how to represent some vowels he frequently omits them and needs further instruction. Similarly, he requires instruction in the spelling of consonant clusters, (for example, *st*, *tr*) and the need to represent nasals in written language. All these teaching points can be taught using word families and can be presented as games.

3. Daniel has serious difficulties with long words and with syllable segmentation. Although he could segment the one-syllable words quite efficiently he had substantial difficulty when trying to encode two-syllable words. His performance on words of three syllables was very poor indeed. He omitted one of the syllables on every single item. It might help Daniel to think of polysyllabic regular words as a collection of one syllable words. Daniel should be able to learn to spell them reasonably well once he has learned how to segment words and been taught to spell each syllable as if it were a separate word (i.e., *trum/pet*).

Phonetic errors and orthographic difficulties

The spelling errors of many older children with spelling difficulties tend to be reasonably phonetic but incorrect (see Cootes and Simpson, this volume). It is helpful to classify the source of these errors for assessment purposes and to provide guidance about the type of remediation needed.

1. *Irregular words:* These words require word specific knowledge and will need to be taught using whole word methods or mnemonics, for example, SHOVEL, THUMB, BEAUTIFUL, HONEST.

2. *Vowel errors,* for example, JAW → *jor*, ROAD → *rode*. It is always best to teach these words in the context of similar word families, such as JAW, DRAW, LAW, PAW, RAW, etc.

3. *Derivational errors:* These errors stem from a lack of understanding that words which are derived from the same root are related in meaning and have similar spellings, for example, AUTUMN AND AUTUMNAL.

Alan, aged 12, made the following phonetic and semi-phonetic spelling errors on the words of increasing syllable length: *appel, pupy, kiten, trafick, colar, tolip, palish, fingger, sigaret, katalog, advencher, radeater, deskavery, atamatick*. He never omitted syllables even on the four-syllable items and very rarely produced nonphonetic spellings. His pattern of spelling indicated that his appreciation of the sound structure of words is intact. However, his spelling errors show that he finds it very difficult to remember what spellings look like, even when spelling easy words such as PUPPY and APPLE.

Second, it is evident that he has not been able to deduce certain common orthographic rules about the English spelling system, such as that words of two syllables which end with the sound [ɪk] are spelled *ic* (*comic, traffic, panic*, etc.) or that most words beginning with the sound [k] begin with the letter *c*.

Alan will need to be taught a number of orthographic rules along with being shown lists of words which share the same spelling pattern (see Cootes and Simpson, this volume). He should be helped to find a way of learning whole word spellings so that he can begin to build up a written vocabulary of words he often uses in his writing. It will also be important to teach him doubling and suffixing rules which, although by no means infallible, will help him to make more informed guesses about spellings he cannot remember. Finally, he should be encouraged to use joined-up writing when practising writing the letter patterns he is being taught so that he can develop tactile memory of the word spellings he finds so difficult to recall. Daniel will also need similar type of instruction when he has resolved his problems with correct identification of the sound level of language.

Unassisted free writing

A sample of unassisted free writing is a particularly informative diagnostic instrument. Most children, can produce quite acceptable spelling attempts by the age of 7 years. If a child aged 7 or over is still struggling to produce a short piece or is producing numerous nonphonetic spellings so that it almost impossible to decipher what he or she is trying to say, spelling skills should be assessed.

The easiest way to obtain a sample of unassisted free writing is simply to ask a child to write about something which interests him or her for a specified amount of time – either five or ten minutes. However, poor spellers often do not know what to write about because they detest writing. It is therefore more helpful to suggest a topic, such as tell the story of *Little Red Riding Hood, Batman* or some other popular film or TV series. I often give younger children a cartoon asking them to tell the story adding any details they like. Error analysis of spelling should be performed in exactly the same way as has already been suggested for the spelling tests. In the case of free writing, the ability to communicate ideas and handwriting should also be examined. Writing speed should also be calculated as number of words per minute (see Taylor, this volume). Further points to keep in mind when assessing free writing are available in Table 6.8.

Table 6.8: Guidelines for the analysis of free writing

Free writing

1. *Intelligibility*
   Easy to understand.....   average....   difficult to understand.....

2. *If difficult to understand:*
   Can writer read what has been written?   yes.....   no.....

3. *Compared to the rest of the class is this piece of writing?*
   Above average .....   Average.....   Below average.....

4. *If below-average perform a detailed error analysis*

5. *Errors: Analysis*

Phonetic:..
....

Semi-phonetic:..
....

Nonphonetic...
....

   Mainly phonetic.....   Partially phonetic.....   Nonphonetic......

The story in Figure 6.1 (see p. 82) was written as a retelling of a story depicted in a cartoon of a boy who sees a dog in a shop window, runs home to fetch his mother, brings her back to the shop so that they can buy the dog and returns home with it. Matthew, who was 9; 10 years at the time of writing, wrote the following (author's interpretation in parenthesis):

> A dreyd (boy) wos (was) wok (walking) Dan (down) the rod (road) and hey (he) srom (saw) the littwe (little) dog a(and) he ust (asked) he (his) muemy (mummy) thetcotd (he could) hat (have) ta (it??) she siead (said) Iway (I will) giv ti (it) the my I hv (have) got a pet dog and wae (went) to bed and I win (went) fol (for) a wcko (walk) and he had a dig dog ahtl (???) hat.....

It is clear that Matthew was still having inordinate difficulty producing writing which could be understood by others. Many of his nonphonetic errors were unintelligible and could only be deciphered because we knew the story content of the cartoon (BOY → *dreld*; SAW → *srom*; WALK → *wcko*; ASKED → *ust*; COULD → *cotd*; IT → *ti*; WENT → *wae*. However, there was also one phonetic (GIVE → *giv*) and one semi-phonetic spelling (HAVE → *hv*). These show that he can sometimes arrive at a good approximation of the speech sounds in the words. Moreover, he has a small vocabulary of words which he can spell correctly and these could be used as a springboard for developing spelling and writing skills.

Donald was 14-years-old at the time of writing the piece in Figure 6.2 and had a spelling age on the Vernon spelling test of 9; 8 years.

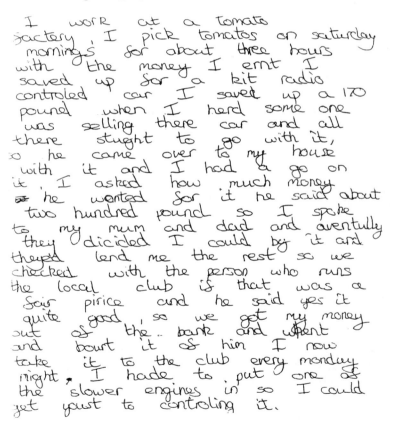

Figure 6.2: Donald's writing; aged 14 years.

This essay about his summer job, written in ten minutes, shows that he has resolved most of his earlier problems with spelling by sound but was having residual problems at the orthographic level, for example, *factery, ernt, controled, herd, stught* (STUFF), *wonted, aventully, dicided, whent, pirice* (PRICE), *bourt, of* (OFF), *youst* (USED). It is apparent that Donald has particular difficulty with irregular words and with homophones (*there* for THEIR, *herd* for HEARD, *by* for BUY) and will need remediation which concentrates on the teaching of spelling patterns and orthographic regularities.

A Case Study of Specific Reading and Spelling Difficulty

To show how assessment of reading and spelling can provide useful information about a child's current problems and indicate which areas are in most need of intervention, the case of Frances is presented. She was 8;8 years old when first assessed and she had a reading age of 6;8 years on the *British Abilities Scales Test of Word Reading* (Elliot, 1992). She was able to read a number of the easier words correctly, but her reliance on partial visual access made her reading inaccurate:

i.e. IF → *of*
      WINDOW → *windows*
      MEN → *man*
      DIG → *dog*
      SPORT → *spot.*

On an experimental single-word reading test in which she performed extremely poorly compared with readers with a 7-year reading age, she made an assortment of visual errors ranging from identifying words by first letter cues only, to a few visual errors which closely resembled the target. Interestingly, the majority of her errors incorporated information about two letters indicating that she was beginning to develop word recognition skills which take letter information into account. However, none of her errors were sound-based errors; her alphabetic skills had not yet emerged.

Frances's attempt to read simple nonwords supported this conclusion. She was only able to read one of the one-syllable nonwords and was unwilling to attempt any two-syllable items. Her errors disclosed that she could decode most of the initial letters and some of the final letters, but was unable to decode most vowels and blends. She made several reversal errors reading PAB as *bid* and SMADE as *seb*. Finally, she made some odd errors reading MUF as *bife* and SKAG as *sculpt.*

The *m* and *b* confusion was one which appeared frequently in her spelling and stemmed from her inability to pronounce both of these sounds distinctly.

Tests of letter naming and letter-sound naming confirmed that Frances still had many gaps in her knowledge of letter-sound mappings. Although she knew the names of all the letters, she did not know the sound of eight letters, namely *o,u, i, r, w, s, r, x* and was likely to have difficulty decoding words which contained these letters. When asked to write the 26 letter names, Frances was able to do so without error. But when requested to write the letter which represented a spoken phoneme, Frances could only produce the correct letter 42 per cent of the time. It appeared from these results that although Frances had competent letter-naming skills, she had not been able to use letter-name information to help her deduce the sounds of the letters, and had not yet formed reliable letter-sound mappings. Frances's poor performance when asked to write the letters which represent individual speech sounds suggests that her spelling would be weak.

Frances's spelling age of 6;2 years on the Vernon Spelling Test confirmed this suspicion. She was only able to spell 6 words correctly and proved unable to produce plausible spellings for words which were not already stored in the lexicon. Her spelling attempts were almost always nonphonetic and could not be read by someone who did not already know the identity of the target. She spelled SICK → *scak*, STORY→ *shroy*, GRASS → *geasa*, BIT → *peat*, DOWN→ *domen*, and EARTH → *ehar*.

One year later Frances was asked to write another cartoon story (see Figure 6.3) in which a dog finds a baby bird which has fallen out of its nest and takes it to his master. She made 16 errors on the 40 words attempted, an error rate of almost 38 per cent. However, although a number of her errors were nonphonetic, *soma* (SOME), *sedr* (SHOWED), *beg* (BEGAN) and *chiren* (CHILDREN), there were also some partially phonetic errors, *bieds* (BIRDS), *biad* (BIRD), *he's* (HIS) and *daid* (DID). Moreover, a number of words were correctly spelled (*tree, down, nest, sing*) including *put* an irregular word which needed word-specific knowledge. Several of Frances's errors suggest that she was trying to remember what the words looked like rather than what they sounded like, e.g. *somn* (SOME) and *bog* (boy).

Apart from the numerous spelling errors, Frances's Fig 6.3. writing shows that she totally disregarded punctuation and would require extensive instruction in its use. In addition, the occasional omission of syllables suggest that she would benefit from being taught to count syllables in words, and to spell longer words syllable by syllable. She could also be asked to play word family games in which she has to identify the syllables and helped to monitor each syllable when trying to generate new spellings.

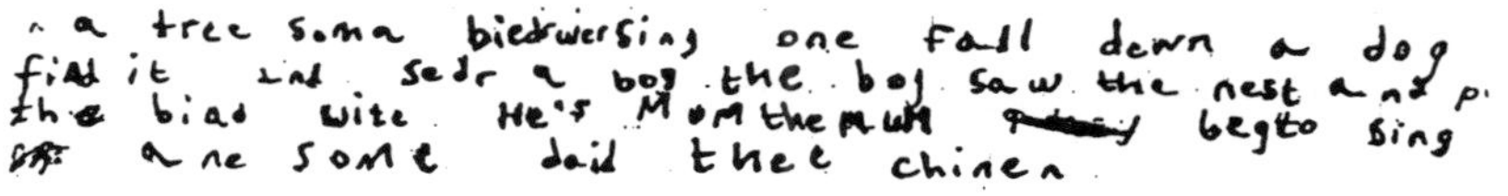

In a tree soma (some) bieds (birds) wersing (were singing) one fall (fell) down a dog (boy) fiAd (found) it and sedr (showed) a bog (boy) the boy saw the nest and put the biad (bird) wite (with) he's (his) Mum the Mum beg (began) to sing and some (so) daid (did) thee (the) chiren (children)

Figure 6.3: Frances's writing; aged 7 years.

Frances had a history of speech difficulties and although no longer receiving speech therapy, had residual articulation difficulties which appeared to influence some of her spelling errors, especially the [m], [b] and [p] confusion mentioned previously. The speech and language therapist's report noted that Frances had difficulty repeating words and nonwords which contained clusters, she confused nasal sounds such as [m] and [n] and she made a number of other phonemic substitutions such as *th* [θ] pronounced as [f], *the* [ð] pronounced as [v] and *r* as [w]. Such errors were also evident in her spelling.

On the *Neale Analysis of Reading Ability (Second edition)*, Frances scored an accuracy reading age of 7;3 years and a comprehension reading age of 7;0 years. From this result it was evident that Frances was able to identify words much better if she had context to help her. Although she could not decode any unfamiliar words, she was able to guess a few words correctly.

Cognitive assessment showed that Frances had great difficulty with word and nonword repetition when compared with children of the same reading age. She also found it extremely difficult to think of words which rhyme with *cat, dog* or *pin*. On the *Bradley Test of Auditory Organization* in which she had to identify the word which sounded different from the others (map, cap, gap, *jam;* or fish, dish, wish, *mash*) she performed poorly compared with other children of the same 7-year reading level. Her difficulties with sound-letter mapping, decoding and reading unfamiliar words and nonwords were understandable given her basic phonological problems.

Conclusions

Assessment of reading and spelling and associated cognitive deficits is a crucial precursor of teaching. By adopting detailed assessment procedures and taking the time to undertake careful error analysis, it is possible to identify precisely the strategies used by each individual, and to discern why they are not progressing normally. The next step is to devise a teaching programme which is tailor made to the child's or student's needs. The assessment procedure suggested above will take approximately 45 minutes to administer, and another hour to score and interpret. Although this may seem a long time to spend on one child, the understanding gained from embarking upon such a diagnostic procedure should in the long run save time for practitioner and student alike.

Appendix 6.1 Standardized reading and spelling tests

Single-word Reading Tests

Jastak, S. and Wilkinson, G.S. (1993) *The Wide Range Achievement Test 3* Wilmington, DE: Jastak Associates, Inc.

Macmillan Test Unit (1985) *Macmillan Graded Word Reading Test.* Basingstoke, Hants: Macmillan Education, Ltd.

Schonell, F.J. (1971) *Graded Word Reading Test.* Edinburgh: Oliver and Boyd.

Scottish Council for Research in Education (1974) *Burt (Rearranged) Word Reading Test.* London: Hodder and Stoughton.

Young, D. (1978) *SPAR Spelling and Reading Tests.* London: Hodder and Stoughton.

Prose Reading

Neale, M. (1989) *Neale Analysis of Reading Ability*–Revised British Edition. Windsor, Berks NFER–Nelson.

Vincent, D. and De la Mare, M. (1989) *New Reading Analysis.* Windsor, Berks: NFER–Nelson.

Vincent, D. and De La Mare, M. (1990) *Individual Reading Analysis.* Windsor, Berks: NFER–Nelson.

Spelling Tests

Jastak, S. and Wilkinson, G.S. (1993) *The Wide Range Achievement Test 3*. Wilmington, DE :Jastak Associates, Inc.

Vernon, P.E. (1977) *Graded Word Spelling Test*. London: Hodder and Stoughton.

Vincent, D. and Clayton, J. (1982) *Diagnostic Spelling Tests*. Windsor, Berks: NFER–Nelson.

Young, D. (1978) *SPAR Spelling and Reading Tests*. London: Hodder and Stoughton.

Young, D. (1983) *The Parallel Spelling Tests A and B*. London: Hodder and Stoughton.

Chapter 7
Assessing Reading Comprehension

Susan E. Stothard

It is common practice in school to assess children's reading ability in terms of their word recognition skills. Children who can read many words in relation to their peers are regarded as good readers whereas children who can read only a few words are considered to be poor readers. There can be little doubt that children who are unable to recognize words have a reading problem; decoding skills are an essential component of reading. However, this method of assessing reading often means that children with other types of reading problems go unnoticed. The goal of reading is not simply to identify each word correctly, comprehension is also important. In each classroom there are some children with hidden reading problems, whose word recognition skills are good, but whose comprehension skills are poor.

During the last decade it has become clear that many children struggle to understand what they have read. It is reported that 9.5–15 per cent of children experience specific difficulties with reading comprehension (Stothard and Hulme, 1995; Yuill and Oakhill, 1991). These children are able to read aloud well, i.e., they have age-appropriate decoding skills; however, their reading comprehension is poor.

This chapter will begin with a short review of theories that have been proposed to explain reading comprehension difficulties in children (see also Stothard, 1994). It will then go on to describe the case studies of two children, Andrew and Katy, who have reading comprehension difficulties, and highlight the pattern of difficulties that underlie their comprehension problems. The next section of this chapter will address the issue of assessment, that is, how can comprehension be assessed. It will outline the important factors that must be considered when assessing comprehension and review some of the standardized comprehension tests that are available commercially.

Finally, the chapter will close with the all important question of remediation and offer some suggestions as to how children with comprehension problems might be helped to overcome their difficulties.

Theories of Children's Reading Comprehension Difficulties

Are comprehension difficulties attributable to inefficient decoding processes?

It has been suggested that reading comprehension difficulties are
attributable to inefficient decoding processes. The main version of
this theory is Perfetti's 'decoding bottleneck' or verbal efficiency
hypothesis (see Perfetti, 1985). According to this theory, if readers do
not recognize words sufficiently quickly and automatically, the
processing required for word recognition will place an additional
burden on memory, and will reduce the resources available for
comprehension. Thus, even when word recognition is not inaccurate, if it is slow and laboured, it may take up resources that are
important for the comprehension of a text. Also, since short-term
memories decay rapidly, if word recognition is slow then few words
will be available in memory when needed and once again comprehension will suffer.

However, research shows that children with specific reading
comprehension difficulties do not read slowly. For example, Stothard
and Hulme (1995) measured the decoding speed of a group of children with specific comprehension difficulties. These poor comprehenders read at a normal speed, their rate of reading being similar to
age-matched controls. Oakhill (1981, unpublished study presented
in Yuill and Oakhill, 1991) also reported that poor comprehenders
are not slow decoders. It appears that inefficient decoding skills are
not a major cause of reading comprehension difficulties.

Are comprehension difficulties due to limitations of short-term memory?

It has also been suggested that comprehension problems might be
associated with poor verbal memory skills. To understand prose it is
necessary to hold information in memory so that the semantic and
syntactic relationships among successive words, phrases and
sentences may be computed and a meaningful representation of the
passage constructed. It follows that poor memory skills might
contribute to reading comprehension difficulties.

Surprisingly perhaps, there is actually little support for this proposal. Several studies have reported that children with specific reading comprehension difficulties have normal verbal short-term memory capacity. For example, Oakhill, Yuill and Parkin (1986) and Stothard and Hulme (1992) found that children with specific comprehension difficulties have normal short-term memory spans and are able to remember a similar amount of information as age-matched controls.

Further evidence that comprehension problems are not the product of short-term memory difficulties comes from studies examining children's memory and comprehension of text. Oakhill (1981, unpublished study reported in Yuill and Oakhill, 1991) studied children's memory of sentences in a free recall task. The children were presented with a series of sentences, one at a time, which they had to recall. Recall was assessed in two ways: a strict verbatim criterion required the child to remember the exact wording of the sentence and a lenient gist criterion required the child to remember the meaning of the sentence, but not the exact words. For example, a child might be asked to remember the sentence, 'The foxes hunt rabbits, and the wolf follows the foxes.' If the child's recall was, 'Foxes hunt rabbits and a wolf follows the foxes', this would be scored as incorrect according to the verbatim criterion. However, because the recall retains the meaning of the original sentence, it would be scored as correct when the gist criterion was applied. When the strict verbatim criterion was used to assess performance, children with reading comprehension difficulties obtained similar memory scores to age-matched controls. However, when the more relaxed gist criterion was used, the poor comprehenders remembered significantly less information than the controls. These findings indicate that poor comprehenders are able to remember the details of sentences in a word-for-word manner. However, their gist memory, memory for the overall meaning of the text, is impaired. In comparison, children with good comprehension skills appear to make a more active attempt to understand. The fact that the poor comprehenders are able to remember the exact wording of sentences indicates that weak short-term memory skills are not the cause of their comprehension difficulties.

Thus, it is clear that children with specific comprehension difficulties do not show deficits on simple memory tasks. Their difficulties do not lie in the storage of information, but rather in the processing of that information to derive meaning. It has, therefore, been suggested that comprehension difficulties might be related to more complex impairments in functional working memory capacity (Yuill, Oakhill and Parkin, 1989). Yuill, et al. (1989) gave good and poor comprehenders a working memory task which involved reading aloud triplets of numbers and then recalling, in order, the final digit in each triplet (for example, 835;402, response: 5;2). They found that the poor comprehenders obtained significantly lower memory scores than the age-matched controls. Yuill, et al. conclude that these findings provide evidence for a 'general non-linguistic working memory' limitation in their poor comprehenders. This, however, seems a very odd conclusion given that this task is quite clearly verbal; the children read aloud and then reported the final item from each triplet.

Stothard and Hulme (1992) also examined whether poor comprehenders have a working memory deficit. The children were given a listening span task; they heard a series of short sentences and had to assess the validity of each by responding true or false. They also had to memorize the final word from each sentence and recall these words in the correct serial order ('Butter goes on bread' (true), 'Giants are small' (false), response → *bread, small*). The poor comprehenders obtained similar scores to age-matched controls and tended to outperform younger children matched for comprehension skills. Taken together, these results make it seem unlikely that working memory deficits are a major cause of reading comprehension difficulties.

Can poor comprehenders make inferences when reading and listening to stories?

Alternative theories of reading comprehension difficulties have looked to processes that are characteristic of skilled readers and suggested that children with comprehension difficulties might be impaired in such processes. For example, comprehension is a constructive, integrative process; skilled readers spontaneously draw inferences to link together ideas and to fill in information that is only implicit. This process is necessary so that an integrated representation of the text can be formed. Consider, for example, the following extract: 'Jane sat under the tree and pulled another present out of her stocking. It was a beautiful golden necklace. She couldn't believe how lucky she was to receive all these presents.' Skilled readers will automatically draw the inference that it is Christmas. Although this information has not been stated explicitly, the words *tree, stocking* and *presents* provide the implicit clues to allow this inference to be drawn.

It has been suggested that children with reading comprehension problems might experience difficulties making such inferences. Oakhill (1982) examined the relationship between children's reading comprehension and their use of constructive memory representations. The children were presented with a series of short stories which they were asked to listen to and try to remember. They were then given a recognition memory task and had to decide which of a series of test sentences they had heard before. There were three types of test sentence: original sentences, i.e., sentences that had been presented before; valid inference foils, i.e., sentences that had not actually been presented but were semantically congruent with the original story and invalid inference foils, i.e., sentences that were semantically incongruent. An example of the materials used in this study are presented in Figure 7.1. Oakhill found that children with comprehension difficulties made fewer errors on the valid inference foils than did age-matched controls, but they made more errors on the invalid inference foils. In other words, the poor comprehenders were less likely to make confusions of a semantic nature. These findings indicate that poor comprehenders are less likely to form constructive memory representations from sets of related sentences.

Original sentences:
The car crashed into the bus.
The bus was near the crossroads.
The car skidded on the ice.

Recognition sentences:
The car crashed into the bus. (original sentence)
The bus was near the crossroads. (original sentence)
The car was near the crossroads. (semantically congruent, valid inference foil)
The bus skidded on the ice. (semantically incongruent, invalid inference foil)

Figure 7.1: An example of the materials used in Oakhill's (1982) study

Oakhill (1984) has also shown that children with reading comprehension difficulties are poor at making inferences when reading. Good comprehenders and poor comprehenders were given a series of short stories to read and at the end of each were asked a set of comprehension questions. There were two types of comprehension question, requiring either literal information, i.e., information that was mentioned explicitly, or implicit information, i.e., information that could only be inferred (see Figure 7.2). The questions were asked twice, first with the text removed, the children being required to respond from memory. The text was then returned and the questions repeated, the children being asked to check the text before answering. When answering from memory, the good comprehenders performed significantly better than the poor comprehenders on both question types. However, when the text was available, the good comprehenders were only better on the inferential questions, both groups making very few errors on the literal questions. Thus, poor comprehenders can scan text to retrieve information that is explicitly stated; however, they find it difficult to retrieve information that requires an inference to be drawn. These findings indicate that children with comprehension difficulties are less able to draw inferences and use relevant general knowledge when reading a story. Failure to draw inferences will prevent the reader from forming an integrated representation of the meaning of a text which, in turn, will hinder comprehension.

John's Big Test

John had got up early to learn his spellings. He was very tired and decided to take a break. When he opened his eyes again the first thing he noticed was the clock on the chair. It was an hour later and nearly time for school. He picked up his two books and put them in a bag. He started pedalling as fast as he could. However, John ran over some broken bottles and had to walk the rest of the way. By the time he had crossed the bridge and arrived at class, the test was over.

Literal questions
1. What was John trying to learn?
2. Where was the clock?
3. How many books did John pick up?
4. What did John have to cross on his way to school?

Inferential questions
5. How did John travel to school?
6. What did John do when he decided to take a break?
7. Why did John have to walk some of the way to school?
8. How do you know that John was late for school?

Figure 7.2: An example of the materials used in Oakhill's (1984) study.

Do poor comprehenders monitor their own comprehension?

Another important characteristic of skilled reading is the ability to monitor and evaluate one's own comprehension. This awareness of the reading process, of the strategies involved and a knowledge of one's own cognitive processes is termed *metacognition*. Skilled readers employ a variety of metacognitive processes during reading: they identify important aspects of the passage, allocate attention to relevant information, monitor their comprehension of the passage and take corrective steps when necessary to recover from disruptions and distraction (Brown, 1980). It is generally acknowledged that these strategies aid comprehension and failure to employ them might be a cause of reading problems.

Indeed, a number of studies have shown that children with specific reading comprehension problems have weak metacognitive skills. For example, Yuill and Oakhill (1991) reported that children with specific reading comprehension problems seem to lack an awareness of the goals of reading. When asked what makes someone a good reader, poor comprehenders were significantly more likely to say that 'not knowing words' was a cause of poor reading than were their age-matched controls. Poor comprehenders appear to resemble younger children in terms of their emphasis on decoding rather than understanding.

Children with specific comprehension problems have also been shown to have difficulties monitoring their comprehension. Yuill, et al. (1989) tested good and poor comprehenders' ability to resolve apparent inconsistencies in a text. Children heard a series of stories describing an adult's apparently inconsistent emotional response to a child's action. For example, in one story a mother is pleased with her son when he refuses to share his sweets with his little brother. This inconsistency is resolved by the information that his little brother is on a diet. Following each story, the children were asked whether the adults should have behaved as they did, and why. When the anomalous and resolving information were separated by intervening sentences, the poor comprehenders were poorer at detecting the anomalies than age-matched controls. It appears that poor comprehenders have difficulty in comprehension repair, being less likely to use resolving information to explain the inconsistencies.

Taken together, these findings indicate that children with comprehension difficulties adopt a passive approach to reading. During reading they are less likely to employ such strategies as re-reading, pausing and self-questioning. In short, they fail to monitor their comprehension. They fail to detect when understanding breaks down and therefore are unable to apply 'fix-up' strategies to restore comprehension. Hence, it is hardly surprising that such children have a very limited understanding of what they have read.

Are the problems of poor comprehenders specific to reading?

An important question about children with reading comprehension problems concerns the specificity of their difficulties. Are the comprehension difficulties specific to reading, or do these children also show relatively poor language comprehension skills? Evidence indicates that children with reading comprehension difficulties also have listening comprehension difficulties.

Stothard and Hulme (1992) examined the listening comprehension skills of a group of children with reading comprehension difficulties. The children were given two tests of language comprehension: a listening comprehension task and the *Test for the Reception of Grammar* (TROG) (Bishop, 1983). The listening comprehension test comprised a series of four short stories that were read aloud by a female adult speaker and tape recorded. The children listened to the stories and were asked a set of comprehension questions at the end of each passage. The TROG comprises a series of 80 four-choice items. For each item, the child is shown four coloured pictures and has to select the picture that corresponds to a test sentence read aloud by the experimenter. For example, the child might hear the sentence 'The girl is pushing the horse' and be shown pictures of a girl pushing a man, a girl riding a horse, a horse pushing a girl and a girl pushing a horse.

The poor comprehenders exhibited marked difficulties on both comprehension tasks, performing at a significantly lower level than age-matched controls. However, they obtained similar scores to a group of younger children who were matched for reading comprehension skill. In other words, the poor comprehenders showed equivalent deficits on reading and listening comprehension tasks. It is clear that these children have a general language comprehension deficit.

The poor comprehenders' verbal ability was examined further (Stothard and Hulme, 1995) by administering a short form of the *Wechsler Intelligence Scale for Children–Revised* (WISC-R) (Wechsler, 1974). The poor comprehenders were found to have a selective deficit in verbal IQ; they obtained significantly lower verbal IQ scores than age-matched controls. However, the raw scores they obtained on the verbal subtests did not differ from those of younger comprehension-age controls. In other words, the poor comprehenders had similar reading comprehension, language comprehension and verbal-semantic skills to a group of younger children whose comprehension was normal for their age. Hence, the poor comprehenders' weak comprehension skills actually appear to be in line with some of their other verbal skills. In this light these children's comprehension difficulties might be thought of as a manifestation of a more general deficit in verbal-semantic skills.

To conclude, the studies reviewed here indicate that children with reading comprehension problems have a variety of difficulties. They have general language comprehension problems, showing deficits on tests measuring vocabulary knowledge and listening comprehension skills. They are also poor at making inferences when reading (or listening) and therefore are unable to form an integrated representation of the overall meaning of the passage. In addition, poor comprehenders have been shown to have weak metacognitive skills; they are unlikely to monitor their comprehension and generally read in a passive manner.

Case Studies of Children with Reading Comprehension Problems

The research reviewed above offers a general picture of children with reading comprehension problems, outlining the average characteristics of groups of poor comprehenders. Case studies of children with reading comprehension difficulties can also be informative. They provide detailed information about individual children and highlight their strengths and weaknesses. This information can often be masked in group data. Here, I present data from two children, Andrew and Katy, who took part in a series of studies investigating reading comprehension difficulties (see Stothard, 1992).

The case of Andrew

Andrew was first seen when he was 8;3 years of age. His teacher considered him to be an average reader for his age. Surprisingly, however, the assessment revealed that Andrew had marked reading comprehension difficulties. On the *Neale Analysis of Reading Ability (Revised)*, Form 1 he attained a reading accuracy age of 8;10 years and a reading comprehension age of 6;4 years. Andrew read very quickly (89 words per minute) and gained a reading rate age of 11;1 years. Therefore, Andrew's decoding skills are good for his age, but his comprehension is clearly limited.

Andrew's general ability was measured by a short form of the WISC-R. Verbal skills were assessed by the Vocabulary and Similarities subtests and nonverbal skills were assessed by the Block Design and Object Assembly subtests. Andrew's nonverbal ability (IQ 106) was average for his age; however, his verbal IQ was weak (IQ 79). Andrew found the vocabulary task very difficult, his ability to define the meaning of words being very poor. For example, he defined BRAVE as *someone who would do it*, DIAMOND as *small thing . . . it's pointed* and NONSENSE as *don't want to listen*. It is reasonable to assume that Andrew's poor vocabulary skills contribute to his reading comprehension difficulties.

To determine whether Andrew's comprehension difficulties were specific to reading, he was administered two tests of language comprehension: a non-standardized test of listening comprehension and the *Test for Reception of Grammar* (TROG) (Bishop, 1983). The listening comprehension task was derived from the *Neale Analysis of Reading Ability (Revised)*, Form 2. The first four passages were read aloud by a female adult speaker and tape recorded. Andrew listened to the passages and at the end of each one was asked the accompanying comprehension questions. The TROG provides a measure of receptive language comprehension skills (see above and Klein, this volume). It comprises 80 four-choice items. For each item four coloured pictures are presented and the child's task is to select the picture that depicts a test sentence read aloud by the experimenter. For each item there are three distracters which are either of a lexical or a grammatical nature. The test assesses the understanding of a range of grammatical contrasts, such as masculine/feminine personal pronoun, comparative/ absolute, and neither X nor Y.

Andrew performed poorly on both measures of language comprehension. On the listening comprehension task he was able to answer just 7 of the 28 questions correctly. Age-matched controls gained an average score of 18.64 questions correct. Similarly, Andrew attained a below average score on the TROG. He scored 70/80 items correct, which is much lower than age-matched controls (average score: 76.5). It is clear that Andrew's comprehension difficulties are not restricted to reading. Rather, he has global language comprehension difficulties.

Thus, it is clear that Andrew had marked difficulties with reading comprehension and language comprehension. Furthermore, his verbal language skills were poor. It might, therefore, be hypothesized that Andrew's weak verbal skills underlie his comprehension difficulties. However, as noted above, reading comprehension is a highly complex activity in which readers automatically make inferences and bring knowledge to bear. It is therefore possible that Andrew has additional problems which reduce his reading comprehension ability. This possibility was assessed by examining his comprehension for different sized units of text.

Andrew was given two cloze reading tests taken from Snowling and Frith (1986). Both texts were adapted from children's nature stories and judged suitable for a reading age of 7–8 years. The first reading task comprised a lengthy story about a beaver. At intervals throughout the text a gap was inserted and three alternative words were given (an extract from this task is presented in Figure 7.3). Andrew was required to choose the word that fitted the context of the story. The appropriateness of the word choices was varied systematically. At each choice point one alternative was 'story-appropriate' (it fitted both the sentence and the story context), one alternative was 'sentence-only-appropriate' (it fitted the immediate sentence context, but was inappropriate in the wider story context) and one alternative was 'inappropriate' (it neither fitted the sentence nor the story context). For example, in the sentence, 'Just then there was another noise and the wolf *disappeared/appeared/threaded*', the choice between the first two alternatives depends upon an understanding of the story beyond that of the individual sentence. Both *disappeared* and *appeared* are appropriate in the sentence context, however, reference to the story context (i.e., that the beavers were already facing the wolf) implicates the former alternative as being correct. The word *threaded* is inappropriate in both sentence and story contexts.

A significant preference for story-appropriate choices indicates efficient text comprehension at a level above that of the individual sentence. A tendency to select sentence-appropriate items suggests that the individual sentences are being processed as separate units, the information contained in successive units not being integrated. Failure to reject inappropriate words suggests that comprehension of even small units of meaning within sentences is impaired.

The second reading task, the Hedgehog Story, followed a slightly different format. Rather than offering explicit word choices, comprehension was assessed by requiring Andrew to identify anomalous words that appeared randomly within the text. The anomalous words were of two types. 'Plausible' words were acceptable in the narrow sentence context, but not in the wider context of the story. 'Implausible' words were inappropriate in both the sentence and story context. For example, consider the following extract: 'The hedgehog could smell the scent of the *electric* flowers. She knew that among them there would be worms, snails, insects and other good things to *see*.' The word *electric* is an implausible substitution for *spring* as it fits neither the sentence nor the story context. In contrast, *see* is a plausible substitution for *eat* as it makes sense within the confines of the sentence, but not in the entire story. Here, preference for implausible as opposed to plausible anomalies implies that comprehension is limited to small units of text.

	darker	
The forest was	earlier	than the river bank and strange noises
	smaller	

	trees	cat
came from the rustling	birds. The frightened	**beaver** could see
	cars	room

	cut
almost nothing at first. Then she	felt a light glinting ahead of her.
	saw

	thin	**in**
It was the fierce	skinny eyes of a tiger glowing	with the
	golden	beneath

	from
darkness. The beaver froze. She was too far	above the water to
	after

	safety		**wait**
dive for	fun.	She could only	whistle for the cat to pass by.
	books		pay

Bold typeface denotes correct word choices

Figure 7.3: Extract from the Beaver Story

Andrew performed well on the Beaver Story task. On the 26 gaps that were analysed, Andrew chose 23 story-appropriate words and 3 sentence-only-appropriate words. This was similar to age-matched controls (average number of story-appropriate choices: 23.4, average number of sentence-only-appropriate choices: 2.6). Therefore, Andrew was able to process the text efficiently and comprehended the story as a whole.

Andrew found the Hedgehog Story more difficult. He correctly identified 12 of the 15 implausible anomalous words, but identified just 2 of the 15 plausible anomalies. He made six false alarms, incorrectly stating that the actual words were anomalous. This level of performance is slightly poorer than that observed in age-matched controls. On average, the age-matched controls identified 3.9 plausible and 11.7 implausible anomalies and made 3.6 false alarms.

These findings indicate that Andrew is able to monitor his comprehension when the task demands this. On the Beaver Story, Andrew was required to choose one out of three words to complete a series of gaps. Andrew's attention was thus continuously focused on the exact selection of words and in effect he was forced to monitor his comprehension. It is possible that this may have stimulated a metalinguistic process that Andrew would not normally use during reading. Indeed, Andrew struggled when he was given a less obtrusive test of text comprehension in which he was required to detect anomalous words that were surreptitiously embedded in the text. Andrew had particular difficulty detecting plausible anomalies, i.e., words that were plausible in the context of the immediate sentence but not in the wider context of the story. It appears that Andrew's comprehension is limited to rather small units of material.

So, Andrew indeed has marked comprehension difficulties. His difficulties are not restricted to reading, his listening comprehension skills are also impaired. Andrew also has poor verbal language skills, in particular his vocabulary is weak. It appears that Andrew's impoverished vocabulary knowledge contributes to his difficulties. It is also apparent that Andrew does not automatically monitor his comprehension. As such he will be less likely to realize when understanding breaks down and will therefore be unable to take corrective action to restore comprehension.

The case of Katy

Katy was first seen when she was 8;1 years of age. She was a child of average ability. Her verbal IQ was 94 and her nonverbal IQ was 92 (short form of WISC-R). Katy found reading difficult. On the *Neale Analysis of Reading Ability (Revised)*, Form 1 she attained a reading accuracy age of 7;2 years and a reading rate age of 7;7 years. Thus, her decoding skills were weak for her age. Katy also exhibited marked reading comprehension difficulties and attained a reading comprehension age of 6;1 years, a lag of some 2 years below her chronological age. Although Katy had a mixed pattern of reading difficulties, it was felt that her reading comprehension problems were the most severe and needed investigation.

Katy was given two tests of listening comprehension skills to determine whether her comprehension difficulties were restricted to reading. She was given a non-standardized test of listening comprehension and the TROG. These tests are described above. Katy performed poorly on both tasks. She answered 9 questions correctly on the listening comprehension test which is much lower than the average score of her peers (average score of age-matched controls: 18.64). Katy's incorrect responses indicated that she had difficulty recalling factual details and also had difficulty making inferences. For example, the story in Passage 2 is about two children receiving a surprise parcel from their uncle. When asked, 'How do you know that Jane and Peter were not expecting the parcel?', she replied, 'Grandpa didn't tell them.' Furthermore, when asked 'Who had sent the parcel?', she said, 'Grandpa.' The story actually makes no reference to Grandpa. It is important to note that Katy's comprehension difficulties cannot be explained in terms of a short-term memory deficit. She attained a scaled score of 9 on the WISC-R Digit Span Test (Wechsler, 1974), which is average for her age.

Katy also obtained a low score on the TROG, answering 72 of the 80 items correctly. Age-matched controls gained an average score of 76.5 items correct. It is clear that Katy's comprehension difficulties are not restricted to reading. Rather, she has global language comprehension difficulties.

Katy's reading comprehension difficulties were further examined by giving her two cloze reading tests: the Beaver Story and the Hedgehog Story. As discussed above, these tests assess comprehension for different sized units of text. Katy found both cloze tasks difficult and it was evident that she rarely monitored her comprehension during reading. On the Beaver Story, she chose 18 story-appropriate words and 8 sentence-only-appropriate words (26 choices were analysed). Thus, the probability of Katy making a story-appropriate choice, given that the inappropriate alternative had been rejected was 69.23 per cent. This is a much lower probability than seen in the age-matched controls (average score: 90.08 per cent).

Katy found the Hedgehog Story especially difficult. It will be recalled that in this task the child has to identify anomalous words that are surreptitiously embedded in the passage. Katy correctly identified just 4 of the plausible anomalies and 9 of the implausible anomalies (mean score for age-matched controls: 3.9 and 11.7, respectively). Moreover, Katy made an extremely high number of false alarms, incorrectly saying that 25 actual words were anomalous (see Figure 7.4 for an extract from her responses). Almost two-thirds of her responses were false alarms. Age-matched controls made 3.6 false alarms on average. Many of Katy's errors seemed to arise because she took a very literal interpretation of the meaning of words. For example, the final part of the story describes a mother hedgehog raising her young babies and then encouraging them to leave the nest to look after themselves. After reading the sentence 'a litter of old hedgehogs was growing inside her', she said that 'litter' was wrong, interpreting litter to mean rubbish. A similar example occurred when Katy read the following sentence: 'the mother drove him away'. Here, Katy said that 'drove' was wrong and indignantly stated that 'hedgehogs can't drive!'

For three months the hedgehog had been warm and <u>snug</u> in her under-ground nest. Now the weather was *fatter* (warmer), she woke from her long sleep and saw that winter had really gone. The hedgehog could smell the <u>scent</u> of the *electric* (spring) flowers. She knew that among them there would be worms, <u>snails,</u> insects and other good things to *see* (eat). As soon as it was dark she would go out and *burn* (find) some food. After such a long sleep, the hedgehog felt <u>weak</u> and very hungry. She <u>poked</u> around in the grass and found a slug and a *stone* (worm). Then, after a while, she found a <u>newt</u>. Quickly she pressed her spines into it and bit into its *metal* (tasty) <u>flesh</u>. All the time, while looking for food, she had to take care that no foxes or badgers <u>crept</u> up on her. By morning she was very <u>sick</u> (tired). So she found a pile of <u>dead</u> leaves under a holly bush and settled down to *play* (sleep). One night, as the hedgehog was <u>tramping</u> off to the stream, she heard a <u>scuffling</u> noise behind her. She found that there was another *tractor* (hedgehog) following her.

Notes:
The words that Katy identified as being anomalous are underlined.
Italicised words indicate anomalous words to be detected. The original words are given in parentheses.

Figure 7.4: An extract from Katy's responses to the Hedgehog Story

The results from the cloze tests indicate that Katy has difficulty monitoring her comprehension. Furthermore, her comprehension is often restricted to small units of text, sentences or phrases, and there-fore she does not comprehend the story as a whole. Her tendency to take the literal meaning of words and her failure to process informa-tion flexibly will cause additional problems. Although these difficul-ties were observed on tests of reading comprehension, it is easy to see how they could cause problems for listening comprehension.

Whether prose is presented aurally or in a written form, the information must be monitored and inferences drawn to maximize comprehension.

Assessing Reading Comprehension

It is clear that reading comprehension difficulties constitute a serious problem. Many school assignments, such as English, geography and history require pupils to read books and extract the relevant information. Children with comprehension difficulties will struggle to complete such tasks and fall behind their peers. Because reading ability is commonly assessed in terms of decoding skills, comprehension difficulties can easily be overlooked or mistaken for laziness. It is, therefore, important to formally assess children's comprehension skills so difficulties can be detected and appropriate help given.

There are two main methods of assessing reading comprehension ability in children: cloze tests and question and answer tests. Cloze tests generally adopt the following procedure. Children are given either a series of isolated sentences or a connected passage of prose to read. At intervals throughout the text, a gap is inserted and a choice of say three alternative words is given (for example, 'The little dog *buried/bit/made* his bone under a stone'). The child is required to choose the word that fits the context of the passage. A variation on this theme involves identifying anomalous words that are embedded within the text (for example, 'It was a very hot day so Jane put on her scarf and gloves'). In question and answer tests, children are given a passage to read and then asked a series of comprehension questions. The questions may be open-ended (for example, 'Why was Peter happy?') or multiple choice. Furthermore, the questions and answers may be spoken or written to allow for group testing.

The two methods of assessing comprehension skills described here have associated advantages and disadvantages and the choice of test will ultimately depend upon the reasons for assessment. Cloze tests have the advantage of being relatively quick and easy to administer as an entire class can be tested at once. They are also quick to score. Therefore, a cloze test is often the most appropriate test when a teacher wants to assess the reading comprehension skills of the whole class. However, cloze tests do have a number of disadvantages. First, they frequently measure vocabulary rather than comprehension skills. For example, the following item is taken from the *Spar Reading Test* (Young, 1978).

'Sensible means *recite; referee; regard; reasonable; resemble; refresh.*'

Although vocabulary knowledge does contribute to comprehension ability, the two skills are not synonymous and it is important to ensure that the test goes beyond assessing the meaning of individual words. Second, cloze tests often measure decoding skills rather than comprehension skills. For example, the *Suffolk Reading Scale* (Hagley, 1987) is designed to show how well children understand what they read. The child is presented with a series of sentences, each with one word missing. Each sentence is accompanied by a list of words and the child has to circle the word that fits the gap.

> The festive occasion ended with a _____ firework display.
> *speculation; spectacular; classified; perpetual; spectacle*

Kate Nation gave this test to a large group of Year 3 and Year 4 children (ages: 7–9 years). She found that performance on the Suffolk Test correlated much more highly with decoding skills than with listening comprehension skills. In Year 3, the Suffolk reading score correlated 0.49 with listening comprehension and 0.79 with nonword decoding (Year 4 correlations: 0.41 and 0.75, respectively). In other words, this test is primarily a measure of decoding skill, not comprehension.

A further disadvantage of cloze tests is a problem that is associated with group tests. When a child performs poorly on a cloze test it is difficult to determine whether the problem is attributable to poor comprehension skills, or whether it actually stems from impaired decoding skills. Tests that do not provide an independent assessment of decoding and comprehension skills make it difficult to identify the cause of the child's difficulty. This problem can be overcome to some extent by administering the test individually and asking the child to read the passage aloud.

Question and answer tests can provide a more thorough assessment of comprehension skills by assessing literal and inferential processing skills. This is especially true for tests with open-ended questions. The major advantage of this type of test is that, when given individually, it is possible to determine whether the child's inability to answer the comprehension questions is attributable to weak decoding skills or impaired comprehension. Some tests give separate scores for decoding and comprehension skills (see the *Neale Analysis of Reading Ability*; 1989) providing a more thorough assessment of reading ability. However, individual tests are time consuming and most teachers do not have the resources to assess the whole class in this manner. Arguably the best solution is to use a group test as a screening device to identify children with difficulties. These children could then be given an individual test.

When selecting or designing a comprehension test there are a number of factors that should be considered. First, as noted above, it is important to ensure that the test actually measures comprehension skills and is not simply a test of vocabulary knowledge or decoding ability. The test should measure literal and inferential processing skills, that is, it should assess memory for details explicitly stated in the text and it should also assess the ability to draw inferences and recall information that is only implied. Some comprehension tests require that the questions are answered from memory (*Neale Analysis of Reading Ability*, Neale, 1989), whereas others allow the child to refer back to the passage (*Wechsler Objective Reading Dimensions*, Wechsler, 1993). Differences in memory load among different comprehension tests do not appear to be important. Oakhill (1984) noted that children with reading comprehension problems still experienced significant difficulty answering inferential comprehension questions even when they were allowed to check their answers by referring back to the actual passage. Finally, it is important to remember that tests that supply separate measures of decoding and comprehension skills provide a more accurate assessment of reading ability. Such tests should be used when possible.

There are now a large number of commercially available reading comprehension tests. The *Neale Analysis of Reading Ability, Revised* (Neale, 1989) is one of the most widely used tests in the United Kingdom. It is a standardized reading test that provides age-related measures of reading accuracy, reading rate and reading comprehension. Percentile ranks can also be computed. The test is administered individually. The child is asked to read aloud a series of short passages and at the end of each one is asked a set of open-ended comprehension questions. The test has two parallel forms to allow for re-testing. The Neale test is suitable for children aged 5- to 13-years and takes about 20 minutes to administer.

The revised version of the Neale has recently been criticized. Gregory and Gregory (1994) have suggested that the Neale underestimates reading ability. They gave a group of 5- to 8-year old children the Neale and *The British Ability Scales* (BAS) *Reading Test* (Elliot, 1992). They found that the average Neale accuracy and comprehension reading ages were lower than the BAS reading age by about nine months and suggest that it is the former test that is inaccurate. Stothard and Hulme (1991) have also outlined some shortcomings of the Revised Neale. First, we noted that Forms 1 and 2 are not equivalent measures of reading ability. Specifically, when given Forms 1 and 2, 7-year-old boys obtained significantly lower scores on the latter form. No such difference was observed for girls. It appears that Form 2 underestimates the reading ability of boys. A further problem with Form 2 is that the comprehension questions are not appropriately graded. In principle, the comprehension questions should become progressively more difficult as the test progresses from Level 1 to Level 6. However, Level 5 is actually more difficult to understand than Level 6. With these problems in mind, it is important to remember that the results obtained from the Neale need to be interpreted cautiously. Furthermore, it should be remembered that Form 1 of the Neale seems to be a better measure of reading skills and should be used in preference to Form 2 wherever possible. Finally, it is worth pointing out that despite these criticisms, the Neale is still useful for identifying children with specific reading comprehension difficulties.

The *Wechsler Objective Reading Dimensions* (WORD) (Wechsler, 1993) test is also an individually administered test of reading ability. The WORD differs from the Neale in so far as decoding and comprehension skills are measured by two separate tests. Reading accuracy skills are assessed by asking children to read aloud a series of words that are graded in difficulty. The reading comprehension test comprises a series of short printed passages, each followed by an orally presented open-ended question. Scoring is based solely on the child's response to the question. This test is designed to test skills such as recognizing stated detail and making inferences. From the WORD, a reading accuracy age and a reading comprehension age can be computed. Standard scores and percentile ranks can also be derived. The WORD is suitable for children aged 6- to 16-years and the reading comprehension test takes about 10–15 minutes to administer. Unfortunately, this test is only available for psychologists to administer.

There are also a variety of group administered tests, such as *Group Reading Test*, ages 9–14 years; *London Reading Test*, ages 10–12 years ; *Effective Reading Tests*, ages 6–12 years; *Reading Ability Series*, ages 7–13 years; *Suffolk Reading Scale*: ages 6 –13 years; these tests are all published by NFER-Nelson. Group tests are useful for screening large numbers of children to identify those children with reading difficulties. However, because they cannot give separate scores for reading accuracy skills and reading comprehension skills it is difficult to identify the exact nature of the child's reading difficulty. There-fore, it is often necessary to follow up group tests with individual tests for those children who experienced difficulties.

Conclusions and Implications for Teaching

The research presented in this chapter clearly shows that children's reading comprehension difficulties are not a trivial matter. Approxi-mately one in ten children experiences specific reading comprehen-sion problems; these difficulties ranging from 7–26 months delay in comprehension skills (Stothard, 1992). There can be no doubt that these children are in need of specialist help.

So, how can children with reading comprehension problems be helped to overcome their difficulties? The research presented in this chapter shows that reading comprehension difficulties are associated with general language comprehension difficulties. Poor comprehen-ders have poor verbal–semantic skills, limited vocabulary knowl-edge, weak inferential and integrative processing skills and poor metacognitive awareness skills. Given that reading comprehension problems typically co-occur with general language comprehension difficulties, the focus of remediation should not be on reading *per se*. Rather, remediation should focus on general language processes and instruction needs to target a wide range of verbal–semantic skills such as vocabulary knowledge, listening skills and expressive language skills (see Stothard, 1994 for a review).

A number of research studies have shown that vocabulary instruction can be an effective means of improving reading compre-hension. In a series of studies Beck and her colleagues (see Beck, Omanson and McKeown, 1982a; Beck, Perfetti and McKeown, 1982b; McKeown, Beck, Omanson, et al., 1985) have shown that vocabulary training can produce significant improvements in chil-dren's comprehension (see also Kameenui, Carnine and Freschi, 1982; Stahl, 1983). For example, Beck, et al. (1982b) taught children a large set of words by a variety of instructional activities such as defining, sentence generation, classification, oral and written production and word speeded games. They found that the vocabu-lary instruction had a number of beneficial effects. Compared with controls, the trained group obtained significantly higher scores on the experimental vocabulary test, and they also made significant improvements on standardized tests of vocabulary and reading comprehension. As similar gains were shown on the vocabulary and reading comprehension tests, it seems that the vocabulary instruction might be responsible for the transfer effects. Teaching children the meanings of words can improve comprehension because knowing the meanings of individual words makes it easier to construct the meaning of the overall passage.

It has also been suggested that teaching children other cognitive strategies such as inferencing skills and metacognitive skills can help improve reading comprehension. For example, Yuill and her colleagues (Yuill and Joscelyne, 1988; Yuill and Oakhill, 1988) argue that reading comprehension can be improved by teaching children how to draw inferences during reading. Yuill and Oakhill (1988) reported that poor comprehenders who had been taught how to draw inferences made significant gains on a standardized test of reading comprehension. However, these findings are difficult to interpret. The inference-trained group did not show significantly greater gains in comprehension than a control group who received standard comprehension exercises. Hence, it is not clear which component of instruction is important. Furthermore, it is possible that the observed gains in comprehension are merely a reflection of practice effects on the reading test.

Training studies that have tried to improve children's metacognitive skills are also plagued by similar problems. For example, Paris and colleagues (Paris, Cross and Lipson, 1984; Paris and Jacobs, 1984) taught children about reading strategies and how to use them. A variety of strategies were taught including comprehension monitoring, summarizing and finding the main idea. Training was successful in so far as the children made marked improvements in both metacognitive awareness and comprehension skills, as assessed by their performance on error detection tasks and cloze tests. However, the training did not produce significant improvements in standardized test scores; trained children were not significantly better than controls at answering questions about previously read stories.

In conclusion, the most effective method of improving reading comprehension skills appears to involve improving the child's underlying vocabulary knowledge. In addition, there is some evidence to suggest that teaching children to draw inferences and read in a more strategic manner can also produce improvements in comprehension. However, further research is needed to confirm the efficacy of this latter approach.

Chapter 8
Promoting Phonological Awareness in Preschool Children

Lyn Layton and Karen Deeny

The centrality of phonological awareness to the development of efficient written language skills has been demonstrated through a range of studies (see Goswami and Bryant, 1990 for an overview and Snowling, this volume). In order to establish a framework for this chapter some of the conclusions from recent research which have particular relevance to preschool, preliterate children are listed as follows:

- phonological awareness at the onset-rime level, evident in rhyming skills, contributes significantly towards alphabetic literacy (Goswami, 1994)
- explicit awareness of the onset-rime division is within the capacity of normally progressing preschool children and is evident in their ability to detect rhyme (Goswami and Bryant, 1990)
- preschoolers can be trained to make judgements about the onset-rime division (Lundberg, Frost and Petersen, 1988)
- children who remain insensitive to the onset-rime division are at risk of reading and spelling failure (Bradley, 1988)

These theoretical positions have yielded innovative and creative techniques for promoting phonological awareness but the practical implications for children in nursery classrooms and other preschool groups do not yet appear to have been fully exploited. As Blachman (1991) wrote of the situation in the US:

> Despite the evidence (confirming the value of explicit training in phonological awareness for the development of literacy skills), activities to build phonological awareness have not routinely been integrated into our kindergarten and first grade classrooms.

The research evidence is now set before practitioners as a challenge to take a fresh look at the foundations from which children start to learn to read and spell. Teachers, in particular, should consider building into the prereading curriculum, activities which will promote *metalinguistic skills* in all children. These are the cognitive skills which call for an explicit reflection on the form of language, for example, recognizing the phonetic similarity between the words: *tea, key, bee* and being able to judge that the word *door* would be an odd one out in this rhyme sequence. Such activities should supplement, but not replace, existing procedures for training the visual skills necessary to process written language which currently appear to dominate the prereading programme. Metalinguistic activities, such as training in rhyme detection, require conscious deliberation. Chanting a succession of nursery rhymes, while valuable as a starting-point, would not be regarded as sufficiently demanding of explicit awareness to stand alone as metalinguistic training.

We are therefore suggesting that teachers adopt a prereading programme that does not leave children to acquire finely-tuned phonological skills by accident. The extra dimension which we are proposing will maximize the benefits of early training for the vast majority of children. It should also create opportunities for professionals to examine and promote important underlying skills in order to prevent the emergence of serious literacy difficulties *before* children embark on literacy instruction. Such an approach could have a positive effect on the acquisition of literacy for all children. The requirements however, beg important questions if the challenges which we have set down are to be met:

- who are the children with poor phonological skills?
- who might take responsibility for:
  - identifying children who do not have age-appropriate phonological skills?
  - developing a structured prereading programme?
- how can teachers promote phonological skills in children identified as being at risk for literacy problems?

Kamhi and Catts (1989) suggest that poor phonological skills have a life-long effect with a variety of manifestations along the way. Thus, in addressing the question of who are these children with poor phonological skills, we should acknowledge that a child might progress from an earlier spoken language difficulty to a later written language problem. In particular, children with a phonological disorder affecting spoken language seem to be most at risk for dyslexic difficulties (see Stackhouse, this volume).

In addition to the children whose poor phonological skills are clearly manifested at an early age in spoken language difficulties, there are other children whose speech and language difficulties remain hidden (Stackhouse and Wells, 1991). Their phonological weaknesses may not be identified in the preschool years because there are very few specific tasks or games which provide opportunities for demonstrating explicit phonological awareness at this early age. It seems that poor phonological processing does not necessarily result in overt spoken language difficulties, or, at least, not those severe enough to come to the attention of a speech and language therapist. Therefore, it would seem unwise, possibly negligent, to assume that children have the necessary prerequisite skills for developing literacy without asking them to demonstrate these skills.

This raises the question of who is to shoulder the responsibility for detecting the subtle phonological weaknesses in this unnoticed group of children in particular. Clearly, they are not coming to the attention of speech and language therapists. However, the nursery and reception classteachers are ideally placed to ask children to demonstrate the skills so crucial for understanding letter-sound correspondence and to initiate intervention programmes for children who demonstrate phonological weaknesses. This could be achieved within the prereading programme which, we have already suggested, should be in place for all young children and which should comprise a repertoire of tasks, both to develop and to assess children's phonological skills.

We need, therefore, not only a programme of activities, but also the expertise of the professionals (principally teachers and speech and language therapists) to implement it. We have implied that the two professional groups assume responsibility for two different groups of children: speech and language therapists are well placed to address the needs of the *noticed* group, and teachers the *unnoticed* group. However, the responsibilities do not, in reality, divide that neatly. Factors influencing which children may fall into unnoticed or noticed groups are many and varied: for example, those who have been referred to speech and language therapy but have failed to attend or are not adequately served by a poorly resourced service might receive scant attention to the skills which serve both written and spoken language.

However the children are divided, it is our contention that teachers and speech and language therapists can share the responsibility for both assessing and facilitating phonological skills. In this chapter we will describe the techniques for promoting phonological awareness in preschool children with identified weaknesses which we have used in our research programme. The programme has a strong practical bias in the design and implementation of phonological training routines. The skill mix of the researchers involved resulted in effective and workable programmes of activities. This pooling of expertise can contribute to the reduction of specific written language difficulties by addressing the pre-requisite skills of children with noticed or unnoticed language difficulties.

Preschool Training Programmes

An awareness of the sound structure of spoken language provides the key to cracking the code of alphabetic literacy. Without the key, the relationship between alphabetic letters and the way in which they combine to produce written representations of the words we say and hear, seems to the reader, random and haphazard. Evidence that children have not discovered the key is available in the so-called bizarre spellings produced by severely dyslexic writers. It was with a commitment to facilitating literacy development in children who might be at risk of developing such problems that our investigation set out to examine the phonological abilities of preschoolers and to enhance these abilities when they were found to be under-developed.

The investigation initially drew on the methods and findings from other studies. Bradley and Bryant (1983) tested 400 4- and 5-year-old non-readers on their ability to detect rhyme and alliteration. The results showed that rhyme detection scores in particular predicted the children's progress in reading and spelling four years later. This finding was specific to literacy development. There was no relationship between scores on the rhyme tests and scores on mathematical tests. Further, there was no effect of differences in measured intelligence (see Muter, this volume, for further discussion of rhyme skills).

As part of the same project, Bradley and Bryant also undertook a training study in order to confirm the causal nature of the relationship between early sound categorization skills and later reading ability. They selected 65 children who, as prereaders, performed poorly on their measures of phonological awareness. These children were trained to match words according to initial, medial or final sounds in 10-minute individual sessions. After one year or 20 sessions the training procedure was extended to test for the effect of linking letters with sounds. Bradley and Bryant concluded that phonological training which made the letter-sound linkage transparent was effective in promoting reading ability. The groups in this part of the research were aged 6 years at the beginning of their training and thus would have been attending primary school where, in Britain, all children are taught to read and spell.

A study conducted by Lundberg, et al. (1988), in Scandinavia, involved 390 6-year-old children. However, these children were preschool and preliterate. In preparation for the study, nursery class-teachers participated in intensive training sessions in which they came to understand the theoretical framework and to acquire skills necessary for implementing metalinguistic routines. In the experimental group, the children, all non-readers, were trained to attend to progressively smaller units of spoken words until finally, they were introduced to phonemes–the smallest units of spoken words which can modify meaning. On the basis of comparisons between the experimental group and an untrained control group the researchers claimed that training prereaders to attend to the sound structure of spoken words promoted reading and spelling ability by making the alphabetic principle clear.

As part of the same study, the preventative power of phonological training was demonstrated. Twenty-five children, judged to be at risk for developing literacy problems on the basis of very low scores on rhyme, syllable and phoneme awareness tests were selected. Post-training, their performance on a range of written language measures was shown to be superior to that of a matched but untrained control group.

It seemed to us that research had already demonstrated that normally progressing preschoolers are on the threshold of discovering the formal properties of spoken words. Moreover, Bradley and Bryant's study confirmed that children who remain insensitive to phonological structures are at risk for developing written language difficulties. Lundberg's work with preschoolers suggested that, under the direction of specifically-trained teachers and in a lengthy training programme, 6-year-old children can be taught to bring this emerging awareness to an explicit level and even attend to phonemes, outside written language instruction (see Hatcher, this volume, for further discussion of training programmes).

The aim of our study was to facilitate written language development in children who are at risk for literacy problems by promoting phonological awareness skills in the preschool period prior to formal reading and writing instruction. It was based on the premise that normally progressing preschoolers can make explicit judgements about rhyme, provided they have had adequate opportunity to engage in nursery-rhyme chanting and other language-based classroom routines. Therefore, we specified the following as important for identifying and enhancing poor phonological awareness in the nursery classroom:

• Preliterate children are seldom asked to make explicit their observations on the structure of spoken language. Therefore failure to perform well on assessment of rhyme judgement, for example, may simply be due to lack of experience.

• Phonological training for children with an identified weakness in this domain should focus on the skills which contribute to the ability to make explicit judgements on the sound structure of words.

• If the identification and support of children with poor phonological awareness is to become standard practice in nursery classrooms the means of achieving this should have regard to the existing class routine, and thus should be manageable by the majority of teachers without extensive in-service training.

• In order to maximize the preventative effect of training any programme to promote literacy support skills should be completed before a child starts formal schooling.

Pilot Study

The aims of our study at this stage were: to examine procedures for identifying rhyme and alliteration awareness in children aged approximately 3;6 years to 4;0 years in a variety of preschool settings; to investigate what teaching staff in these groups understand about the importance of rhyming activities for the acquisition of literacy; and to establish what skills are generally believed to underpin early reading and writing and how these skills are encouraged within the framework of the preschool group.

The children in these groups, where nursery rhymes were valued, were asked to recite the five nursery rhymes, identified by Maclean, Bryant and Bradley (1987) as being within the repertoire of most English-speaking children: *Jack and Jill; Twinkle Twinkle Little Star;*

Humpty Dumpty; Baa Baa Black Sheep and *Hickory Dickory Dock*. They were also asked to make judgements relating to rhyming and alliterative words. The results showed clearly that the children were having difficulty in disregarding the meaning of the words. That is, they were simply unused to being asked to respond to the sounds of words.

Teachers' views on nursery rhymes, phonological awareness and prereading skills were collected from staff in these groups and those of nursery classes attached to primary schools, in structured interviews. Responses were supplemented by observations of activities, particularly those which focused on language use, during the normal routines of the preschool groups. In general, we found that teachers tended to regard visual skills as particularly important for reading. Language activities such as nursery rhyme chanting were valued, mainly for the opportunities which they provided for social exchange. It did not seem that teachers were fully aware of the significance of rhyme knowledge for later literacy development.

However, many games already used by the groups had the potential for promoting phonological awareness, and we took the opportunity to modify these and to try them out on the children. These activities were collated to form a structured resource pack for classroom use.

Main Study

The aims of the main study were to identify poor phonological awareness in preschool children and to promote written language development before school entry and the start of formal literacy instruction.

Two hundred and fifty children, all native English speakers, in the nursery classes of 21 Local Education Authority schools in the West Midlands of England were randomly chosen for inclusion in the study. The population was divided to facilitate the implementation of the investigation, with the schools in one LEA ahead of those in the second by one term. These represent two cohorts. Three schools in the first cohort elected to repeat the study with a new intake of children and collectively, these became the third cohort. A final total of 240 children was available for assessment and the average age of the children at the time of assessment was 4;5 years.

Phase 1–Identification

Observations made during the pilot phase suggested that it was important to establish that children were not failing to make phonological judgements simply through lack of experience. We therefore decided to preface phonological testing with an *experience* phase. This involved the implementation of the *class-based activities* (referred to above as a *resource pack*) in the nursery, under the direction of the teacher or nursery-nurse.

The group activities followed the progression suggested by Lundberg's study (Lundberg, et al., 1988). The first activities were intended to promote general listening or attention and included a variation on 'Simon Says'. Rhythm activities followed in which the children were encouraged to beat out the sound patterns in phrases and words. The children were introduced to the concept and label *word* so that they would be able to interpret: 'Which *words* sound the same/different' or 'Which words rhyme?' The word game section concluded with an activity asking the children: 'Which word is wrong?', 'Why is this word wrong?', in e.g. 'Jack and Jill/Went up the road?' A range of rhyming activities then included games to elicit rhyming judgements and the production of rhymes.

Procedures using the same format were introduced for words with the same onset. Activities in these sections conceptualized a word as a train in order to identify the beginning of a word. Other games included 'I-Spy', but the teachers were supplied with the words to use so that we could be sure that they were using the whole onset of the word and not just the sound of the initial letter (for example, *ch-air, sp-oon*) . The popular 'Tray Game' was also included, in which the teacher shows the children items on a tray all having the same initial sound. The children are then given extra items and they must judge whether these can be included, according to the onset of the word.

The experience phase did not feature activities calling for explicit phoneme awareness because, despite Lundberg's claims that 6-year-old non-readers can be trained to make judgements at this level, it is generally believed that such awareness spontaneously develops only in connection with reading and spelling and is rarely discovered in preliterate children.

The programme was conducted over a 42-day period on a daily basis. All the materials which supported the games were supplied, and the teachers attended two informal meetings as preparation for their part in the study.

It should be emphasized that the programme was intended to familiarize the children with the notion of disregarding the meaning component of spoken language in order to reflect on its formal structure. However, it was not intended to be a rigorous training procedure but a usable teaching resource. Therefore, certain principles, derived from both theory and practice, guided its design and production:

- The games should be regarded by teachers as relevant and appealing, and should be easily fitted into existing slots during the nursery day, for example, during 'Talk-time'.
- The combined effect of the games should orientate children towards making phonological judgements by encouraging them to attend to the linguistic form of familiar words rather than their semantic associations.
- The cognitive and linguistic demands imposed by the games should be limited as far as possible. Therefore, the vocabulary was constrained by a number of factors, for example, the receptive vocabulary of the average 4-year-old; concepts which could be unambiguously illustrated; phonological complexity and memory loading.

The children who had participated in the activities were assessed when they were about 4;6 years. Each child was asked to recite the five traditional rhymes (listed above) which had featured in the Maclean, et al. (1987) study. They were then asked to judge which two words rhymed with a target word and which word was the odd-one-out. Again, the vocabulary which featured in the test was carefully controlled to reduce contamination of results by other variables. The words were illustrated to reduce the memory loading, but the significance of the illustrations was deliberately understated so that, for example, the children were not shown the illustrations until they had repeated each word. The same odd one out format was used to measure alliteration detection; the key feature of these words being that all but one had the same onset. There were ten items in each test and scoring was 1 for each correct item. Thus, each test had a maximum score of 10.

The results shown in Table 8.1 suggest that rhyme detection, as measured by the tests devised for this study, was more likely to be within the capacity of this age-group than alliteration detection. This confirmed observations made during testing when it was decided to regard performance on the rhyme detection test as the key indicator of phonological awareness. Analysis of the final results suggested that this decision was well-founded.

Table 8.1: Comparison of the three groups of schools on the phonological awareness tasks

	N*	Nursery Rhyme Knowledge (n)		Rhyme Detection (n)		Alliteration Detection (n)	
		Mean	SD†	Mean	SD	Mean	SD
Group 1	131	7.107	2.689	5.992	3.901	4.244	3.014
Group 2	90	7.656	2.801	6.034	4.141	4.409	3.319
Group 3	19	8.053	4.217	7.105	3.838	4.053	4.679
Total	240	7.388	2.531	6.096	3.830	4.291	2.968

* This is the total number of children for each group. The actual number for the tests is, in some cases, slightly smaller.
† Standard deviation of the sample.
n Maximum score for each test = 10

Table 8.2: Correlation matrix* of the three tasks

	Nursery Rhyme Knowledge	Rhyme Detection	Alliteration Detection
Nursery Rhyme Knowledge	–		
Rhyme Detection	.451	–	
Alliteration Detection	.344	.581	–

* All correlations are significant at p< .001

Maclean, et al. (1987) established that the nursery rhymes which we used in our study are popular with English-speaking children. Moreover, knowledge of these rhymes is known to be predictive of phonological awareness. Therefore, we included this measure to provide some evidence of the validity of our other two tests. Table 8.2 shows that scores from both the rhyme detection test and the alliteration detection test correlate significantly with each other and with those indicating nursery rhyme knowledge. However, the correlation of nursery rhyme knowledge with alliteration detection is lower than that with rhyme detection.

As Frith (1995) points out, many factors, for example, poor motivation or attention may affect performance on phonological tests despite all efforts on the part of the testers to set up tests as games. To control for this we tested the children who performed at or below chance level on the rhyme detection test on a non-verbal ability test:

The *Coloured Progressive Matrices* (Raven, 1984). Frith acknowledges that although people at all intellectual levels can experience difficulties with phonological processing a 'very low IQ would depress scores on any test, including phonological tests' (Frith, 1995). Consequently, only those children with a measured score at or above the 50th percentile were considered for further involvement in this study. Using these criteria, 41 children were targeted for further intensive phonological training which formed the focus of the second phase of the investigation.

Phase 2–Training

Another programme of activities was designed for the targeted group to follow over a 30-day period. In line with the remediation approaches suggested by Bryant and Bradley (1985) and by teachers working with children with severe dyslexia, it was considered appropriate that children requiring additional phonological training should receive one-to-one attention. This decision was further justified after considering the possibility that, for this group, a failure to set up accurate representations of spoken language might lie at the heart of their difficulty with rhyme detection. Therefore, we felt that it is essential that these children should be given enhanced opportunities for listening and perceiving accurately, through individual instruction.

Half of the group was assigned to a control group where the children received one-to-one training in semantic categorization skills without any special reference to phonological factors. Otherwise their training programme was equivalent in terms of length and application to that administered to the experimental group.

The programme for the experimental group followed a step-wise progression with the first activities intended to establish the skills involved in making explicit comparisons between words, for example, each child was required to judge whether two words were the *same* or *different*. As poor short-term memory often co-exists with poor phonological awareness (Baddely and Gathercole, 1992), games to promote memory functioning followed. These procedures attempted to support weak auditory memory skills by teaching multisensory strategies, for example, verbal rehearsal (saying words we want to remember) as suggested by Gathercole (1993) and verbal imaging (deliberately setting up and attending to mental pictures). New words and rhymes were introduced around the theme of Humpty Dumpty and friends, and the more advanced activities mirrored those which had featured in the previous group-based phase of the study.

Initial feedback from the nursery teachers who were responsible for implementing the individual routines suggested that children enjoyed the games and responded positively to them, and the programmes were completed for the majority of children. However, in a hectic nursery classroom with minimal staffing, one-to-one training on a daily basis created pressures and some teachers felt that they would be unable to sustain the level of support as a routine approach to enhancing phonological awareness in children with specific weaknesses. The focus of the next phase of the investigation was, therefore, to consider how an alternative means of delivering the same intensive training could be provided.

Phase 3 –Alternative training provision

In line with current trends towards training classroom assistants to support children with a range of special needs and the 'Parents as Partners' philosophy, classroom assistants or parent-volunteers implemented the pack of activities and the children's parents were asked to reinforce classroom exercises. This aspect of the study did not include an experience phase as it was conducted in nursery classes where teachers were already familiar with the aims of the project and with the notion of phonological awareness. For these classes specialized listening activities, developed from the experience phase of the investigation, were already a feature of the prereading programme. Researchers, using the assessment techniques developed in connection with the earlier phase of the investigation, identified children with poor phonological awareness. These children then worked through the activities with non-teachers–volunteers or classroom assistants–who, during the previous half-term, had attended weekly training sessions led by the researchers, in order to become familiar with a modified version of the activity pack which aims to promote the skills underpinning rhyme awareness.

The long-term aim of this phase of the research is to facilitate literacy development for those children who, at the age of 4, were at risk for reading and spelling difficulties on account of under-developed phonological awareness. Their reading and spelling performance will be evaluated when they are between 6 and 7 years of age. By this time the children will have been learning about written language for approximately two years and we would expect that those with well-established awareness of the sound structure of spoken language will be recognizing and utilizing associations between sound patterns and spelling patterns. In contrast, children whose poor rhyme detection skills did not receive any attention might be experiencing particular difficulty with alphabetic literacy.

Meanwhile we are reminded of Blachman's concerns about phonological awareness training activities not being routinely integrated into our 'kindergarten and first grade classrooms...' (Blachman, 1991). Therefore, a parallel aim of the study has been focused on the practical issues surrounding the introduction of explicit phonological awareness tasks into the nursery routine. We have taken the opportunity to examine the feasibility of phonological training routines in the ordinary classroom, and to consider the implications of our work for regular classroom practice.

Implications for Classroom Practice

Classteachers in the study welcomed the opportunity to look more closely at the language skills of their pupils during those activities intended for groupwork. They noted that many of the activities are not, in principle, substantially different from games which young children already know and enjoy, for example, nursery rhyme games and beating rhythms. Some teachers even developed their own versions of activities. In one school a teacher who had taken a particular interest in the work being conducted in the nursery noted that Year 1 children who were struggling with literacy found the division of spoken words into syllables difficult to grasp. She formed this group into a band, with musical instruments, and assigned to each child the name of a grocery item which had the same number of syllables as those in his or her name. The children were then required to beat out their special numbers, chanting either name or grocery item, and marching to reinforce the syllabic rhythm.

In general, the teachers in the study recognized that what the programme demanded was a change of emphasis so that, for example, lack of nursery rhyme knowledge may be regarded as evidence that a particular skill is under-developed and should not be taken simply as an indication that a child is reticent or unstimulated. On a practical point teachers enthusiastically supported the initiative whereby trained classroom assistants were engaged to work closely with children identified for special attention.

Classroom assistants coped well with implementing the intensive programmes and those with wide experience of working with young children valued the insight which it gave them. In two cases the assistants reported that they had been surprised that particular children had been selected for special training, that is until they had asked the children to carry out the tasks and so to demonstrate certain skills. This caused one assistant–also a day-nursery supervisor who had practised the games with younger children–to comment, 'J may well have problems which we would never, otherwise, have known about...'

Elsewhere, reception teachers who had piloted the general experience activities with their classes in preparation for the planned publication of the resource pack, were questioned on the competencies which support phonological awareness: they appreciated that spoken language skills are informed by the same processes which direct phonological judgements. Similarly, they expected that a child whom they regarded as generally unstimulated would be disadvantaged in all language areas. What seemed to be lacking was an acknowledgement that children from linguistically stimulated backgrounds with no obvious spoken language disorder or delay can nonetheless fail to develop awareness of rhyme; that many children who fail to develop rhyme after appropriate experience will not respond to more-of-the-same; and that preparation for alphabetic literacy through effective phonological training may require the radical examination and stimulation of prerequisite skills.

This approach would seem to require of teachers an insight which, in many cases, they do not demonstrate. For example, they need to recognize and make explicit the segmented nature of spoken language. Furthermore, they should distinguish unambiguously between spoken word segments and the individual letters which make up written words: an alarming number of early years' teachers fail to differentiate between phonemes and graphemes, particularly in connection with initial sounds or initial letters: one teacher asked her class to give examples of words which start with the same sound as *Eddie Elephant* and her own example was *eye*. The assumption that preliterate children can readily associate one letter with a range of phonemes is perpetuated in many published resources and we have particularly noted *g* for *giraffe* and *o* for *owl* among classroom materials. In short, for the purposes of promoting phonological awareness as a prerequisite skill for the acquisition of reading and spelling–and as a criterion for choosing materials–teachers must be aware of the cognitive demands which underpin apparently simple activities. This suggests that the teachers' own knowledge base may need to be extended so that they can adopt a *spoken language perspective* when preparing young children for *written language learning*.

This has obvious implications for initial teacher training. However, we should also consider how collaboration between teachers and speech and language therapists can provide opportunities for stimulating a greater understanding of the links between spoken and written language, and how such collaboration can be formalized (see Wright, 1992).

Teacher–Therapist Collaboration

Catts (1991) has identified a key role for the speech and language therapist in facilitating phonological awareness in the classroom. He recommends that, along with class-teachers, speech and language therapists should be centrally involved in the design and evaluation of literacy programmes because of their unique understanding of the processes involved. This is particularly important when children have spoken language impairments. Stackhouse (1989) emphasizes the need for therapists to act in an advisory capacity with regard to the reading and spelling development of children with identified spoken language disorders and has discussed how literacy skills can be developed through routine speech and language therapy activities (Stackhouse, 1992b).

Catts cites examples of speech and language therapists adopting a directly instructional role for teaching normally progressing children about the sound structure of spoken language. Furthermore, his recommendations include a role for teachers in identifying weaknesses in the phonological awareness of preschoolers, using a checklist developed by therapists. In this way, teachers could identify the hitherto unnoticed group and then implement intervention programmes in collaboration with a therapist. In short, collaboration which involves a sharing of knowledge and skills between teachers and speech and language therapists is essential for promoting both spoken and written language development (Popple and Wellington 1996).

Policy change and collaboration

In Britain, the National Curriculum sets out the expectations for attainment in key areas for all pupils, and attainment targets include those for speaking and listening skills in the early stages of formal schooling. It is generally believed that this new focus on spoken language proficiency is reflected in, and responsible for, teachers' growing awareness of disorders and delays in development, and a related increase in the number of referrals from schools to speech and language therapy departments. It may be that a change in policy at a national level has created the impetus for improved liaison between many professionals concerned with early development, especially teachers and therapists. In addition, the recent Code of Practice on the Identification and Assessment of Special Educational Needs has its own emphasis on partnership and co-operation which will surely provide the climate and enhance the opportunities for collaboration, in respect of children with severe, long-term and complex difficulties.

Whereas legislation and policy change may provide the impetus for the development of new approaches, the details of how these might be achieved will be left to practitioners to work out. We know that where therapists are supporting statemented pupils in mainstream education there is often a spin-off effect as therapists assume an informal advisory role and less seriously affected pupils benefit indirectly from having such expertise in school. Elsewhere, a particular example demonstrates how the skills and experience of teacher and therapist might be pooled in planning a response to the joint demands of the National Curriculum and the Code of Practice for the Identification and Assessment of Special Educational Needs. Hereford and Worcester Local Education Support Service has collaborated with the local National Health Service Trust Speech and Language Therapy Department to produce a resource pack for use in the classroom. The initiative arose out of a series of exchanges between support teachers, classteachers and therapists during which many classteachers identified the need for more resources and information to address spoken language problems. The pack is intended, in the first place, for use with children whose spoken language difficulties, including poor phonological skills, tend towards the milder end of any continuum of needs and who thus might be our hitherto unnoticed group (see Hayden, 1995).

Conclusions

In this chapter we have argued for the early assessment and focused training of the skills which support alphabetic literacy development. The study described sets out to tackle these issues by developing class-based routines, assessment techniques and a training programme for children with apparent difficulties with making phonological judgements.

This study is ongoing and as yet we do not have the complete picture of the effectiveness of the early training. However, we remain convinced that children's phonological skills should be examined in the early years, before the beginning of formal literacy instruction. In this way, children with a disposition towards literacy difficulties, arising in connection with phonological weaknesses, can be identified and provided with the type of early enrichment which can nurture prerequisite skills. These skills also underpin spoken language proficiency and so the combined expertise of teacher and speech and language therapist are desirable. We have shown how collaborative measures were effectively deployed in developing a resource pack for promoting phonological awareness, and for implementing the training programme. We now look forward to the day when the teacher/therapist skill-mix routinely informs and directs the enhancement of early literacy skills. Perhaps then, fewer children, with or without a history of overt spoken language disorders, will struggle to become efficient readers and spellers.

Acknowledgements

The research described in this paper was funded jointly by the Department for Education and the Oak Foundation, and was conducted by the School of Education, University of Birmingham in conjunction with Hereford and Worcester Dyslexia Association.

Chapter 9
Practising Sound Links in Reading Intervention with the School-age Child

Peter J. Hatcher

Since the early reports of Elkonin (1963) and Zhurova (1963), numerous studies have shown a relationship between phonological skills and learning to read. Children who are good at perceiving sounds within words, for example, indicating that the spoken word *cat* can be broken into three sounds and *crest* into five sounds, learn to read more efficiently than those who are not good at such tasks. The relevance of this to teachers and speech and language therapists is that children may benefit from being taught phonological awareness before, or as part of, the learning to read process. Recent research suggests that children benefit most from phonological awareness being taught in conjunction with reading and spelling and that the gains outweigh teaching that does not include such training. The chapter will begin with a brief account of the evidence linking phonological awareness and reading. The results of an intervention study (Hatcher, Hulme and Ellis, 1994) and the teaching programme that was employed will be presented. Finally, the chapter will describe how Cumbrian teachers are being trained to use the *Sound Linkage* programme to enhance the effectiveness of their teaching procedures.

Phonological Awareness and the Acquisition of Literacy

The relationship between phonological skill and the process of learning to read has been demonstrated through measuring the two skills at the same point and after an interval of time (see Goswami and

Bryant, 1990, for a review of the evidence). A predictive relationship between phonological awareness and spelling has also been shown (Bryant, MacLean, Bradley, et al., 1990; Cataldo and Ellis 1988; Juel, Griffith and Gough, 1986).

The evidence in support of a predictive relationship between phonological awareness and literacy is very strong. However, it is not sufficient to imply that the relationship is causal, i.e., that phonological awareness directly contributes to progress in learning to read. Although IQ and early reading level have been accounted for in many of the predictive studies, there remains the possibility that other factors may be responsible for the relationship. Data from training studies, where progress in literacy is measured after children have undertaken work on phonological awareness, provide more convincing evidence. With the notable exception of a study by Lundberg, Frost and Petersen (1988), the majority of training studies have found that phonological awareness training is most effective when it is combined with the teaching of reading (Ball and Blachman, 1991; Bradley, 1988; Bradley and Bryant, 1983; Byrne and Fielding-Barnsley, 1989; Cunningham, 1990).

A problem with the combined reading and phonological training studies is that we cannot be sure that it is the combination of the two elements that is important. It may be that the reading element on its own, or the phonological training, has been particularly effective in these studies. In an attempt to resolve this issue, Charles Hulme, Andrew Ellis and I carried out a study in which three groups of children were given training in either visual reading strategies, phonological awareness or a combination of reading and phonological awareness. Compared with the progress of a control group who received no special intervention within the study but nonetheless continued to receive the same type of support that they would have been offered anyway, the reading with phonological training group made most progress in reading and spelling over a 20-week period of intervention. This finding supports the view that phonological awareness has most effect on progress in learning to read when it is combined with training in reading (Hatcher, Hulme and Ellis, 1994).

The Cumbria-York Study

The purpose of our study was to compare the effects of three forms of structured reading intervention on children experiencing difficulty in learning to read. A total of 128 7-year-old children with reading quotients of less than 86 (poorest 18 per cent of readers) on the *Word Recognition Test* (Carver, 1970) were divided into four groups of 32. The four groups were matched on IQ, reading ability, age and sex and were randomly assigned to one of three experimental teaching conditions, reading with phonology (R+P), reading alone (R), Phonology alone (P) or to a control condition (C) at time 1 (T1). Following a 20-week period of intervention, the children were re-assessed (T2) on the same measures of reading, spelling, maths and phonological awareness that had been administered at T1. In order to determine whether the effects of the intervention were long-lasting, measures of reading and spelling were taken again, nine months after the period of intervention (T3).

The measures of reading included a test of early word recognition (words commonly found in children's early reading books), the BAS *Word Reading Test*, a test of single-word reading (Elliot, Murray and Pearson, 1983), the *Neale Analysis of Reading Ability*, a test of text reading accuracy and comprehension (Neale, 1989) and a test of nonword reading that included items such as *um, bac, blod* and *unplint*. We used *Schonell's Graded Word Spelling Test* (List B) to measure spelling (Schonell and Schonell, 1956) and the BAS Basic Number Skills test (Elliot, et al., 1983) to measure arithmetic.

We used four measures of phonological processing to monitor the children's development of phonological skills. These included a modified version of Bradley's (1984) *Sound Categorization Test* and tests of phoneme blending, segmentation and deletion. The sound categorization test was used to measure children's ability to recognize rhyme and alliteration in spoken words. The test consisted of 30 sets of four words. Within each set, three words contained a common sound that the fourth lacked. In the first 10 sets the distinctive sound was the last consonant. For example, children were asked to indicate 'the odd one out' in pin, win, *sit*, fin. In the second set of ten items the distinctive sound was the medial vowel, as in lot, cot, pot, *hat*. The final ten sets of words constituted an alliteration oddity task with the distinctive sound being the first consonant, as in ham, *tap*, had, hat.

The Phoneme Blending Test measured children's ability to blend a sequence of sounds into nonwords. The test consisted of 30 sets of two to seven sounds (for example, *a,b,r,e,l; h,u,p,t* and *i,d,o,c,t*) which were presented to children at the rate of two sounds per second.

The Nonword Segmentation Test consisted of 30 sets of nonwords, each consisting of between two and seven phonemes. For this test, we required the children to segment the nonwords into separate sounds and to push a coin forward as they spoke each sound. For each item, we gave the children the number of coins corresponding to its constituent sounds.

Finally, we used a modified version of Bruce's (1964) *Word Analysis Test* to measure children's ability to delete sounds from spoken words. In section one of the test, the sound to be deleted was the first one in a word. A typical question was 'what word is left if the *j* sound is taken away from the beginning of *jam?*' In sections two and three, the sound to be deleted occurred respectively at the end and in the middle position of words. Typical questions were, 'What word is left if the *d* sound is taken away from the end of *card?*' and 'What word is left if the *p* sound is taken away from the middle of *spoon?*' In section four of the test, the position of the sound to be deleted was varied.

During the period of intervention, the experimental groups received forty 30-minute teaching sessions over 20 weeks. Children in the control group received the teaching that they would normally have received in school. The 93 children in the three experimental groups were taught by 23 teachers who had been released from their normal duties for training and to implement the teaching. Each of the teachers worked with between two and nine children and generally taught the same number of children (one to three) from each of the experimental groups. The children in the *reading and phonology* group were taught to use visual reading strategies (after Clay, 1985), phonological awareness and how to make the link between sounds and the written forms of words (Hatcher, 1994). Details about the reading with phonology programme are provided in the next section. The *reading alone* group received the same reading training as the reading and phonology group, apart from the omission of any reference to letter-sound association activities and phonological awareness. These children received no phonological training or phonological linkage activities. The *phonology only* group undertook the phonological awareness training without any reference to reading.

The aim of the study was to assess the differential effectiveness of the three training programmes in enhancing progress in acquiring literacy. The results for text reading, spelling and maths are presented in Figure 9.1. The results for the other measures of reading were similar to those for text reading.

It was found that on each of the four literacy measures, early word recognition, word reading, text reading and nonword reading, the reading and phonology group made greater progress than the control group. In every case apart from one, the other treated groups failed to make similar progress. The equivalent success of the read-

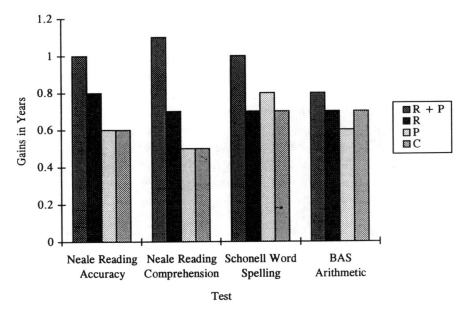

Figure 9.1: Average gains in reading, spelling and arithmetic for the four groups, reading and phonology (R+P), reading alone (R), phonology alone (P) and control (C), following the period of intervention

ing alone group on the early word reading test could be attributed to the ease with which children's first words can be learned through visual, logographic strategies (Frith, 1985; Seymour and Elder, 1986) or selective association (Gough and Juel, 1991). The success of the reading and phonology group in learning to read and spell clearly could not be attributed to the reading element of its training alone. Neither could it be attributed to the phonological element. The phonology alone group did not make significantly greater progress than the control group on any of the measures of literacy. It did, however, make significantly greater progress than the control group in developing phonological awareness. At T2, the phonology alone group performed better than the other groups on a composite score derived from the measures of sound deletion, sound blending, non-word segmentation and sound categorization (see Figure 9.2).

The results support the view that phonological training is most effective in enhancing progress in literacy when it is combined with the teaching of reading and writing. Two other important points must be considered. The training effect was specific to literacy and not attributable to factors such as teacher expectations. None of the treated groups performed better than the control group on the maths tests at T2. Also, with reading, but not spelling, the effect was long lasting. The reading with phonology group continued to outperform the control group on text reading accuracy and comprehension at T3. These findings are in keeping with a study by Iversen and Tunmer (1993) and with research that has found phonic methods to be more effective than methods that omit phonic teaching (Adams, 1990).

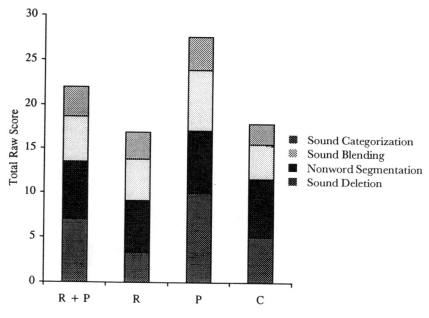

Figure 9.2: Average raw-score gains in phonological ability for the four groups, reading and phonology (R+P), reading alone (R), phonology alone (P) and control (C), following the period of intervention.

The results of our study are educationally, as well as statistically, significant. Inspection of Figure 9.1 shows that the reading with phonology group made over a year's progress in text reading accuracy and comprehension between T1 and T2 (7.43 months), although the teaching lasted for just 20 weeks. This amounts to gains of approximately 1.7 months for each month of elapsed time. In contrast, the control group made gains of just 0.9 months per month.

The Reading with Phonology Programme

The purpose of this section is to provide an overview of the reading with phonology programme. As already noted, it combines a highly structured reading programme, modelled on work by Clay (1985),

with systematic activities to promote and link phonological awareness to reading and writing. In that sense, it goes beyond the traditional Reading Recovery approach.

The first four sessions are taken up with the assessment of children's reading and writing. This is done through reading text and
through a series of diagnostic tests, including measures of concepts
about print, letter and word recognition, writing, spelling and the
ability to hear sounds in words. Based upon the data obtained,
teachers are able to identify children's reading strengths, and areas of
reading confusion and weakness. They are also able to identify
teaching goals that are likely to maximize the children's reading
progress.

Each of sessions 5 to 40 follows a similar format and consists of
three main sections. The first and last sections involve reading text
and the middle section involves writing and work on words, letters
and sounds.

Section One : Reading text and recording children's reading behaviour

Each session begins with children reading a book (or books) that can
be read with at least 95 per cent accuracy (one error or less in 20
words). The purpose of this is to provide children with the opportunity to rehearse known words in as many different contexts as possible and to read with fluency and phrasing. The teachers are
expected to praise children for aspects of their reading that are
being consolidated. For example, if a child corrects an error for the
first time, the teacher would make a positive comment about that
point.

Having read an easy book, children read the book that was introduced during the third part of the previous session. While they are
reading, the teachers use a coding system to record the children's
responses to between 100 and 200 running words. Clay (1985) refers
to this as taking a running record of children's reading. If a book is
found to have been read with 90 to 94 per cent accuracy (commonly
called the instructional level of reading) teachers introduce another
book from the same level at the end of the session. Where children
have read books fluently and with greater than 94 per cent accuracy
on two or more consecutive sessions, teachers introduce a book at a
higher level at the end of the session.

Teachers are provided with approximately three to four books at
each of 20 levels of text difficulty. Often, more books are required at
each level, particularly at the initial shared-reading levels. For this

reason, teachers are provided with a list of about 1200 books categorized according to the 20 levels of the New Zealand Ready to Read series of books (New Zealand Department of Education, 1987).

In addition to helping determine a book's reading level, the running record provides data about children's reading behaviour. This enables teachers to determine whether children have exhibited appropriate directional movement, i.e., whether they have read from left to right and from the top to the bottom of the page. It also enables them to consider the errors the children have made. Of particular interest, in this regard, is whether children realize that they have made errors and whether they attempted to correct them. Teachers look for evidence of children using the meaning of the text, the structure of the sentences, the visual appearance of words and letter-sound relationships to guess at unknown words. They also look for evidence that children have been using these strategies in combination. Of equal importance is evidence that enables teachers to praise children for implementing skills they are acquiring or consolidating. Having completed the running record, teachers select one or two teaching points that they believe are likely to be maximally effective and work on them with the children. At a very early stage of learning to read, children might spend time acquiring a sense of print directionality, or the ability to finger-point to words while they are reading. Children who are more advanced in their reading are encouraged to search for semantic, syntactic, visual and letter-sound clues, to cross-check clues when reading unknown words in text and to correct their own errors. The essence of this level of work is to encourage children to question whether what they are reading makes sense, whether it sounds right and, of particular importance, whether their attempts at unknown words correspond to the letters sound sequence of the printed words.

Section 2: Letter identification, phonological training, writing and phonological linkage activities

Letter identification

Where necessary, the middle part of every session begins with children learning the names and sounds of letters. This is accomplished through a multisensory approach (feeling, writing and naming) and through the construction of individual alphabet books containing pictures and words associated with each letter.

Phonological training

The isolated phonological training involves a graded sequence of 70 activities (Hatcher, 1994) derived from the work of researchers such as Lundberg, Frost and Petersen (1988) and Yopp (1988). The *Sound Linkage* activities are divided into nine sections. These are:

i)   identification of words as units within sentences
ii)   identification and manipulation of syllables
iii)   phoneme blending
iv)   identification and supply of rhyming words
v)   identification and discrimination of phonemes
vi)   phoneme segmentation
vii)   phoneme deletion
viii) phoneme substitution
ix)   phoneme transposition

The grading of the activities in this way is important. One of the requirements for children to be able to manipulate letter-sound relationships in literacy is for them to be able to isolate phonemes within words (phoneme segmentation). On entry to school, some children are not aware that the sentence 'Can I have a biscuit, please?' contains a number of separate words, let alone that the word *can* contains three sounds *c-a-n*. For such children, it is more important to develop lower order phonological skills, for example an awareness of words and syllables, than to attempt to associate letter-shapes with sounds that they cannot discriminate within words. One of the early *Sound Linkage* activities requires children to push plastic counters into a line of squares marked on a card (see Figure 9.3a) while simultaneously saying each word of a sentence. For example, given four counters and the sentence, 'That is my bike', children are expected to push the counters into the squares while simultaneously saying each of the four words. Once children are able to complete such activities with 80 per cent accuracy, they are encouraged to listen for, and to manipulate, syllables in words. Tasks within this section include children clapping in time with rhythmic rhymes (for example, 'One, two, three, four, five, Once I caught a fish alive.'), blending syllables to form common words (for example, *te-le-vi-sion* to *television*), syllable segmentation using plastic counters, and syllable deletion (for example, deleting the word *farm* from *farmhouse* to leave the word *house*).

After becoming proficient at manipulating syllables, the children progress to blending sounds into words. Phoneme blending is generally easier for children than phoneme segmentation and may be

a)

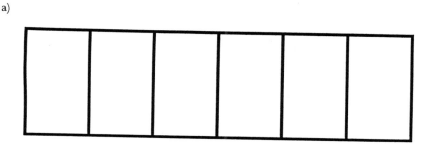

Figure 9.3a: Diagram of boxes used for pushing counters while segmenting sentences or words
Source: *Sound Linkage*, (Hatcher, 1994).

b)

Figure 9.3b: Pictures for blending the words b-oy and s-ea.
Source: *Sound Linkage*, (Hatcher, 1994).

c)

Figure 9.3c: Pictures for discriminating two of three words (doll, tap, table) with the same initial sound.
Source: *Sound Linkage*, (Hatcher, 1994).

d)

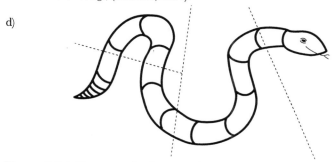

Figure 9.3d: Picture used, prior to work on phoneme segmentation, to introduce the concept of 'breaking things up'.
Source: *Sound Linkage*, (Hatcher, 1994).

carried out without an awareness of phoneme units. At first, children are simply shown two pictures and asked to identify which of the two they think teachers are trying to say. For example, in Figure 9.3b they would be expected to choose the picture of a *boy* rather than the picture of the *sea* when teachers articulate the sounds *b-oy*. The blending activities progress to manipulating five sounds to produce words such as *c-ar-p-e-t*.

An awareness of phonemes may be reached through an awareness of rhyme as, initially, children find it easier to segment words into onset-rime units (for example, *c/an*, *m/an* and *p/an*) than they do to segment them at any other point. The ability to segment final (*ca/n*) and medial sounds (*c/a/n*) emerges later. For this reason, after the phoneme blending activities, children progress to the identification and supply of rhyming words. One of the rhyming tasks requires them to complete rhymes such as:

Mrs Brown
went to town
with her face painted
- - - -

Another requires them to identify which of three words rhymes with a stimulus word. For example, given the stimulus word *house*, the word *mouse* would be the correct response from *monkey, dog, mouse*.

The introduction to individual speech sounds (phonemes) is undertaken by getting children to vary the speed with which they say words such as *fish, sneezing* and *superman*. With the aid of pictures they are then encouraged to listen for specific sounds at the beginning (e.g., *ssss* in *snake*, and *ffff* in *fan*), at the end, and in the middle of words. Following success with this type of activity, children are asked to discriminate between words on the basis of their initial, end and medial sounds. For example, when presented with a set of three pictures: *doll, tap* and *table* (see Figure 9.3c), they are asked to touch the two pictures with the same sound at the beginning. A related but more difficult task requires them to indicate which of four words ends with a different sound. For example, *shoot* would be the correct response given the words *knife, shoot, scarf* and *leaf.*

By this time children should be ready to complete phoneme segmentation exercises such as indicating the beginning, end or medial sound of a target word. For example, they might be asked to indicate what sound the word *window* begins with. After being introduced to the concept of breaking-up words through cut-up pictures of, for example, a snake (see Figure 9.3d), children progress to segmenting words while simultaneously pushing counters into a line of squares. For example, for the word *lock*, children would be given three counters and expected to say *l-o-ck* slowly, while simultaneously pushing the counters into the squares.

The ability to delete or substitute phonemes within words and to transpose phonemes between words normally develops after children have begun to read. Exercises in these sections of the programme include deleting sounds from words, for example, *g* from *gold*, to produce another word *old*, changing sounds within words, for example, the *a* to an *ee* sound in *battle*, to form the word *beetle*, reversing the sounds of words, as required to change *sail* to *lace* and transposing the initial sounds of words, such as *d* and *t* in *down train* to produce *town drain*.

Writing a story

Another key activity for children within Section 2 of the reading with phonology programme is writing a short story. The story consists of one or two sentences and is written on the bottom page of an unlined exercise-book that has been turned through 90 degrees. The top page is used as a practice pad. One of the aims of the writing activity is to help children add to the list of words that they can write fluently.

Teachers generally use the multisensory approaches described by Clay (1985) and by Bryant and Bradley (1985) to help children acquire an initial sight vocabulary. Clay's procedure of trace and say; imagine and say; look and say; and write and say, draws children's attention to the overall appearance of words. Bryant and Bradley's approach of look and say; write and say the letter names, and look and say, draws children's attention to words being formed of sequences of distinct letters. In either case, children are encouraged to write the words in as many different settings as possible (such as using sand, chalk, paint, steamy windows, plastic letters, large crayons and felt pens, etc.), as well as in their story, and the word would be added to a list of words that is accessible to both the teachers and children.

Once children have acquired a reasonable sight vocabulary and are able to recognize speech sounds within words, they are introduced to phoneme segmentation through *phonological linkage* activities such as Bradley's (Bryant and Bradley, 1985) plastic letter technique. Bradley's technique involves choosing a word from one of a set of words known to a child (for example, *hen* from *hen*, *men*, and *pen*) and encouraging the child to form the word with plastic letters. The child is then encouraged to make further words from the same set until such time as he or she realizes that it is only necessary to change the first letter of the word. This type of work runs parallel with the phonological awareness exercises where children segment words using counters and the card with the line of squares on it.

Once children are proficient at perceiving sounds within words and are able to identify letters by name or by sound they are introduced to the notion of using sounds to write words. Naturally, this fits in well with the writing-a-story activity. Using simple phonemically regular words that children wish to write in their stories, teachers draw boxes for each sound segment of a word on the top page of the children's writing-a-story book. They articulate the words slowly and encourage children to either push counters into the boxes or to listen for a sound, think (and possibly practise) how it would be written and consider which box it should be written in. Initially, children might only be able to write the first or last sound. The correct sequencing of letters is attended to after children are able to write each of the letters in the right box without too much trouble.

Cut-up story

Once children have completed their written story, they are encouraged to re-read it. If necessary, they are asked to point to each word while doing so. If one-to-one reading and finger pointing is difficult, teachers write the stories on card and cut the card into language units (e.g., phrases or words) for the children to reassemble. The children then either check their responses by placing the segments on top of or below the teacher's model, or simply read the words aloud. The cut-up story activity remains a part of each session until firm one-to-one finger pointing has been established.

Section 3: Introduction to a new book

Being introduced to a new book

The last segment of each reading and phonology session involves children reading a new book. When introducing a new book (capable of being read by children at the instructional level, i.e., with 90 to 94 per cent accuracy), teachers assist the children in discussing the plot and draw their attention to any unusual language within the book.

Attempting to read the new book

After the book has been introduced and with support being given when difficulties are met, the children are encouraged to read the stories on their own. Teachers will almost certainly derive a teaching point from the children's reading. For example, their attention to letter-sound relationships is encouraged during this activity. Finally, teachers and children read the books together to encourage fluency of reading.

Reading progression within the reading and phonology programme therefore follows Clay's (1985) cycle of consolidating children's reading strengths with material that can be read with more than 94 per cent accuracy, working to overcome confusions and learning new skills with text that can be read with 90 to 94 per cent accuracy and identifying the set of skills to be taught at the next level through a running record of children's responses to text at that level. Most importantly, it also includes additional phonological and phonological linkage activities that are linked to the children's writing and reading.

Reading intervention in Cumbria

Although it is desirable for the teaching approaches used in our study to be adopted by people working on their own, it is likely that some teachers will need training and support to put them into practice. Many have had no formal training in the teaching of reading, and the provision of the broader curriculum occupies much of their day. Following our research, and in line with the requirement that schools should implement a structured programme of work before children can be considered for statutory special educational provision (DFE, 1994), Cumbria Education Authority is supporting the training of teachers in the use of our procedures. The training is provided by tutors and myself, and I also act as the Coordinator. Each trainee undertakes a 14-week course involving three days of inservice work, five half-day tutorials and the teaching of two reading-delayed children. It is hoped that most of Cumbria's infant, junior and primary schools will eventually have access to a reading intervention trained teacher.

During three days of inservice work, teachers acquire the skills to assess children's literacy needs and to design a first lesson plan (see Figure 9.4). On the first day, videotapes of a typical reading intervention assessment, and of a lesson, are shown to the teachers. The task of learning to take a running record of a child reading is taught through a series of graded exercises. These involve teachers listening to a tape of a child reading from a prepared text, with up to 10 per cent errors in it, while looking at the correct version of the text and coding the reading behaviour heard on the tape. The coding symbols are introduced at the rate of one per exercise and then practised in successive exercises. After being introduced to the concept of

	Book level ( ) and suggested titles	Reading items or strategies, one or two only, to be taught if an opportunity arises
1. *Reading easy books* (books than can be read with greater than 94 per cent accuracy), or *shared reading*	1 2 3	

2. Where applicable, *book to be read at the instructional level* (90-94 per cent, accuracy) with the teacher taking a running record. The book should have been introduced and read by the child before the first session.

Book level ( ) and suggested title

3. *Letter knowledge*	Identification (letter to be practised)	Formation (letter to be practised)
4. *Phonology*	Activities to be undertaken from Sections 1 to 9 of *Sound Linkage*	
5. *Writing a story* (letter or word to be practised) Phonological linkage (see Section 10 of *Sound Linkage*) where applicable		
6. *Cut-up story* (state the objective)		
7. *Introduction to a new book* at the instructional level (90-94 per cent accuracy) *Attempt at reading and shared reading*	Book level ( ) and suggested title	

Comments

Figure 9.4: Blank lesson plan for the first 35-minute reading intervention session

phonological awareness and the structure of the *Sound Linkage* programme, the teachers work in groups of four to practise the administration of tests among themselves. On the second day, working in the same groups, they undertake the assessment of a reading-delayed child. They are then introduced to the relationship between the assessment data, the teaching strategies, the format for each lesson and subsequent record keeping.

At the end of the first two days, each group of four teachers is assigned a set of teaching strategies to study before the third day of training. These include strategies for recognizing words and letters, writing and cutting-up stories, manipulating sounds in words, reading books, text reading and the analysis of the running record. Group members are also asked to compile a provisional first lesson plan for the child they have assessed. The third day of training, which takes place nine days later, is undertaken in three regional groups each with 16 teachers and two tutors. Working in their small groups of four, teachers reach agreement on a summary of their allotted teaching strategies. These are discussed with colleagues in the other groups. A similar strategy is adopted with respect to the four sets of first lesson plans. By the end of the third day, the teachers should have developed a good understanding of how to derive a first lesson plan, an awareness of the main teaching strategies and confidence in discussing issues with their colleagues. In addition the three regional groups will have produced 12 sets of assessment and first lesson plans for the school that supplied the children for the practice assessments on day two of the training.

During the period of intervention, each tutor supports eight teachers. They observe them giving at least one lesson, and run five half-day group tutorial sessions. During the tutorials, the teachers observe videotapes of each other teaching. In order to ensure that teachers provide quality feedback and are receptive to receiving it, they are encouraged to judge lessons against objective criteria (see Figure 9.5) from the start of the course. Like the first lesson plan, the adoption of these criteria is essential if teachers are to develop appropriate skills in a short period of time.

Reading with Phonology: a Field Study

During 1994, forty-three teachers completed a 14-week training course as described above. They included teachers who normally work with children with special educational needs, headteachers and class teachers. Released from their normal teaching duties they spent

Teacher.......................................   Session no ......   Date ..../..../....

Indicate as appropriate (✓, ✗ or ?).

1. Evidence of good liaison: school ( ), class ( ) and parent ( ).

2. Quality of reading environment:

    room ( ), lighting ( ), desk space ( ), temperature ( ), noise ( ), other..................( ).

3. Appropriate completion of: assessment documents [ ], summary strategy
    documents [ ], first lesson plan [ ], subsequent lesson plans [ ] and running
    records [ ].

4. Lesson Format	Correct order	Time taken	Appropriate allocation of time
a) Re-read familiar book	[ ]	( ) }	
b) Running record	[ ]	( ) }	9 mins [ ]
c) Letter identification	[ ]	( ) }	
d) Phonological activities	[ ]	( ) }	
e) Write story	[ ]	( ) }	
f) Cut-up story	[ ]	( ) }	17 mins [ ]
g) Introduction to new book	[ ]	( ) }	
h) Attempt at reading new book	[ ]	( ) }	
i) Shared reading of new book	[ ]	( ) }	9 mins [ ]

5. Quality of lesson

	(✓, ✗) or	(emerging)
a) Made appropriate use of books from list provided	[ ]	( )
b) Carried out running record appropriately	[ ]	( )
c) Praised appropriate emerging reading behaviours	[ ]	( )
d) Followed criteria for changing book level	[ ]	( )
e) Integrated reading and writing	[ ]	( )
f) Made appropriate use of phonology and phonological linkage	[ ]	( )
g) Reviewed previous learning	[ ]	( )
h) Selected one or two maximally effective teaching points	[ ]	( )
I) Generalized learning using a range of materials	[ ]	( )
j) Encouraged over-learning of skills	[ ]	( )
k) Minimized time wasting	[ ]	( )
l) Taught for independence	[ ]	( )
m Exhibited good use of questioning	[ ]	( )
n) Encouraged integration of meaning, syntax, auditory and visual reading strategies	[ ]	( )

Figure 9.5: Reading intervention quality control sheet

approximately forty 35-minute teaching sessions on each of two children and eight 35-minute sessions, on each of the children, collecting pre-and post-intervention test data. The children were selected for the training on the basis of their difficulty in acquiring literacy skills. No control was exercised over factors such as IQ. Seventy-eight of the children were from primary schools (average age 7;3 years at the start of the programme) and eight were from secondary schools (average age 12;9 years). Six of the secondary school children had statements of special educational need and one had an IQ of less than 55. During the teaching sessions, the children followed the reading with phonological training programme described above.

The children's gains in literacy skills were very encouraging. The 7-year-old children, who were about 18 months delayed in their reading at the start of the intervention, made average gains of 8 months in word reading and 11 months in spelling over the 3 months of intervention. For each month of intervention, this represents gains of 2.67 months for reading and 3.67 months for spelling. These gains numerically exceed those made in our original study and, while it is not possible to make a direct comparison, suggest that it is likely that the teachers benefited from the more finely structured training programme employed on this occasion.

The secondary children, who were about 72 months delayed in reading at the start of the intervention, made gains of 9 months in word reading, and 5 months in spelling over the same three-month period. For each month of intervention, this represents gains of 3 months for reading and 1.67 months for spelling. These findings suggest that the reading with phonological awareness teaching procedures can help older children and also children with moderate and possibly even severe learning difficulties.

In keeping with observations made by teachers who took part in the original research, the teachers noted that the children's listening skills and confidence also appeared to have increased. Many reported that their colleagues, and the children's parents, had independently noticed such changes. One parent was reported as saying, 'I now have a son who wants to go to school and is enjoying every moment.' This is a gain that cannot be underestimated and again supports the effectiveness of the reading with phonological awareness teaching programme.

Sound Linkage – its effects at an individual level

While group results are crucial for evaluating the effectiveness of a teaching programme, a case study can provide an understanding of what is happening to an individual as they proceed through the programme. David, a child with severe reading difficulties, provides a good example of how reading and phonological awareness training bring about change during the course of a sequence of teaching sessions.

David's slow progress in acquiring literacy was apparent before he was six. At 5;9 years he was not only delayed in his literacy attainments relative to his friends, but he exhibited poor articulation of some words (for example, *taktor* for TRACTOR), spoonerisms in his speech, (such as *par cark*) and was slow in his verbal responses to questions. He was also tearful about going to school. On the positive side, he was noted to enjoy modelling, drawing, book illustrations and being read to by his mum.

Some six months later, according to his performance on the *British Ability Scales* (Elliot, et al., 1983), David was found to exhibit average general reasoning skills. However, he performed at a below average level on the visual IQ scale and on subtests that measure the ability to remember a series of spoken numbers, to copy a series of shapes and to read single words. Aged 6;3 years at the time of testing, David was credited with reading at less than the 5-year level. He was also noted to be poor at phonological awareness tasks. While able to blend syllables, he did not appear to be able to blend phonemes into words, to detect the odd word out in a three-word rhyme-oddity task or to segment words into phonemes.

At the time of the pre-intervention assessment, when he was 6;7 years, David knew most of the concepts about print but he was not able to point to words as they were read or to make a return-sweep at the end of lines of print. Neither was he able to name or give the function of punctuation marks. He was able to articulate the sounds commonly associated with 19 lower- and 16-upper case letters, to write a few words, such as *in, it, tom* and *me*, and to use initial- and final-sounds when writing unknown words (for example, *rn* for *ran*). He tended to write upper- and lower-case letters indiscriminately, to mirror-write some letters, to muddle the order of letters in words and to omit spaces between words. He wrote *tehD the-ost* (see Figure 9.6a) for the sentence, 'The bear frightened the ghost.' David was able to read about six words from the *Early Word* reading test. He articulated two of the words, *went* and *stop*, after naming the letters according to their sound (*wuh-eh-nuh-tuh*). He was now able to blend three phonemes into words. Not surprisingly, perhaps, David tended to rely on pictures as clues to text reading.

teno – – – – – – – –

frightened te h – ost.

the bear   the ghost

Figure 9.6a: Example of David's writing prior to this intervention

I see the cat

Figure 9.6b: Example of David's writing with support in the first week of intervention

Figure 9.6c: Example of David's writing after 12 sessions.

I play with ny dog and I play ball with him. His name is Nelson.

Figure 9.6d: Example of David's writing after 36 sessions of interventions.

After the pre-intervention assessment, David received thirty-six 35-minute teaching sessions. During the first few sessions, his teacher followed a multisensory approach to building a basic sight vocabulary, encouraged David to finger-point while reading, to finger-space when writing or re-assembling cut-up stories and to segment spoken sentences into words using counters. He also learned to name and to form letters. After 12 sessions, David was able to point to words as he read but still needed prompting to leave spaces between words when writing. He had progressed from writing simple sentence structures, such as, 'I see the cat', to more complex forms, such as, 'If its a badger you can see, please tell me', (see Figures 9.6b and 9.6c). He was also using initial sounds as clues in his reading and being prompted to use end sounds. The use of capital letters and full-stops were also being taught.

David continued to exhibit difficulty in attending to sounds in spoken words. By session 24, he had only just mastered the ability to identify medial words in sentences of four words, to tap the syllabic rhythm of poems and to blend three phonemes into words. Nevertheless, his concentration and confidence with phonological awareness tasks had improved. He was also becoming more confident with text, looking carefully at the ends of words as well as their beginning and correcting some of his errors. However, picture and meaning clues continued to be his preferred option. By session 36, David was enjoying rhyme. By then, he had also begun to use plastic letters to form onset-rime groups such as *like, bike, pike* and *hike*. His writing had also shown further improvement (see Figure 9.6d).

After the 12-week period of intervention, David was re-assessed on the attainment measures employed at T1. On the *Sound Linkage* test of phonological awareness, he was credited with being able to segment words into phonemes (score 6/6) and with some ability to delete phonemes from words to make new words (3/6). He did not exhibit these skills at T1. His spelling had improved dramatically. He was able to write unknown words using sequences of four sounds and, aged 6;10 years, was credited with an average performance (6;8 years) on the Schonell spelling test. He was also able to write sentences and to leave spaces between words.

David's word reading was also found to have improved significantly. His reading age of 6;5 years on the Burt test was again within normal limits. He continued to exhibit weaknesses, however. He exhibited difficulty in naming letters (such as *p, b, d, g, t, j*) and in giving the sounds associated with certain letters (such as *p, b, d, q*) and in reading text. Consequently, his teacher felt that David would need to follow the programme of reading intervention until he had reached a higher level of text reading and was no longer dependent upon her for encouragement and support. There is no doubt, however, that the reading with phonological training programme had had a significant impact upon his progress in acquiring literacy during the 12 weeks of intervention.

Procedures and points arising from practice

As well as commenting upon the benefits of the teaching programme for the children, teachers commented upon their own gains. The structured programme of literacy training was much appreciated. They referred to their increased confidence in teaching reading and to the benefits of the course to their schools. They noted that many of the diagnostic tests, the running record, the notion of children reading books at the instructional level and a number of the reading and sound linkage strategies had been adapted for normal class teaching by their colleagues, as well as by themselves.

Their progress did not come easily, however. It required much hard work and a willingness to adopt novel teaching procedures. A major factor for teachers is that they have to abandon their classes, for a significant amount of time, and adapt to working with individual children. With classes of 30 children or more, they do not normally have time to carry out fine-grain analysis of phonological processing, reading and writing skills and to integrate their findings in a purposeful manner within a structured teaching programme. In order to help them adjust to this way of working, the materials have been made as explicit as possible.

The adaptation to fine-scale analysis is particularly difficult in the abstract area of phonological processing. Teachers may not know anything about phonological awareness, and in some instances may themselves exhibit limited phonological awareness. Teachers used to teaching consonant blends as units may have difficulty in appreciating that the word *crest* contains five sounds (*c-r-e-s-t*). Similarly, when segmenting words into phonemes, it is difficult for them to keep consonants as phonetically correct as possible (for example, segmenting *spot* as *sss-p-o-t* and not *suh-puh-o-tuh*).

It is also difficult for some teachers to think about the learning process, such as the role of long-term memory in learning. Initially, they have a tendency to cover learning points as they occur. This can be confusing and result in recent learning interfering with earlier learning. If a teacher helps a child with each aspect of a sentence he or she wishes to write, rather than writing the difficult words for the child and concentrating on one or two important points, the child may only remember the last point covered. It is also important to make teaching points as clear as possible and to build on children's existing knowledge. Where teachers always refer to letters by sound, as in *i-nuh-guh* when spelling *ing*, they may not appreciate that this is phonologically confusing. The pronunciation is not phonetically correct and the sound of the letter *i* in *ing* is not the same as it is in *Friday*. For that reason, it is better to refer to letters by name when committing the spelling of words to memory.

Just as adapting to this type of work is not easy for the teachers, the training involves tensions and anxieties for the tutors. They have to adapt to working with adults, giving them the freedom to make errors with their material. So far as possible, the tutors help teachers to assimilate the necessary skills through the use of short-term goals that are related to the criteria for a successful lesson. By tutorial 2 for example, teachers are expected to be able to allocate approximately the right amount of time to each of the three main components of a teaching session and to demonstrate reliability in their ability to take a running record.

The process of helping teachers is facilitated by sharing the tutorial teaching criteria with them. It is also helped by the tutors modelling the approach that they wish the teachers to adopt with children. When video-tapes are being watched, the tutors learn to look for and reinforce teaching strengths and to allow time for others, using the criteria, to raise points of concern. They may prompt discussion of unrecognized errors. In adopting this approach, they have to strike a balance between ensuring that teachers stick to the agreed structure of the programme and encouraging them to challenge ideas. They have to be both forceful and restrained. Given the reported results and the feedback from teachers, it seems likely that the provision of trained tutors, in combination with a finely structured programme of support, enhances the effect of explicitly linking reading and phonological awareness training with reading-delayed children.

Concluding Remarks

Explicitly linking training in phonological awareness with the teaching of reading is a powerful tool for helping children to overcome their reading difficulties. Our recent data suggest that this is the case for children of secondary as well as primary age and for children with a range of learning difficulties. A 14-week training programme designed to help teachers deliver the *Sound Linkage* programme can increase its effectiveness and its applicability in a wide range of settings.

Chapter 10
Teaching Spelling to Children with Specific Learning Difficulties

Claire Cootes and Sarah Simpson

Spelling in an orthography such as English is by no means a straight-forward task. In the first stages of spelling, the child must come to realize that it is possible to analyse the speech sounds of a spoken word and to write these down using a set of letters that they must also learn. Later, the child must revise these first guesses at the spellings of words, and learn how speech sounds (phonemes) are conventionally written in the English spelling system, by sets of letters (graphemes). An awareness of the complexities of the English writing system will guide our discussion in this chapter which will look at the teaching of spelling from the perspective of the learner. We shall focus on how an individual's strengths and weaknesses and his or her learning strategies can be identified, and on how to proceed with the teaching of spelling in the light of that knowledge.

Spelling, however, is only one literacy skill and it is difficult to isolate consideration of its development from that of reading. We begin, therefore, by discussing the interaction of these skills and the changing nature of their influence on each other over time. The normal acquisition of literacy, and the way in which reading and spelling are acquired in overlapping, but not altogether parallel steps, is clearly described by Uta Frith in her stage model of the development of literacy (Frith, 1985). According to Frith, reading is first approached logographically, with the child relying on whole word recognition. She calls this the logographic stage of development. The next phase, the alphabetic, is reached first for spelling. Now, words are written through the sounding out of one phoneme at a time. This paves the way for the alphabetic stage in reading, in which phonic strategies are added to whole word recognition. This step is essential to facilitate the decoding of new words that the child has not seen before. Reading then becomes the pacemaker for the final orthographic stage, in which the child automatically recognizes the spelling conventions of English embodied in printed words. This knowledge is thought to generalize and to provide the more specific skills required for spelling–writing words according to orthographic rules.

From a developmental perspective, Bryant and Bradley (1985) suggested that children having difficulty in the acquisition of literacy skills may be failing to use 'the right skill at the right time'. Their research with poor readers suggested that it was the merging of skills required for reading with those required for spelling, which was problematic for such children. The key to remediation for Bryant and Bradley lies in teaching poor readers to apply their skills more effectively. To this end they advocate an approach in which both phonological sensitivity and alphabetic knowledge are worked on together, so that the child is encouraged to categorize words according to both the sounds and the letter strings that they have in common. In this way the child can be encouraged to make the crucial connection between the phonological structure of a word and its visual form. The teaching of reading and spelling must therefore go hand-in-hand and should not be separated.

To illustrate some of the problems the specialist teacher may meet, we begin by describing two children with spelling difficulties. The first child was having problems in the alphabetic phase of development, the second was failing at the later, orthographic phase.

Spelling problems in the alphabetic phase

Simon was 7;6 years old when he was first seen. He was a highly intelligent boy (Full Scale WISC III = 131) who had developed no reading or writing skills whatsoever. There was a history of dyslexia on both sides of the family, and assessment revealed that although his spoken language and verbal reasoning were excellent, Simon's phonological awareness was very poor indeed.

Simon received four hours a week of individual tuition for the next academic year during which progress was slow. At the end of the year he was able to produce the following:

> I was woking bowe the hise stret. wen a man in a tes shiort soing on it NASA space station [Simon asked for help with this phrase] soid you have been electid to go on a space miscord I was overwelord with ocsit-mont so I said okey and the come on then he said so we dox of. wen we

got to the mojol. I saw were foms I would be. But wen they told me that we were going to soturn all thorts of being foms floo out of my hed.Wen I got on the space mojol I have a bit of norvsnis. But wen I rmemb thet I was going sature the necst thing I hord was....

Simon translated his writing as follows:

I was walking down the High Street when a man in a T shirt saying on it NASA Space Station said, 'You have been elected to go on a space mission.' I was overwhelmed with excitement, so I said, 'OK,' and then, 'Come on then,' he said. So we took off. When we got to the module I saw how famous I would be. But when they told me that we were going to Saturn, all thoughts of being famous flew out of my head. When I got on the space module I have a bit of nervousness. But when I remember that I was going to Saturn the next thing I heard was...

It can be seen that he has learned to spell several common words such as *have, was* and *were,* and it is clear that he is beginning to transcribe speech sounds, for example in his spellings of FLEW → *floo*, WHEN→*wen*, ELECTED→*electid*, NEXT→*necst*. He is clearly entering the alphabetic phase. However he is not using his letter-sound knowledge to monitor spellings of the common irregular words which he has learned as individual spelling patterns. Thus, he writes HOW as if he were selecting a word randomly from his store of learned spellings, demonstrating his natural insensitivity to the sounds in words. Also many of his spellings are not phonetic:

OVERWHELMED → *overwelord*
FAMOUS → *foms*
REMEMBER → *rmemb*

These kinds of errors show that he has difficulty using phonological strategies competently. Furthermore, children of 8-years-old who have good phonological awareness are usually aware of word boundaries, but Simon makes two word boundary errors in this piece of writing:

HIGH STREET → *hise stret*
T SHIRT → *tes shiort*

Simon's imaginative and mature use of language is evident in phrases such as 'overwhelmed with excitement', and 'all thoughts of being famous flew out of my head', but his writing is painfully slow. It is not difficult to imagine how frustrated he must feel at his poor ability to commit ideas and thoughts to paper.

The problems which arise in teaching a child like Simon are immediately apparent. An inherent weakness in phonological awareness is not easily remedied, and his ability to compensate through the use of visual strategies does not always serve him well. The sheer struggle to become literate can seem quite daunting for a child with these difficulties, and the greater the discrepancy between general cognitive ability and literacy skills, the greater the frustration.

Spelling problems in the orthographic phase

Max is a 17-year-old boy of above average ability whose difficulties with literacy have been charted over time. He now reads well but still has serious problems with spelling. His spelling errors include:

ANXIETY → *angsiaty*
PHYSICIAN → *phisition*
THROAT → *throught*
OBVIOUS → *oveose.*

These examples are good phonic approximations of the target words and show that Max now has considerable knowledge of spelling conventions. However, it would appear that he has become over-reliant on following his speech sounds, applying alphabetic principles rather than learning when and where to employ different orthographic (i.e. spelling) conventions.

Further evidence of Max's over-reliance on the sound of words is seen when his free writing is examined. Here his spelling is even more error prone, as not only is he ruled by how individual words sound, but also by the rhythm of a sentence. For example, the loss of the word boundary in FROM MY ANGLE → *fromy angel* and THE BOAT DRIFTED AIMLESSLY ROUND *the boat drifted aimless lyround,* where he misplaces the suffix *-ly* in order to preserve a particular intonation and expression in the sentence. Max is also particularly sensitive to stress patterns, marking stressed syllables with capital letters even when using a word processor, e.g., *beFore, aGain.*

As is often the case, structured remedial teaching in the early stages was focused on spelling for Max, rather than on reading and was heavily phonically based. This is likely to have led to a heightened awareness of phonics at the expense of orthography. As a late and reluctant reader he has failed to apply his visual attention to the detail of letter sequences in words and is now having difficulty progressing to the stage of the proficient speller (the orthographic stage). His spelling strategies demonstrate the influence of earlier teaching and his use of compensatory strategies which are not altogether successful.

The Remediation of Spelling Difficulties

Approaches to intervention and remediation will inevitably reflect the theoretical framework of the particular programme employed or teacher involved. It is difficult to know whether such intervention is best aimed at remediating the cognitive deficit (i.e., strengthening the weakness) or at promoting an alternative cognitive strength in order to compensate for the deficit. To some extent, this depends on the stage of development the child has reached and also upon the severity of his or her difficulties. Intervention can be planned only in small steps, therefore, and the sensitive teacher should be prepared to modify his or her approach as the child progresses (or fails to progress).

Some general principles to guide and inform practice at the alphabetic level

Linking phonology and orthography

The now classic longitudinal study conducted by Bradley and Bryant (1983) was one of the first to emphasize the importance of combining the training of phonological skills with the teaching of reading. In this study they showed that oral and written work could be integrated by employing plastic letters for the child to manipulate and build words. Children working in this way were better able to forge explicit links between reading and spelling. Moreover, children whose phonological skills were trained by linking the sounds and letter patterns that rhyming and alliterative words shared, made and maintained a better rate of progress than children working within just one modality. Similar claims have been made by Hatcher, Hulme and Ellis (1994) who found that training poor readers in phonological skills in isolation from reading and spelling skills, is less effective than training which makes explicit links between these skills (see Hatcher, this volume).

Level of segmentation

If the teaching of spelling in the initial stages is to be informed by theoretical understanding, then it is important that early spelling strategies be taught in a way which is known to be developmentally appropriate. Goswami and Bryant (1990) describe three separate levels at which words can be segmented; into syllables (*cat-er-pill-ar*), intra-syllabically into onsets and rimes (*c-at*), or phonemes (*c-a-t*). They argue that segmentation at the level of the syllable and onset/rime is possible before the onset of literacy, but that phonemic segmentation occurs as a result of exposure to an alphabetic script. It follows that if onset/rime segmentation places fewer demands on the learner than phonemic segmentation, it is more appropriate to work with these units rather than adopting a traditional phonic approach which concentrates on the synthesis and segmentation of single sounds at the expense of larger units.

Once some basic sound/symbol correspondences are established, work should move away from the single sound level and be focused at the level of onset and rime as far as is possible. In addition, from an early stage the child should be encouraged to look for consistent spelling patterns rather than attempting to translate individual letters to sounds. Goswami (1994) stresses the importance of encouraging a child to learn new words by analogy with those already mastered, and emphasizes the need to look for consistency in spelling patterns rather than phonic regularity. For example, the ostensibly irregular spelling pattern *ight* is a remarkably consistent pattern in that *igh* gives the long *I* sound without exception, and occurs in 90 other words.

Further rationale for teaching at the onset/rime level is offered by Tunmer (1994). He notes that it promotes the identification of individual phonemes, that short vowels are more stable when produced as part of a rime, that it facilitates learning of consonant blends and that it is a useful way to raise the awareness of orthographic units which are greater than single sounds mapped to single letters.

A practical scheme which is firmly based in these theoretical principles is the *Phonological Awareness Training Programme* (PAT) by Jo Wilson (1993). This scheme works explicitly with onset and rime, uses the concept of learning through analogy and recognizes the need for dyslexic learners to combine the skills used for reading with those used for spelling. In addition it is highly structured, provides opportunities for practice and overlearning and promotes active participation by requiring the children to generate word lists for themselves. It is particularly useful with the older student (7+ years) who has already been exposed to a basic phonic scheme.

A structured, sequential, cumulative and multisensory programme

Thomson (1991) stresses the need for a remedial programme to be structured, sequential, cumulative and multisensory allowing the pupil to build one skill upon another. In order to be well structured, a remedial programme should be based on a detailed assessment of the individual student's performance in all aspects of literacy, cognitive style and phonological awareness.

An important part of any assessment procedure will always be the analysis, for diagnostic purposes, of both reading and spelling errors (miscue analysis). Students' reading errors in either a single-word reading test or a prose reading test should never be marked simply as right or wrong. Their incorrect attempts should be recorded (either in writing at the time, or for the less experienced teacher, from a cassette recording), so that the type of errors that are being made can be looked at in detail (see Goulandris, this volume). A preponderance of any particular type of error is an indication of the strategies being used, and of particular likely weaknesses. For example, if a child regularly substitutes another similar word (GLISTENING → *gleaming*; STOOL→*spoon*) the teacher might conclude that he or she is not making use of phonic strategies, perhaps because of poor phonological awareness. Instead the child may be relying on visual cues and not focusing on the detail in the word. If, however, the child reads common irregular words such as HAVE as if they were regular (rhyming with *save*), an over-reliance on phonics and poor visual skills would be indicated. Similarly spelling errors should be categorized: does the child make mainly phonetic errors, such as BOX → *bocks*? Are the errors bizarre - bearing little relationship to the sound of the word, such as WINDOW → *wingth*?

Whether the strategies being used in both reading and spelling appear to indicate poor phonological awareness, or alternatively (and less commonly) poor use of visual cues, teaching methods must balance the need for training in areas of weakness while making maximum use of compensatory strengths. A multisensory approach offers the opportunity to do this. It will encourage the child to integrate information from auditory, visual, tactile and kinaesthetic channels, and so to make that important connection between reading and writing. It will use methods which link sounds, symbols and writing patterns as well as those which employ the child's stronger sensory channel as a means of supporting a weaker channel. Such a programme will also ensure that the child is fully engaged, and so promotes active learning.

No matter where the child's strengths and weaknesses lie, it will be necessary to make links with his underlying spoken language skills and to make material to be learned as relevant and meaningful as possible. For this reason work may be introduced at the level of the single word, but quickly needs to be raised to the level of the sentence. Words to be learned need to be incorporated into sentences, and sentences into short dictations. The child then needs to be encouraged to discuss these, to visualize them, to listen to them, to repeat them and finally to write them and to read them. It is important to ensure that dictation passages are composed of words with spelling patterns covered in the teaching programme to date.

A scheme which lends itself well to a structured and multisensory approach is *Spelling Made Easy* by Violet Brand (1984). This scheme groups words into graded *word families*, and provides both word lists and dictation passages. It offers a well organized programme which is a popular and useful resource, easy to adapt to suit the individual learner's needs. In following such a programme, pupils should be given plenty of opportunity to overlearn and generalize the points taught, with regular review and revision built in to encourage automaticity.

Two particular cases illustrate some of the points raised here. Kim was assessed as a student with visual weaknesses and auditory strengths and learned her word families by combining the words into easily memorized little poems. Will, on the other hand, was a boy with considerable visual strengths and poorly developed auditory skills, and he preferred to learn his word families by drawing elaborate comic strips to illustrate the action-packed and highly imageable dictations which he made up. Both students followed a teaching programme adapted to meet the particular strengths and weaknesses revealed by a thorough diagnostic assessment.

Good teaching practice

In addition to the specialist teaching techniques mentioned, normal good teaching practice needs to be remembered. If the child is to be well motivated it is important that he or she be encouraged to participate actively in the learning process and to feel consulted and involved. Activities should be fun and relevant. Sessions should be well paced and kept to a reasonable length. A variety of tasks tapping a range of skills should be offered, along with opportunities for practice and integration of skills. Success should be ensured through adequate opportunities for overlearning, but boredom avoided. The role of affective factors such as interest, motivation and self-esteem should not be underestimated.

A spelling programme

The starting point for a spelling programme will depend on the results of qualitative assessment. As each child's needs and knowledge base will be different, it is important not simply to work systematically through a list of spelling patterns. It is frustrating for a student to be taught something he already knows; equally, there may be unexpected gaps in knowledge which need to be covered. Progress, and the extent to which new material has been accommodated can be observed in free writing exercises.

As a first step, an understanding of the distinction between vowels and consonants is essential for students of all ages because so many orthographic conventions in English depend on this concept. Plastic letters are useful as a teaching aid, particularly in the early stages and for the younger child. Once some basic sound symbol correspondences have been established, the pupil can move on to some simple consonant-vowel-consonant (CVC) word building, for example, *b + ad, b + in,* and from here to simple two syllable words, such as *bandit* using the pupil's increasing sound symbol knowledge.

Generally only one spelling pattern should be introduced in a one hour lesson. The pattern taught in the previous lesson should be revised, and other rules should be referred to regularly. The opportunity should be given for the student to *hear* the words with the particular spelling pattern being taught; to *say* the words; to *use* the words orally in a sentence (in order to ensure that meanings are known); to *write* the words. There is a danger when concentrating on the written form of words, of forgetting that even some simple CVC words may be unfamiliar to children. For example, *ban, pun, rick, latch* may be the equivalent of nonwords. Our present focus is the teaching of spelling, but most courses of tuition will have a broader base in literacy, and a good balance should be struck, ensuring that all areas are covered in each lesson.

Writing may take the form of labelling pictures, writing to dictation, or including specific words in sentences or funny stories made up by the child or by the teacher. It can be quite fun for both teacher and child to compose a story, using for example, all the *igh* words, and then to compare notes afterwards. Stories and pictures are both excellent memory aids in that they make strong visual links between words which share a spelling pattern. These short stories can also be used for dictation passages, as long as the other words used are within the ability range of the child.

Teachers often find it difficult to decide which rule to do next. There is, of course, no pre-ordained order, especially if one is teaching on an individual basis. The following is a suggested order only, and is based on the complexity and usefulness of the teaching points. It should also be emphasized that these are spelling guidelines rather than rules, and that there are a number of exceptions to most of the points given. It is perhaps useful to think of the concept of orthographic regularity in terms of a continuum. If a word has a large number of 'neighbours', such as *station, nation, elation,* it is more regular than one, such as *friend* which has not. The most important words to teach are those whose patterns are most usefully generalized, and those which, as a result of their high frequency are indispensable, even though they do not neatly fall into patterns, such as *have, some,* etc. Naturally, highly irregular, low frequency words will only need to be taught to the advanced student.

A suggested order for teaching at the alphabetic level, with some teaching tips

We suggest that teachers refer to resources commercially available teaching when devising an individual teaching programme. Commonly used ones include The PAT scheme (Wilson, 1993) and Spelling Made Easy (Brand, 1984) already referred to. Useful worksheets can be found in *Rime Time* (Bellamy and Dart, 1995), *Making the Alphabet Work* (Hardwick, 1994) and Folens Publishers materials.

We report here a useful order for teaching the various spelling concepts, together with some teaching tips.

Single consonants

Single consonants and their sounds need to be taught in a logical sequence, avoiding teaching those which look or sound alike in too close proximity; teach sounds which occur most frequently first, for example, *s, t, n, d.* Using coloured plastic letters to form an alphabet rainbow on the table, select letters and think of words which have the sound in initial and then final position; a bag full of small objects beginning with particular letters can be useful. It might be a good idea to start with the initial letter of the child's name.

Short vowels

The letters for short vowels *a, e, i, o, u* should be taught alongside single consonant sounds/letters–the larger onset/rime units being introduced as soon as possible. To reinforce the concept of vowel letters, these can be written by the child in a different colour from the consonants. Take care not to cause confusion by teaching similar sounding short vowels at the same time. Brand (1984) suggests the following order - *a, o, i, e, u.*

It is usually inappropriate to teach more than one short vowel in a lesson. Start off with VC words where appropriate - *it, in,* then CVC words -*sit, pin.*

Consonant digraphs

Consonant digraphs are pairs of consonants that represent a single sound, namely, *th, sh, ch*. These need to be taught in initial position before final position where they are more difficult for the child to hear clearly.

Consonant blends

Consonants blends represent clusters of two or three consonants: *sp, st, sm, sn, sl, sw, sc, sk, tr, tw, dr, br, bl, gl, gr, fl, fr, cr, cl, pr, pl, spl, spr, str*. Like digraphs, these should be taught in word initial position before final position (*-nd, -nt, -mp, -st, -sk, -nk, -ct, -ft, -lp, -ld,*). When teaching digraphs and blends in final position it is a good idea to treat them as part of the rime unit, i.e. *h + and, p + ink*.

-ck following a short vowel

One of the most satisfying spelling rules to teach is that *-ck* always follows a short vowel; *-ck* never follows a consonant.

Suffixes

Once final consonant digraphs, (e.g. *sh*), final consonant blends, (e.g. *st*) and *-ck*, (e.g. *pick*), have been taught, it is a good idea to introduce the suffixes, *-ing* and *-ed* (such as *wished, rusting, packing*). This allows the child to write a large number of longer words quite early on in the programme.

The "flossy" rule

The flossy rule, that after a short vowel the sounds [f], [l] and [s] are each written with a double letter, *ff, ll, ss* is a much less satisfactory set of rules than *-ck* because of irregularities in the pronunciations of preceding vowel sounds, depending on dialect (for example, *class* and *mass, staff, gull* and *pull, doll* and *roll*).

The exceptions should also be taught at this stage as they are high frequency words (*if, of, yes, bus*, etc.).

Vowel digraphs

Vowel digraphs are letter strings containing two letters to depict a vowel sound, such as *ai, ay, oa, ow, oi , oy, ee, ea, au, aw*. When teaching *ai* be careful to select words with the long *a* sound e.g. *pain, rain*. Some words containing the digraph have different pronunciations, such as *-air* and *-ail*; these should be taught at a later stage.

It is important that groups of words sharing both sound and spelling pattern should be introduced together. The *oa* words; *Joan, toad, foal, road, coast, toast, foam, oak, moan, groan, loaf, stoat, goat*, etc., are rather good for making up a silly story.

Vowel modified by r (ar, or, er, ir, ur,)

This should be taught for vowels in stressed position, for example, *farm, form, fir, burn*. The unstressed endings (for example, coll*ar*, visi-t*or*, bak*er*) can be taught later. Do not teach more than one vowel +r form in a lesson.

Silent e

The rule should be related to simple CVC words, such as *cap/cape, pip/pipe, hop/hope, tub/tube*. As for *ai* (above), it is a good idea to avoid words containing *r* and *l* (for example, *mare, pale*) to begin with, as these words will not sound like others in the group.

c followed by i, e, y

This rule describes the fact that *c* gives an '*s*' sound when followed by *e, i*, or *y*, as in *city, cell, Lucy*. This is very reliable for reading, but more complicated for spelling, as it is difficult to know whether to use *s* or *c*.

Start off with simple words like *face, mice, nice, race, space*. In most such cases, *c* will be used, as *se* will give the sound '*z*', e.g. *hose, nose*. In initial position, start with *cell, city*, moving on to more difficult words like *circle* and *circus* at a later stage.

g followed by i, e, y

The guideline that *g* followed by *e, i*, or *y*, sounds like '*j*' parallels the *c* rule (above) but is much less reliable because the exceptions are high frequency words (*get, give, girl, gift, gear, geese, giddy, gig, giggle, girth*).

k + e or i

The '*k*' sound with '*e*' or '*i*' after it has to be written as *k*, as in *kid, Kent*, etc. This rule follows naturally from the *c* rule.

w modifies a following vowel

The letter *w* will change the sound of vowels that follow it. For exam-ple, *w* + *a* gives a short '*o*' sound , as in *wash*, *w* + *ar* gives '*or*', as in *warm*, *w* + *or* gives an '*ur*' sound, as in *worm*.

Each of these should be taught on separate occasions, but the pupil should be aware of the general principle that *w* affects the following vowel sound.

-tch and -dge after a short vowel

Both of the spelling patterns *tch* and *dge* are reasonably regular. The exceptions to -*tch* are few but common—*rich, which, such* and *much*. The -*dge* rule can be explained almost rationally (unlike so many English spelling patterns), as follows. The letter *j* is very restricted in its use (note its high value in Scrabble). It never comes at the end of a word. The 'j' sound in word final position is written -*ge*. But -*e* (silent e) makes the previous vowel long - *age, huge*. So, after a short vowel, a final 'j' sound must be written *dge* (distancing the *e* from the vowel).

Consistent letter strings

Some letter strings have consistent pronunciations and should be introduced as such. These are the spelling patterns -*alk, -ight, -ckle, -ttle*.

gu + e, i, y

The letter *u* keeps the 'g' hard in words like *guess, guest, guilt, guitar, guide*. This follows from the *soft g* rule above.

The -ed ending

The verbs whose past tense is formed by adding -*t* are relatively few, (*crept, kept*, etc.) and they usually involve a change of vowel sound, as in *mean → meant*. So it is better to assume an -*ed* ending even if a 't' is heard, as for example in walk*ed*.

Common endings

Finally, it is necessary to teach other common endings such as -*ly*, -*tion, -ful, -ous*, etc.

Coping with irregular words

Alongside this structured phonic teaching, the child will need to be taught some of the more common irregular words and some vocabulary which is either topic specific or of direct relevance (for example, family names, address etc.). The methods advocated for this vary, and some experimentation may be necessary to establish which is the most successful for the individual learner. *Simultaneous Oral Spelling* (SOS) and *Fernald Tracing* are multisensory methods which have proved the most popular, although Brooks (1995) suggests that a third method *Words in Words* may be more effective for certain learners.

The *Simultaneous Oral Spelling* (SOS) method is a multisensory method and is a variant, devised by Bradley (1981), of the Gillingham and Stillman method (1956). The procedure for this method is simple, but should be followed precisely. The child is shown the word to be learned (visual input), and the teacher then reads the word which the child repeats (auditory input). Next, the child writes the word (kinaesthetic feedback), saying the name of each letter as it is written (oral feedback). The child then says the word again, and checks that the word has been written correctly (visual feedback). The word is then covered and the whole process repeated at least twice more. In order to provide reinforcement and an opportunity for overlearning, the child is encouraged to practise the word over the next week.

Bryant and Bradley (1985) advocate the use of SOS and emphasize its value in helping the learner to chunk words and to become familiar with sequences of letters and with patterns of movements attached to these sequences. Similarly, Thomson (1991) reported a study comparing teaching through SOS with teaching using a visual method (Look-Cover-Say-Check). He found that dyslexic children learned more effectively using SOS while normal readers learned equally well with either method.

An alternative method is the tracing method described by Fernald (1943). This method differs from *Simultaneous Oral Spelling* in that its primary focus is on movement rather than on individual sounds. The child decides which word is to be learned, and the teacher then writes this word. The child traces the writing with a finger, and at the same time says each syllable aloud. Preferably cursive script should be used as this facilitates word-specific kinaesthetic feedback. The process is repeated until the child is able to write the word from memory.

Words in Words (Brooks, 1995) is more of a mnemonic technique than the other two strategies, and has not received a great deal of attention in the past. However it is a particularly useful method for learners with considerable and persisting phonological difficulties. For example, a particular student, Annabel, struggled with a phonic approach to spelling until she was 14. The *Words in Words* combined with mnemonic technique provided the breakthrough she so badly needed. The teaching of sound-letter correspondences was abandoned in favour of using words within words and her spelling took off quite dramatically. Here are a few examples of words she was taught (identified initially on the basis of her own need):

- business: I get the BUS to business
- mystery: I've lost MY STEREO–it's a mystery.
- pirates: pirates don't pay the RATES

- piece: a piece of PIE
- minutes: miNUTes
- familiar: famiLIAR
- comparison: comPARISon
- health: He, (Al) enjoys good health.
- believe: don't beLIEve a lie.

Some general considerations when working at the orthographic level

The persistence of spelling difficulties as opposed to reading difficulties

It has long been observed by teachers in the field of Specific Learning Difficulty that many students who have overcome some of their initial difficulties, and have progressed from the initial logographic stage of literacy to the alphabetic stage, then fail to progress to the orthographic stage. Such students may be at a relatively basic level, may have reached a functional level of literacy, or may even be reading fluently and automatically, but they continue to display considerable difficulties in spelling and in the organization of their written work.

The explanation put forward for this discrepancy between reading and spelling skills, is that these skills make different demands of the student. Reading is categorized as a recognition process, spelling as a retrieval process. Reading is viewed as the more basic skill involving the recognition of words based on partial visual cues or phonic knowledge at single word level, or inviting the use of a range of additional language skills at text level. Spelling on the other hand is a more demanding skill. In the early stages spelling is experimental and relies on an ability to segment words into their constituent sounds and map these to symbols. Errors will reflect the child's imprecise phonological awareness and level of knowledge of basic orthographic conventions, for example, WENT → *wet*, BOAT → *bot*, ARM →*rm*. Spellings will become increasingly accurate as orthographic knowledge is acquired, but a phonologically based approach has considerable limitations in a spelling system such as English. This 'assemble by sound' approach needs to be complemented by a whole word approach, where precise spellings information is retrieved from the lexicon.

Frith and Frith (1980) observe that if spellings are to be accurately retrieved, they must first be adequately represented and stored in the memory of the speller. However, as Snowling (1985a) points out, a student who is not approaching literacy with well integrated skills, will not have adequately stored orthographic knowledge and will therefore be forced to spell words according to the way they sound–not a very satisfactory course of action with English orthography where the relationship between sounds and letters is so complex.

Moving forward from phonics

Diagnostic teaching assessment should indicate whether students with continuing and intransigent spelling difficulties have failed to grasp basic phonic principles, or whether, as is often the case, they have developed an over-reliance on sounds and a lack of appreciation of, or facility with, orthographic conventions. That is, they have failed to integrate strategies appropriate for reading with those appropriate for spelling. For students who, though initially slow to grasp phonic principles, have become too reliant on a sounding out approach to reading and spelling, a programme emphasising alphabetic strategies will not be appropriate.

Students who are relying too heavily on phonological strategies for reading and spelling benefit from a programme in which explicit attention is paid to the orthographic representations of words rather than to their sounds in isolation. Within such a programme, they will be encouraged to approach words analytically.

A metacognitive approach

Tunmer (1994) endorses the three kinds of remedial strategy that we have already outlined, namely systematic rather than incidental instruction, using writing as a way of supporting phonological coding and using common elements in word families as opposed to relying on individual sound-symbol correspondences.

However, a fourth suggestion made by Tunmer appears to be most relevant in considering the needs of the student working at a higher level. He advocates that for these students it is important to move away from the skill-and-drill approach and to adopt instead a metacognitive approach to instruction. A metacognitive approach is one which encourages the development of problem solving strategies, rather than focusing on the training of specific skills. Borkowski (1992) outlines such an approach in general terms and explains how it teaches children to monitor and regulate their own performance, to take more responsibility for their own learning, and to devise ways of organizing a framework of knowledge onto which new knowledge can be mapped.

An older student, or one working at a higher level, may learn most effectively by adopting an analytical approach; one which requires engagement with the task at a cognitive level. Such an approach will also ensure that the student pays conscious attention to the spelling patterns within words.

Suggestions for teaching at the orthographic level

Although there are more rules, regulations and conventions in the English language than may at first be appreciated, as with the conventions already discussed, it is important to regard the following as guidelines rather than rules.

Syllables and syllable division

In order to attack, and so read or spell, unfamiliar multisyllabic words, it is helpful to be able to divide them into syllables (Cox and Hutcheson, 1988). As students with Specific Learning Difficulties have been described as having difficulty in phonological awareness, it is to be expected that they may have difficulty in segmenting words into syllables. They will therefore benefit from explicit teaching in this skill.

The number of syllables in a word equates with the number of beats, for example, *cat* = one syllable, *bandit* = two syllables and *elephant* = three syllables. A syllable is a sound or group of sounds produced on one push of air; it may be represented by a single letter, such as *I, a* or a group of letters, such as *me, strength*. Each syllable contains a vowel which in the written form may be composed of one or two letters (*a/gain, ad/mit*). In order to determine how a word might be read or spelled it is helpful to know the six types of syllables that can be identified.

The six kinds of syllables for use in written English are:

- closed syllable (VC) i.e., one in which a short vowel (V) is followed by a consonant (C) or consonants. It may be a word, for example, *up, act*, or part of a word, *ab/sent, rib/bon*.
- vowel-consonant-e syllable (VCe), i.e., one in which a vowel is followed by a consonant which in turn is followed by *e*. The *e* is silent and makes the vowel preceding the consonant long. It is often at the end of a word, for example, *ride, in/hale, re/pose*.
- open syllable (V or CV), i.e., one which ends in a vowel, and that vowel is usually long, for example, *o/pen, cra/zy*.

- double vowel syllable (VV), i.e., one in which two vowels (or a vowel + a semi vowel, or a vowel + *gh*) make one sound, for example, *coat, day, cow, high*.
- consonant+le syllable (Cle) i.e., one in which the final *e* is silent. It is always at the end of a word, for example, *ta/ble, han/dle*.
- *r*-controlled syllable (Vr), i.e., one in which the vowel is neither long nor short and is followed by an *r*, for example, *arm, term, girl, form, turn*.

Guidelines for adding suffixes

Suffixes in English serve to change the syntactic function of a word:

- + *ful* changes a noun to an adjective : *beauty, beautiful*
- + *ly* changes an adjective to an adverb: *beautiful, beautifully*
- + *ed* = past tense: *walked*.

Practice in using the same root word with different suffixes will also heighten awareness of syntax.

There are three guidelines to be learned:

1. Doubling rule

i) words of one syllable

If a word ends in one vowel letter followed by one consonant letter, double the consonant before adding a suffix beginning with a vowel, for example, *clap + p + ing*.

BUT

- do not double the consonant if the word has two vowel letters together, for example, *read + ing*
- do not double the consonant if the word already has two consonant letters together, for example, *bend + ing*
- do not double the consonant if the ending being added begins with a consonant, for example, *sad + ness*

The point of doubling the consonant then is to maintain the short vowel sound.

ii) words of two syllables

If the stress falls on the second syllable, double the consonant before adding an ending beginning with a vowel, for example, *begin+n+ing*

BUT

- Do not double if the stress falls on the first syllable, for example, *gallop+ing*.

A useful tip for training awareness of stress placement is to ask the pupil to imagine he is making a heartfelt speech. From time-to-time he will wish to emphasize his words by thumping the table. It is almost impossible to thump the table except on the stressed syllable. In this way, the pupil can test the words he wishes to spell, for example, *orbit*, *budg*et, *hinder*, (first syllable stress), oc*cur*, out*wit* (second syllable stress).

2. Adding suffixes to words ending in silent e

Drop *e* when adding a vowel suffix, for example, *make → making*.
Keep *e* when adding a consonant suffix, for example *safe → safely*.

3. Adding suffixes to words ending in y

If the word ends in a consonant + y, (*carry, beauty*), change *y* to *i* + suffix: e.g. *carry → carried, carriage; beauty → beautiful, beautify*.

BUT

- keep *y* after a vowel: *stay → stayed*
- keep *y* when the suffix begins with *i*: *hurry → hurrying*

Sometimes these three rules can be successfully practised through word-sums–*clap+ing, safe+est, sad+ness, hurry+ed*. However, teachers should be aware that some pupils will learn the rule, put it into practice for the purpose of the exercise, and fail to modify their own spelling. It is therefore essential keep checking whether the pupil can read back the words he is creating in the course of such exercises, and can write these words to dictation following practice with lists of word-sums. In addition, teachers should discuss the nature of the spelling rules with their pupils, so adopting the metacognitive approach outlined above.

Prefixes and their meanings

Prefixes modify the meaning of words and do not affect syntactic function. If prefixes such as *dis-, mis-, in-* and *un-* are taught as detachable units having a particular effect on meaning, the pitfall of doubling letters in the wrong place, for example, *misstake, dissappointment*, is less likely to arise. Some older pupils respond well to historical explanations for the spelling of words such as the Latin prefix *ad-*

when combined with words such as *ad+count, ad + credit, ad + point*, has led, through assimilation, to *account, accredit, appoint* –hence the double consonant.

Homophones

Some words, in spite of sounding the same, have different spellings. These are called homophones, for example, *reign, rein, rain*. Homophones illustrate quite clearly why reliance on sound-symbol correspondence simply will not work in English. Teaching the spelling of homophones can be most effective when mnemonics are added, for example, emphasizing their meaning, syntax, or distinctive visual features.

* BUY/BY? Buy you (u) a present.
* FIR/FUR? Draw a fir tree round the I in fir.
* THEIR/THERE? Teach through syntax: the, a, my, their + noun (or noun phrase).
* TO/TOO? Heightened sensitivity to spoken English will show that these are not homophones at all–*to* has a much shorter t+schwa sound. Children need some convincing of this, but once grasped no recourse to either meaning or syntax is necessary.

Conclusions

Young dyslexic children have difficulty reflecting on the sounds in speech, in producing and identifying rhyme and alliteration–in short in separating language sounds from language meaning.

In order to help these children to take the first steps towards the acquisition of literacy in an alphabetic language, the teacher must train them through multisensory techniques to link sounds with symbols, and to follow their speech sounds. For many children such training is successful and the alphabetic stage of literacy is reached (albeit rather later than for the child without specific learning difficulties).

However, as English is far from truly alphabetic, other problems await the teacher as the child develops. Poor attention to sound in the early years often leads to poor attention to the detail in written language later. This is just about acceptable for the purpose of reading (although such children are notoriously inaccurate readers), but it simply will not do for spelling, for which much more explicit lexical knowledge is required. Overreliance on sound becomes as much of a handicap to the dyslexic teenager as was his failure to identify with it in the first place. Furthermore, the phonological deficit in some children is so marked and so apparently intransigent that it seems more sensible to give up on the phonic route to spelling altogether.

To allow children to master the vagaries of English orthography, the teacher needs to harness other metacognitive skills: an awareness of regular orthographic patterns and knowledge about the structure of words and their morphology. The cognitive style of the individual must always be borne in mind, but the teacher must be aware that this will change over time rendering former teaching strategies inappropriate.

Chapter 11
Developing
Handwriting Skills

Jane Taylor

Writing systems have been developed by mankind for communicating thoughts and ideas in a permanent way. A great variety of languages and their corresponding scripts are used in different parts of the world today, and to be able to use these effectively, the codes as well as their written forms must be mastered. Handwriting is a physical skill and requires a high degree of perceptual-motor co-ordination. The purpose of this chapter is to examine some of the difficulties experienced by children learning to write, and to suggest strategies for helping both the beginner writer and the child whose handwriting is a cause for concern.

When learning to write, the child's task is to master 26 small and capital letters, the numerals 0–9 and basic punctuation. To promote the acquisition of skilled writing, specific teaching and training is required. For children who are failing with their handwriting, accurate diagnosis of the causes is a necessary precursor to remediation. In addition, it is necessary to ensure that sufficient time is given to the practice of this skill, with appropriate monitoring of performance, until legible, fluent and attractive writing can be produced with ease.

Underlying Deficits which Cause Handwriting Difficulties

There are a number of reasons why a child may be experiencing handwriting difficulties. Let us begin by considering some of these.

Developmental dysco-ordination syndrome (DCS)
Pupils with DCS, previously referred to as clumsy, are children who experience considerable problems in acquiring everyday motor

skills. They may experience gross motor difficulties such a sensory motor deficits, poor postural tone, sequential and motor planning difficulties, poor balance, poor eye tracking, inability to cross the midline, poor body image and confusion of directionality and laterality. Developmental milestones have frequently been delayed and the child is poor at PT and sports.

A child who has DCS may find the gross motor control required to maintain good writing posture and correct tool-hold difficult to sustain. Fine hand/eye co-ordination skills may also be affected in these children. They therefore have difficulty in learning correct letter formation, both in achieving the correct movement pattern for each letter and in using the writing instrument competently. The *Test of Motor Impairment* (1982) now revised as *Movement Assessment Battery for Children* (ABC) (Henderson and Sugden, 1992) is a useful diagnostic tool to pinpoint areas of difficulty. A checklist is provided to help the classteacher to identify those children with movement difficulties. A more detailed test can be administered to give information on the degree and precise nature of the motor impairment. The child who demonstrates movement difficulties should be considered at risk, and the problems which he or she experiences should be recognized. Suitable programmes to increase skills in the diagnosed areas of weakness should be considered to be an essential part of a school's policy for Physical Education.

Visual perceptual and visual motor difficulties

Many children with developmental dyscoordination syndrome also have poor visual perception which make the acquisition of handwriting skills more difficult. Gardner (1982) in his *Test of Visual-Perceptual Skills* defines visual perception as 'the ability to give meaning to what is seen'. He suggests that there are seven areas which can be identified:

- *Visual discrimination:* the ability to match or determine the exact characteristics of two forms when one of the forms is among similar forms
- *Visual memory:* the ability to remember for immediate recall, all of the characteristics of a given form, and to be able to find this form from an array of similar forms
- *Visual-spatial relationships:* the ability to determine, from among a number of identical forms, the one single form or part of a single form that is going in a different direction from the other forms

- *Visual form constancy:* the ability to see a form, and to be able to find that form, even though the form may be smaller, larger, rotated, reversed, and/or hidden.
- *Visual sequential memory:* the ability to remember for immediate recall, a series of forms from among a larger set of forms.
- *Visual figure-ground:* the ability to perceive a form visually, and to find this form hidden in a conglomerated ground of matter.
- *Visual closure:* the ability to determine, from among a number of incomplete forms, the one that is the same as the stimulus form, i.e., the completed form.

The test examines each area and the scores give a very clear indication of a child's strengths and weaknesses.

Another useful test, which ascertains a child's ability to copy a presented form accurately is *The Developmental Test of Visual-Motor Integration* 3R (Beery, 1989), often known as **VMI**. A sequence of 24 geometric forms is presented to the child for him or her to copy. If a child demonstrates problems with visual or visual motor perception he or she should be considered at risk, and ways in which help can be given in the classroom to strengthen specific areas of weakness need to be assessed.

A child with visual perceptual problems may find it difficult to recall the shape of a specific letter, the sequence of the movement pattern of a letter and the sequence of letters in a word. Pausing to recall how to spell a word can make writing jerky. Such children may reverse letters or fail to see similar patterns in letters. They may have difficulty regulating the slant or appreciating the regular height of letters, and find it difficult to maintain an even space between letters and words.

If the child has serious problems, either with motor coordination or visual perception, then it may be necessary to seek advice from a physiotherapist and/or an occupational therapist.

Dyslexia

Children with dyslexia or specific learning difficulties experience difficulties processing written language and may also have problems with numeracy. Because they find learning to read, spell or express thoughts on paper difficult, they write fewer words. They also complete fewer arithmetic assignments. It is therefore not hard to see that actually, they practise their writing less than their peers. They are also discouraged by how laborious they find handwriting to be and by the unattractive outcome of their efforts.

A test such as the *Aston Index* (Newton and Thomson, 1982) or the MIST (see Hannavy, this volume) could be used by the classteacher to screen for written language difficulties, as these children will need appropriate help to improve their literacy skills in addition to spending time on mastering handwriting skills.

Attention Deficit Hyperactivity Disorder (ADHD)

Children with ADHD are those who 'differ from their peers in the degree to which they appear to be able to sustain attention in tasks and play activities'. They also display extreme difficulties in starting and finishing schoolwork and other activities. By the very nature of this underlying difficulty, children with ADHD are likely to have problems in focusing sufficient attention on the detail which mastering handwriting requires in the early stages of learning to write.

Physical handicaps

Children with handicaps such as cerebral palsy and osteogenesis (brittle bones) are likely to require specific help to acquire handwriting skills. They may need to bypass handwriting altogether and adopt alternative means of communication such as word processing.

Other reasons for handwriting difficulties

Some children fail to pick up elements of handwriting for less clearly defined reasons. There may perhaps have been insufficient teaching, learning and practice at a vital stage in learning to write, or the standard of handwriting which a teacher expected may have been considerably lower than the child's potential standard. On the other hand they may simply have missed handwriting instruction lessons for a variety of reasons, such as illness or change of school. A systematic handwriting policy should be developed in schools to ensure that the at-risk child does get sufficient support and time to enable him to develop fluent and presentable handwriting.

Ergonomics

Before embarking on handwriting instruction, the teacher must be aware of the physical environment in which the child is expected to write. It is necessary to consider:

- Whether the height of the table and chair fit the child. Brown (1989) suggests that, as a rule of thumb, the height should be half the height of the child and the chair seat should be one third his/her height. However, Lewis and Salway (1989) point out that sitting the 'small older child' on two stacked chairs produced more mature behaviour. The alternative is to use adjustable furniture or a foot stool. The present trend is to consider whether a healthy back is more efficiently maintained if the chair seat slopes slightly forward.

- The use of a sloping writing surface on which to write. An angle of 20 degrees is the most comfortable (Brown, 1989). A sloping surface improves the position of the wrist, head and hand in relation to the writing surface. Strain may also be reduced in this position.

- The type of tool to be used. The child should be offered a variety of pencils and pens from which to select the one which feels most comfortable and suits his or her style of writing best. For example, shafts of different shapes and diameter, pens with different width tips.

- The stage at which the change from pencil to pen is to be made.

- The size and type of paper to be used and whether it should be lined or unlined. The number of lines to be used. The width between lines.

- The surface on which the child writes. This should not be too hard. For example, the child can rest his work on a large piece of card. The table or desk should be uncluttered.

- The child's sitting position. The child should be taught to adopt a good posture with feet flat on the floor, bottom well back on the chair, hips slightly flexed, a straight back and the non-writing hand stabilizing the paper.

- The position of the paper. The right-handed child should have the paper tilted 10–20 degrees to the right and the non-writing hand should be placed on the paper above the writing hand. The left-handed child should have the paper tilted to the left at an angle of about 30 degrees. The top right hand corner should be in line with the child's navel. The non-writing hand should be placed above the writing hand. The writing hand should be below the writing line so that the child can see the letters as he writes them.

- It is very important that left-handed children are encouraged to have their paper correctly positioned every time they write as this will not restrict the writing arm as it moves towards the body across the page. They need to be reminded that as they write they should move the paper up rather than moving their writing arm down, thus maintaining the hand and arm in the optimum position. They should sit on the left of a right-handed child. If the child has a hooked grasp then the paper should be in the right-handed position.

- The grasp which the child uses. The ideal grasp is considered to be the dynamic tripod grasp (Schneck and Henderson 1990). The use of an additional shaped grip, which can be fitted onto the shaft of the writing tool, may facilitate an improved grasp. Once the grasp is automatic, the grip can be abandoned.

- Ideally the light source should be to the front of the child; from the left for the right hander and from the right for the left hander. The child should be taught to appreciate the importance of these underlying ergonomic principles.

The Early Stages of Learning to Write

Before embarking on teaching handwriting, it is desirable that the teacher identifies those children who are likely to experience difficulties in the early stages of learning to write, to ensure that they are given sufficient supervision. It is also necessary to check that the child has had adequate prewriting experience. Colouring is a valuable activity as it requires accuracy of fine motor movements of both the fingers and the wrist. If prewriting patterns are used, these should relate to letter shapes.

Before a child embarks on a handwriting programme the teacher might find it helpful to observe how the child:

- Draws a person (Naglieri, 1987). Michael (1984) suggests that the ability to draw a person should be an indicator of whether the child is ready to begin writing. He states, 'unless the child is able to draw a clear head which relates to legs and arms, there is little point in teaching writing until the child has matured.' However, in the author's experience some children who have shown poor body concept in their drawings have learnt, with appropriate teaching, to write successfully. Nevertheless, a child who shows inconsistency in his 'draw a person' should be considered at risk. Nicky was one such child; he was a right-handed child with ADHD when seen at 7;3 years. Figure 11.1 shows that his drawing of a person was fairly rudimentary. His handwriting performance is shown in Figures 11.2 and 11.3.

Name ...Nicky................... Date .28..2..95......

Figure 11.1: Nicky's 'Draw a person'. Nicky is 7;3 years, right-handed and has developmental coordination disorder

- Copies a circle, a cross, a square, a triangle and diamond. Sheridan (1975) states that a child should be able to copy a circle at 3 years of age, a cross at 4 years, a square at 5 years and a triangle at 5-and-a-half years. Many of the letters have movements similar to these basic shapes. If a child is unable to draw a triangle he may find letters with diagonal lines i.e. *k v w x z* difficult to write and should also be considered at risk.
- Writes the letters of the alphabet.

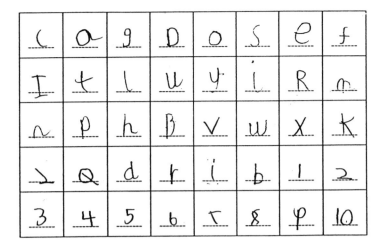

Figure 11.2: Nicky's letter formation

Figure 11.3: Nicky's free written expression

The teacher needs to confirm whether vision and hearing tests have been administered and that there are no problems. In addition, the child should be able to:

- understand the language of instruction e.g., above, next to
- recognise letters by matching in the very early stages of learning to write
- identify the names and/or the sounds of the letters

Mastering the formation of letters and numerals

Learning about letters and numerals can be made fun and interesting. Children should be encouraged to observe the variety of styles used for letters and numerals, for example in magazines, on advertisements or on food packets. They should learn to appreciate the similarities and differences between letters and should be taught that letters fall naturally into groups. For instance, they may be divided into letters with ascenders (tall letters), letters with descenders (letters with tails) and x height letters (middle size letters) (see Figure 11.4). Alternatively, as letters with straight lines occur in more than half the alphabet, letters with straight lines could be put into a group.

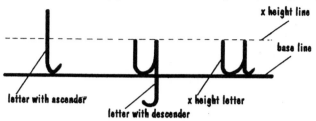

Figure 11.4: Examples of how letters can be grouped

As an exercise, plastic or wooden letters can be sorted into their proper groups and then placed correctly on a line. Spending time on these tasks should familiarize the child with the letters. Once having appreciated that letters fall into groups, the child can begin to learn their similarities and differences. For example, the letters *a, d, g,* are all based on the letter *c.* Appreciation of this fact lessens the amount of information which has to be remembered. It will also enable children to become self-critical about the shape of the letters as they are written, and will help them to monitor whether the letters they have produced match the model given.

In the initial stages of learning to write, children should be encouraged to trace over or to copy a model. They should not be expected to copy from a distance, for example, from a white board. Letters which end on the base line should be taught from the beginning with an exit stroke to facilitate the natural progression to a joined script. It is important, even at this early stage, to make the child aware of the relative height of letters and that they should be correctly positioned on an imaginary base line. A tracing exercise is the next step. Cover a set of enlarged letters in plastic with the starting position and directional changes clearly marked. The child is expected to trace over the model until the movement pattern is well established. Ramsden (1992) suggests that initial learning of letter shapes can be practised with the index finger of the dominant hand on the outstretched open palm of the non-writing hand. The middle-size letters start at the top of the palm, letters with ascenders from the top of the fingers and descending letters go on down below the wrist to complete the tail.

To reinforce the patterns associated with well-formed letters, children can use their index fingers to write the letters in a sand tray, before working on paper. Once children can produce each letter confidently, then they can practise on a blank sheet of paper. Michael (1985) suggests that children should be able to write all the letters of the alphabet before they are expected to express themselves in writing. As soon as they start to write words, then a baseline should be used for guidance. To minimize failure, children should be supplied with paper which has the base and x height line indicated. This type of paper should be used until a child's handwriting is consistent and completely automatic (see Figure 11.5).

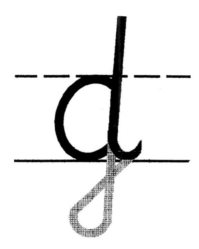

Figure 11.5: Illustration to show how the shape of the letter c forms part of the letters *a, d, g*. Base and x height line indicated.

Verbalization of the movement pattern of a letter as it is written acts as a reinforcement and can enhance learning. For example, as a reminder of the shape of the letter *d*, the child could be asked before beginning to write, to say, '*d* starts like a *c*.' During the writing of the letter, the route the writing instrument will take can be verbalized,

'I start in the middle, back round, up to the top, straight down and flick.'

The use of verbalization is particularly useful for children with perceptual-motor and/or co-ordination problems who may be able to compose at a greater length than they can write down by themselves. In such cases, alternative methods of recording than writing should be considered, at least in the short term. These methods might include dictating to an adult or into a tape recorder, or using a word processor.

Developing a cursive script

The progression from single letters to joining letters is easy if the child has learned to use appropriate exit strokes from the beginning.

When the exit stroke is extended it becomes the entry stroke of the next letter. However, if the child does not use any exit strokes then he may need to practise this first before attempting to master the diagonal joins. Exit strokes should be approximately 45 degrees from the base line.

There are three basic joins:

1. Horizontal join
    The letters *o, r, v, w* can exit with a horizontal join (see Figure 11.6) The letters *f, t* can exit from the cross bar (see Figure 11.7).

Figures 11.6: Horizontal joins

Figure 11.7: Horizontal joins from cross bar

2. Diagonal join
    The exit strokes of letters *a, c, d,e, h, i, k, l, m, n, t, u, x, z* are extended to become the diagonal join (see Figure 11.8).

Figure 11.8: Diagonal joins to x height letters and to letters with ascenders and descenders

3. Diagonal join extended to a round letter
    The letters *a, c, d, g* require the diagonal stroke from the preceding letter to be extended (see Figure 11.9).

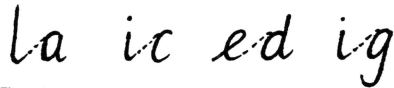

Figure 11.9: Diagonal joins to oval letters

In addition there are some letters which need not be joined. For example, the tails of the letter *g, j, y, q* can be left unjoined or can be extended to form a diagonal join (see Figure 11.10).

Figure 11.10: Diagonal joins from letters with descenders

Similarly the joins from the letters *b, p, s* can be left unjoined or can be joined from the bottom (see Figure 11.11). For those children who confuse the letters *b* and *p*, learning to write an open *b* and *p* may be helpful (see Figure 11.12).

Figures 11.11: Diagonal joins from closed *b* and *p* and from *s*

Figures 11.12: Open *p* and *b*

A natural pause is made after three to four letters. At this point a horizontal movement is made by the forearm in order to progress across the page, so joining all letters is not essential. For those children who have spatial and orientation difficulties, learning to start all letters from the base line and then to join all letters within a word may be more appropriate. It is important that the entry stroke leads up to the base line at an angle of about 45 degrees.

Fluency

Fluency is essential for automatic, legible handwriting and should be incorporated into every teaching programme. Fluency can be developed by spending time on producing letters at speed. This can be achieved by asking the child to write the same letter legibly, as many times as possible in a given time. Ten to fifteen seconds is a suitable period for this exercise. The child then ticks the *good* letters, that is the well-formed ones, again reinforcing the child's self-critical skills. Once a number of letters have been learned the child can be asked to write out one or two words which contain those letters. They can then progress to writing a sentence once all the letters are known, but should check letter formation at the end of each task.

Capital letters

Capital letters will need to be learned but as there are fewer directional changes, they tend not to cause too much difficulty.

Numerals

The correct movement patterns of the numerals 0–9 should also be learnt. Numerals should be the same height as capital letters.

Monitoring progress

A self-monitoring system can be introduced to maintain a continued focus on letter formation. The young child may have an individual chart which is ticked once a letter is mastered. The older child could use a more detailed chart to include information on letter formation, slant, alignment, the relative size of letters, spaces between letters and words. For example, having learnt the letters *i, t, l,* they could be asked to indicate on the chart,

'My straight lines are straight and parallel?' YES/NO.

This system should encourage children to become more aware of the details of handwriting which still require continued practice, and enable them to monitor their own progress. Such systems could also be used by the teacher.

Progress should be regularly evaluated. Evaluation might consist of checking letter formation, administering a copying or a speeded writing test. Alternatively, a free-writing test in which the child is asked to commit ideas to paper within a time limit can be given. This piece of work will provide the teacher with a good deal of information for monitoring handwriting, spelling, punctuation, grammar and use of language (see Goulandris, this volume).

Assessment of Handwriting Difficulties

In order to assess the nature and causes of a child's difficulty with handwriting, samples of letter formation, copying and free writing should be collected and dated. The following checklist provides a useful guide to the points that need to be checked:

- Posture, paper position, tool-hold and pressure.
- Alphabet knowledge: The names of letters should be known. Common confusions are b/d, m/w, u/y, f/t, g/j, p/q, i/j/l.
- Letter formation: This can only be done by watching the child write the letters. It is necessary to identify those letters which are incorrectly or poorly formed.
- Formation of numerals: It is necessary to identify those numerals which are incorrectly formed.
- Relative height of letters: Letters with ascenders, letters with descenders and x height letters should all be the correct height.
- Slant of straight lines: Straight lines should be straight and parallel.
- Alignment: Letters should sit on the line correctly.
- Space between letters and words: The space between letters and words should be even.
- Size of writing: The writing should not be too big or too small.
- Correct use of capital letters and punctuation: A sentence begins with a capital letter and ends with a full stop.
- Joins: If letters are joined it is important to check that the joins are made correctly.

Handwriting speed

A considerable time in school is spent writing. Some children are able to produce legible, attractive handwriting at speed whereas for others, it is always a laborious task. It is useful for the teacher to know the writing speed of a child compared with the class average as this has implications for written tasks which the child is expected to produce. This information may be derived from an evaluation of copying speed. The familiar sentence:

The quick brown fox jumps over the lazy dog

can be used for this purpose. A simpler sentence may be more appropriate for younger children. The children are first asked to copy the sentence in their *best* handwriting. This task is timed. Then they copy the sentence for three minutes in *fast* writing. There are no national norms for writing speeds but research in New Zealand and England indicated an average speed of between 77 and 82 letters per minute for 11-year-olds.

Written expression

A free-writing sample can also be useful for establishing the normal range of performance within a class or school irrespective of national norms. Alston (1995) describes one method of evaluating written output, grammatical competence and expression. The child is requested to write about any of the following topics:

* my favourite person
* someone I know very well
* something in which I am very interested

For example, the free-written expression from a dyslexic boy, Luke, aged 12;1 years is shown in Figure 11.13.

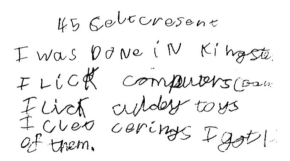

Figure 11.13: Luke's free-written expression at 12;1 years

Ideally the children should write for a twenty minute period, but the actual time should be noted if the full period of writing is not possible. Writing can be assessed under five headings:

1.   Handwriting.
2.   Spelling.
3.   Punctuation.
4.   Grammar.
5.   Logical, stylistic and expressive writing.

Seven- to 10-year-old children from a Cheshire Primary School (86 girls and 82 boys) were asked to write for a 20-minute period. The mean number of words they produced per minute by children in different age groups is shown in Table 11.1 (Alston, 1995).

Table 11.1: Writing speeds of primary school children during a 20-minute free-writing exercise

Age of children (in years and months)	Mean (words per minute)	Standard deviation
7;10	3.76	1.91
8;10	5.63	2.61
9;10	5.98	2.22
10;10	7.64	3.14

Older children have been studied by Dutton (1992). In this study the children were asked to write *My Life History* in a 30-minute period. Writing speed was one aspect which was examined and the results are summarized in Table 11.2.

Table 11.2: Writing speeds of senior school children during a 30-minute free-writing exercise

Age of children (years)	Mean (words per minute)
13;00	12.7
14;00	14.4
15;00	15.9
16;00	17.1
17;00	18.4

The results suggested that girls tend to perform at a better level than boys. Luke had difficulties writing under timed conditions. Ideally, the teacher should examine untimed and speed samples as well as a sample of free writing to ascertain whether the child has specific difficulties:

* maintaining legibility when writing at speed or when involved in free-written expression
* slower than average writing speed
* written expression difficulties which are affecting output

For example, compare Figure 11.14 showing five minutes of Luke's written work at the age of 14 years, with Figure 11.15 showing his copying performance when he had more time to concentrate on legibility.

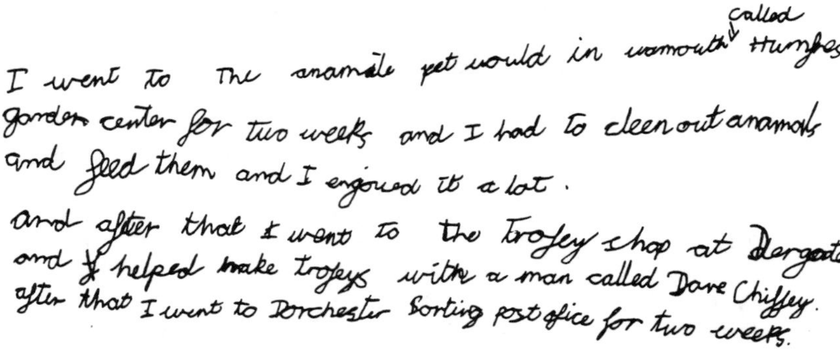

> *I went to The anamile pet would in wamouth called Humfes*
> *gorden center for two weeks and I had to cleen out anamols*
> *and feed them and I enjoued it a lot .*
> *and after that I went to the Trofey shop at Dergate s*
> *and I helped make trofeys with a man called Dave Chiffey.*
> *after that I went to Dorchester Sorting post office for two weeks.*

Figure 11.14: Luke's free-written expression in five minutes at 14 years

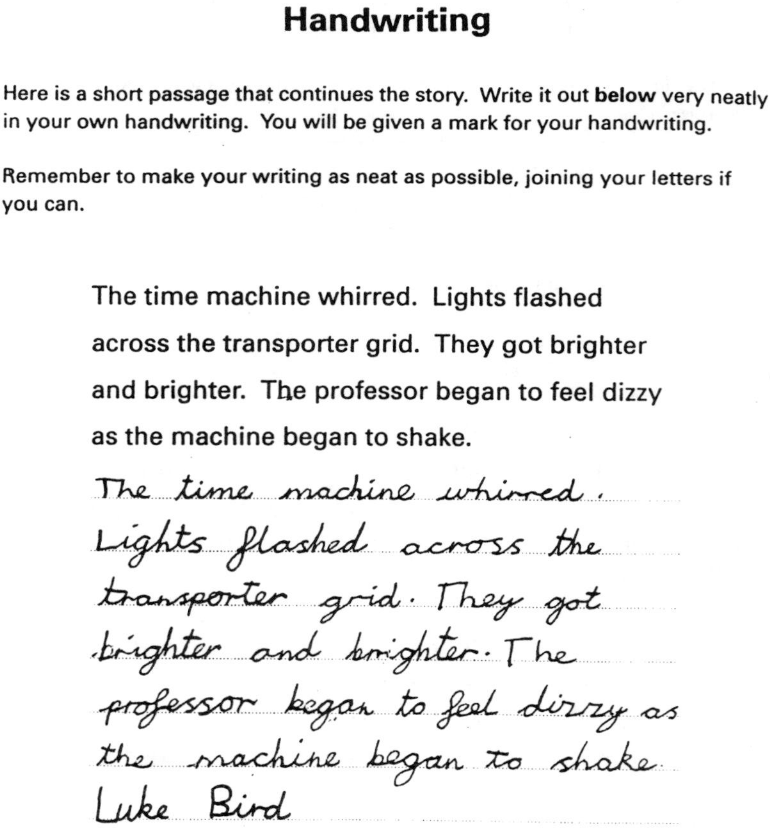

Handwriting

Here is a short passage that continues the story. Write it out **below** very neatly in your own handwriting. You will be given a mark for your handwriting.

Remember to make your writing as neat as possible, joining your letters if you can.

> The time machine whirred. Lights flashed
> across the transporter grid. They got brighter
> and brighter. The professor began to feel dizzy
> as the machine began to shake.

> *The time machine whirred.*
> *Lights flashed across the*
> *transporter grid. They got*
> *brighter and brighter. The*
> *professor began to feel dizzy as*
> *the machine began to shake.*
> *Luke Bird*

Figure 11.15: Luke's copying performance

Involving children in the assessment of their own handwriting

In a survey of first year secondary pupils' attitude to their own handwriting, Whitmarsh (1988) found that 85 per cent of children wished that they could write better and 88 per cent thought that being able to write was important. Children are much more likely to make an effort to improve their handwriting if the teacher does not start by criticizing what is incorrect, but praises all that can be done well. Children should be asked if they know, or have previously been told, what is problematic with their handwriting. This changes the emphasis from one of authority to one of partnership, of discovering together where the problems lie.

Handwriting can be considered to be rule-based. The following rules can be presented to children for them to select the one which they think identifies a problem area for them.

1. All letters except *d* and *e* start at the top.
2. Oval letters should be closed and watertight.
3. Letters with straight lines should be straight and parallel.
4. The relative height of letters should be uniform.
5. Letters should be correctly placed in relation to the baseline.
6. The space between letters should be even.
7. The space between words should be even.
8. Letters which end at the top join horizontally.
9. Letters which end on the baseline join diagonally.
10. A sentence should begin with a capital letter and end with a full stop.

The particular difficulties which a child is experiencing should be discussed and itemized with teaching objectives listed. The teacher may have to use some discretion if there are too many faults. The child's chance of success will be greater if they are expected to work on only one or, at the most, two items at a time. Teaching is likely to be more positive if children are encouraged to identify their own errors.

Implementing a Teaching Programme

Before embarking on a remedial handwriting programme, the teacher should check that there are no underlying problems with the child's vision and hearing. If the medical records indicate that the child has seen a speech and language therapist, physiotherapist or occupational therapist this should alert the teacher to possible earlier difficulties with speech and language, movement sensory-motor or perceptual difficulties which may still persist. The teacher may wish to seek advice of the other professionals or to liaise with them about the teaching programme.

Improving posture and paper position should be the starting point of any remedial programme. It should be explained to the child that, as handwriting is one of the most complex physical skills which we learn, attention must be paid to organizing the body to achieve maximum efficiency, just as one would in any sport.

The rules of handwriting used to identify the difficulties can now form the basis of the teaching programme. The teaching approach for the child who has failed to master handwriting skills should be similar to the approach already described for the beginner writer. The use of rules should be seen as a technique to focus the child's attention on the detail and therefore to make handwriting practice more meaningful.

Rule 1:   Once the inaccuracies of letter formation have been identified, each letter must be worked on as already described.

Rule 2:   Oval letters must be closed. This is achieved by ensuring that the letters *a d g q* are begun at approximately the one o'clock position and are not written as a round *o* with an exit stroke.

Rule 3:   The child is asked to use a fine red pen to mark the straight lines on a sample of his writing. They should then be able to observe if the slant is regular.

Rule 4:   The child is asked to divide a set of plastic letters into three groups, letters with ascenders, letters with descenders and x height letters. Alternatively, the child is asked to write out all the letters of the alphabet and then to write them out again in their specific groups. This will highlight which letters are not placed correctly on the base line. The letter *j* is often placed in the letters with ascenders group.
            Lined paper, with the base and x height lines indicated, will assist the child to work on improving the relative height of letters.

Rule 5:   Discussing the purpose of the base line and how letters and words should be correctly aligned should assist the child to identify those letters which are incorrectly aligned.

Rule 6/7:   The child is asked to measure the distance he or she leaves between letters and words. The correct amount of space which should be left between letters/words is then discussed. The space between letters is often uneven because the joining stroke is irregular. The space between words should be approximately the size of two of the child's small *o*'s. The child is asked to write either a word or a sentence checking the spaces between the letters or words, and ticking those spaces which are even.

Rule 8/9:   See section 'Developing a cursive script' earlier in this chapter.

Rule 10:   The child needs to appreciate the reasons for punctuation.

A list of resources that teachers may find useful for promoting handwriting skills is given in Appendix 11.1.

Ideas for teaching writing-related skills

Punctuation, paragraphs and presentation

Many children with handwriting problems have difficulties with punctuation, paragraphs and the presentation of written work. They need specific instructions and constant reinforcement. It is useful to paste a model of what is expected by the teacher for each subject in the front of the exercise book. The child can then refer to this when he or she needs reminding of what is expected in that subject area.

Copying from a distance

The underlying deficits which often create handwriting difficulties may also mean that other skills such as copying, drawing and labelling diagrams neatly are also a struggle. Alternative methods to copying should be considered. For example, an able writer could make a carbon copy for a poor writer or a photocopied handout could be given.

Instruction on labelling techniques should also be given. For example, emphasizing the need to use a ruler when drawing the indicating lines. Some children find it very difficult to write neatly without a guide line. It can be helpful to provide them with a line on a piece of card which can be placed under the diagram and would provide a guide line (see Figure 11.16).

Note taking

Children should be taught note-taking skills, and a personal shorthand, such as + for *and, posv* for *positive*. A list could be devised by each subject teacher.

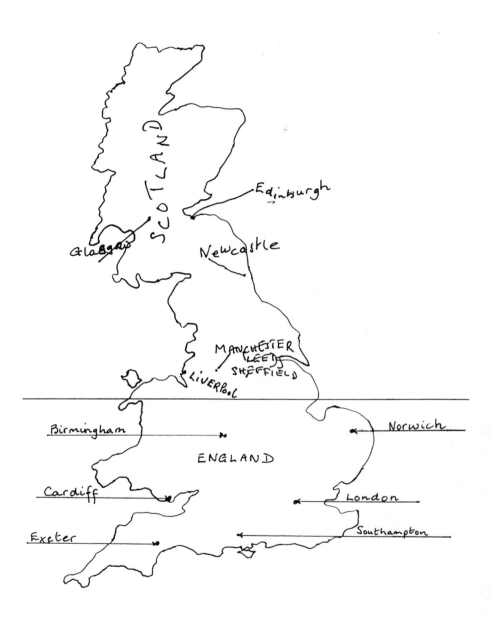

Figure 11.16: Map showing untidy and neat labelling

Keyboard skills

For children with slow, laborious handwriting the advent of word processing is a great boon with presentation being so much better than any handwritten work. There is the added facility of a spell checker and cutting and pasting text which can greatly enhance the quality of written output. Keyboarding is a physical skill and therefore the child who is likely to be using word processing on a regular basis should be provided with proper instruction and given sufficient time to master touch typing. A good example of a teaching programme that introduces keyboard skills in a systematic fashion whilst also reinforcing spelling concepts is provided by Ros Kinloch in her *Easy Type* approach (Kinloch, 1994).

Concluding remarks

In order to fulfil the requirements of the national curriculum, every school needs to develop a structured handwriting policy. In addition, ways in which additional support can be given to those children who are struggling with handwriting skills will need to be devised. Details of some useful publications containing further ideas are given in Appendix 11.1.

In conclusion, practice does not always make perfect. Time spent on providing a meaningful teaching programme in the early stages of learning to write, together with regular monitoring of progress should enable most children to acquire fluent, legible and attractive handwriting. Speed may always be a problem for some. For those children whose handwriting does not meet the demands of the writing situation, alternative methods of communication should be considered and instruction in these given.

Appendix 11.1

TEACHING HANDWRITING SKILLS- Resource List

Alston, J. and Taylor, J. (1990) *Handwriting Helpline*. Manchester: Dextral Books.
Deterding, G. and Scheib, B. (1992) *Steps to Literacy*. Hitchin, Herts: Hames Nisbet.
Myers, P.W. (1993) *Movement into Writing*. Bolton, Lancs: Jarvis Print.
Pickard, P. (1986) *Handwriting–A Second Chance*. Wisbech, Cambs: LDA.
Sassoon, R. (1983) *The Practical Guide to Children's Handwriting*. London: Thames and Hudson.
Sassoon, R. (1994) *Helping with Handwriting–Key Stage 2 and 3*. London: John Murray.

Tasker, D. (1995) *Helping with Handwriting – Key Stage 1 and 2*. London: John Murray.

Taylor, J. (1979) *Writing is for Reading Book 1*. Available from Willowbank, Watery Lane, Weymouth, Dorset DT3 DP5

Taylor, J. (1981) *Writing is for Reading Book 2*. Available from Willowbank, Watery Lane, Weymouth, Dorset DT3 DP5

Tiburtius, S. (1994) *Write on Target*. Manchester: Dextral Books.

Wendon, L. (1993) The Letterland Handwriting Programme. Barton, Cambs: Letterland, Ltd.

Chapter 12

Involving Parents in Helping their Children Overcome Reading and Spelling Difficulties

Sybil Hannavy

The success and approval that children experience when attempting to communicate with adults powerfully motivates them in developing speech. Most children approach reading with the same eagerness with which they learn to speak. Those who falter in the early stages need the kind of guidance and support which will ensure success and this is more likely to occur if both the home and school are involved.

But what kind of support? The practice of sending books home for parents to hear their children read has become widespread in Britain. However, parent listening or sharing does little to help children most at risk of reading failure. Parents of these low-competence readers usually do not know how important their help can be, nor how best to give it. In contrast parent training studies which involve explanation and modelling, as well as monitoring and correction, have been found to improve poor readers' competence as well as their enthusiasm for reading (Toomey, 1993).

This chapter describes an eight-week programme, the Forward Together Recovery Programme which contains many of the features found in parent training studies. It was piloted in Cambridgeshire in 1985 and can be used by parents of children in their fifth or sixth term at school (or later in the case of more severe problems) who are having difficulty 'taking off' in reading.

Before using the Forward Together Recovery Programme children are first given the *Middle Infant Screening Test* (Hannavy, 1994). This test highlights any weaknesses in listening and spelling that relate closely to the child's reading difficulty. Teachers can use the results of this test to focus parents' attention on the specific areas in which their children need help, such as recognizing letter sounds, segmenting sounds within words and writing letters and words. The programme attempts to create a situation in which children experience success with reading and writing and are being nudged towards independence. The way this is done is to share carefully preselected and enjoyable texts with them. Knowledge of letter sounds and the ability to focus on the initial sounds of words is also developed separately through games and writing.

Programme Considerations

Parents as partners

Fundamental to the *Forward Together Recovery Programme* is the assumption that parents of children who are experiencing difficulty with literacy should become partners in their children's educational progress. Parents are therefore invited to make a commitment to help their children daily for eight weeks and to attend nine weekly group meetings for discussion and guidance. It is made clear that they are not teacher substitutes; they are able to develop a unique two-way relationship which can have very positive effects on their children's learning and attitudes, particularly at this stage in their learning development. They should feel this is a joint venture in which they have a special contribution to make.

Parents are helped initially to understand something about their children's problems and about the learning process by examining their children's written work on the *Middle Infant Screening Test* with their teacher. They also hear a tape of their children reading and, finally, they themselves are put into the situation of being beginning readers.

Selecting children

By the fifth or sixth term in school, teachers will know which children are falling behind with reading and writing, but they need to find out which letter-sounds the children know, what stage they have reached in segmenting sounds within words, and whether they are able to write some words from memory.

The *Middle Infant Screening Test* was designed specifically for this purpose. It is a pencil and paper test and teachers can use it for up to

20 children at once. The results also give a class profile which indicates how the poorer children compare with the class average. Children with more severe problems can be given the test in Years 2, 3 or 4, as appropriate.

At this age, children are generally not aware that they are lagging behind their peers and have not, therefore, developed the negative attitudes to literacy which older children tend to have. They still enjoy stories, like being read to and are happy to share books. Their lack of confidence has not yet hardened into a belief that they cannot read. They are willing to try, and they respond quickly to success, although they have got stuck in inappropriate reading and writing behaviour and need to be moved on. By Year One, teachers recognize such children and know that they would benefit from daily individual help, but usually learning support is available only for children with very severe difficulties. It is a good time to draw on the capacity of parents to help at home.

Selecting parents

Parents of low-achieving children are often those who have little contact with teachers. They are not confident in dealing with schools or in helping their children educationally, and they tend to be negatively perceived by teachers. Often such parents themselves had difficulty learning to read and write and their anxiety about their children can be mixed with guilt about their own inadequacy in literacy. The experience of successfully helping their children boosts their own morale.

In fact, there can be considerable obstacles to communicating with such parents, and both teachers and parents might blame one another for this. If schools want to avoid increasing inequality by giving most of their attention to the more easily approachable parents, they have to accept that it is necessary to actively seek out disaffected parents. A school on a large council estate described their method of selection as follows:

> We avoid selecting parents who are obviously struggling to cope, as we feel that it really would be detrimental to the child if the scheme was not run in a relaxed manner. If Mum has a large family or is working then she may well not have the time or, more importantly, the patience to participate in the scheme. A casual chat on the first parents' evening to determine the home situation is our first step and a list of possible parents is drawn up. Careful monitoring of the parents' attitude is essential. You can soon pick up signs of difficulty and if there are problems we step in and preselect the books going home or slow down the writing and phonics programme.

When parents work full-time or shifts, schools must ask whether it would be possible for them to attend any of the meetings. The teacher or another parent can keep them up to date on missed meetings, or in some cases partners, grandparents or older siblings can attend in their place. If parents cannot stay for an hour, their needs are dealt with first so that they can leave early. In practice, the time for meetings which most parents and teachers prefer is an hour before school closes. If this straddles the afternoon break, then teachers need cover for only three quarters of an hour. Group dynamics seem to work best if there are at least four and not more than eight parents, although some teachers run successful groups of ten.

When considering which parents are likely to cooperate with the programme, teachers have found it useful to overestimate rather than underestimate their willingness to take part. Often parents whom they feel will not cooperate in fact do, once their trust is won. It is also important to allow for a certain drop-out rate. Most groups remain intact but sometimes parents do drop out and teachers must realize that neither they nor the parents need feel guilty if this happens. Rather, teachers need to assure parents that their children will continue with the programme at school.

To some parents however, the identification of a special educational need may be alarming. Schools can reduce the possibility of alarm by informing parents when their children first start school that the children's progress is continually monitored and if, after four terms, they are falling behind, then one of the options available to them will be an eight-week home acceleration programme. If the programme has become part of school policy and parents hear good reports about it, they usually welcome the opportunity to participate.

When children suitable for the programme are identified, the class teacher may approach parents individually or alternatively organize an initial evening meeting for both parents. At this meeting, teachers need to ask and discuss suitable times for weekly meetings, and whether parents want to take part. At this stage many schools find it useful to let parents from previous groups relate their experiences. If parents are given a handout such as that shown in Figure 12.1, they realize from the beginning that the school is offering them time and expert guidance and, in turn, will expect a certain degree of commitment. When approached in this way, parents usually accept the invitation to take part in the programme.

The five most important points to make to parents in the first few meetings are that:

- their children lack confidence in reading and writing
- the daily help and encouragement of parents will almost certainly boost confidence and accelerate progress
- parents will be carefully guided through a structured home-help programme
- their attention will be drawn to their own children's specific difficulties
- at the end of the eight weeks, their children will be retested so that parents can judge their progress

Forward Together

The aim of this programme is to support children who would benefit from more help with reading, handwriting and free writing.

Your commitment will be:
- to attend nine weekly meetings for guidance and discussion, every .... from ......(time) to ......(time);
- to contact school if it is not possible for you to attend a meeting, or to arrange for someone else to attend instead;
- to work with your child for 15 to 30 minutes daily where possible;
- to report on progress made, at each weekly session;
- to contribute towards/pay for the cost of the Activity Book to be used throughout this programme.

Our commitment will be:
- to guide you carefully through a structured home-help programme;
- to provide our time, expertise and support, enabling you to continue the programme at home;
- to monitor your child's progress within school.

Figure 12.1: Handout used by Priory Park Infants School, St. Neots, Cambridgeshire

How the Programme is Structured

The programme covers the following specific skills, and uses multi-sensory learning techniques as well as games to encourage development. Tasks are modelled by the adult for children to imitate, and the aim is to develop what Clay (1985) calls a 'self-improving system' in which children check and assess their own work.

Reading

Children choose freely from a range of books which have been pre-selected by teachers according to the following criteria:

- picture on each page with one or two lines of text;
- language which is predictable, containing some rhyme, rhythm or repetition;
- appealing story.

The 'prepare, pause, prompt, praise' method is used to build children's confidence in using decoding skills and contextual cues:

- adult and child first look through the book and the adult reads some of the text in order to familiarize the child with it before attempting to read alone;
- when children do not know a word, the adult pauses for five seconds before prompting, so that children know that they are expected to try and work out the word by themselves;
- if after five seconds the children still do not know the word, they are prompted to leave it out and read on, then return to it later, or to look at the picture, or try the first sound: if this doesn't work the adult supplies the word;
- children are praised for responding to a prompt, or for attempting a word by themselves, or for self-correcting.

Gradually children learn how to attempt words without being prompted. They are also encouraged to respond personally to what they read, and to re-read favourites. During the eight weeks, they often read 30 or 40 books. Parents learn to examine children's books critically and appreciatively. First of all they must bear in mind their children's reading ability and choose texts which are constructed in such a way as to support the reader by means of cumulative repetition, rhyme, and a sense of rhythmical forward movement. The story also needs to bear the reader forward: children should want to know what is going to happen next but a plot is not essential. For instance, in *My Cat Likes to Hide in Boxes*, by Eve Sutton and Lynley Dodd (Picture Puffin/Penguin), a series of humorous cat situations is presented in the form of cumulative repetition and rhyme, and children generally love this book. Illustrations are important in elucidating the text, but need also to be attractive, to add nuances to the text, and to invite browsing. Lastly parents, aware of their children's personalities and interests, will know what will interest them, whether it be fact or fiction.

These insights come gradually over the eight weeks. At this stage parents are still trying to understand how children learn to read. They are invited at the first meeting to read a mystery sentence:

lxttxxx xxx xxx xxx xxly clxxx xxed xxx rxxxxxg xxrds

While guessing at unknown words, they discover that they are using contextual, semantic and phonemic cues. Important points can be made, such as the fact that they scanned the sentence and were given time to tease out its meaning. Many remark on how uncomfortable they felt at being put into the type of problem solving situation which early readers experience, and this helps them realize how the 'prepare, pause, prompt, praise' method informs and encourages their children.

The teacher will have taped each child reading a few pages of a freely chosen book. Parents first listen to the taped reading. They find this interesting, and their responses reveal much about their expectations. They are often surprised at how the initial preparation has helped their children cope with an unfamiliar book.

In the second meeting, discussion is invariably lively. Many parents say that the hardest part of the activity is learning to *wait* for five seconds ('pause') before prompting. They are right. In sitting back and relaxing while their children attempt unknown words, their role has shifted from that of anxious teacher to that of observer and facilitator.

Children sense they are being nudged towards independence and sometimes resist this. Parents air views about ways of overcoming this resistance, and within weeks children are showing increased confidence, as is apparent from the parents' remarks:

> 'takes his time and thinks before he attempts a word.'
> 'uses meaningful alternatives.'
> 'flourishes on praise and encouragement.'

The last remark is common. One mother, at the end of the project, exclaimed that she had never praised her child so much; another that she now talked *to* not *at* her child. As one school put it:

> Our main aim at the meetings is to encourage the parents to be supportive. They often don't see the need for praise–their first reaction is to chastise the children and 'tell them off'. Changing their attitude to the children's performance is the biggest single bonus of the scheme. Also the children's motivation to learn improves as a result of close links between home and school.

Handwriting

At the second meeting parents look at their children's tests. Teachers point out what the children *can* do as well as suggesting areas where they could improve. Handwriting is examined and the handwriting programme described. Parents learn that letters are grouped according to movement. They learn that children need to get the correct movement 'into their fingers', using a routine of writing in flour or sand, and then with felt-tip pens, before finally using a pencil. At the meeting parents practise using these and other media themselves. They will encourage their children to concentrate on those letters which need to be improved. Children will assess their work, awarding good letters a star or a smiley face. Positive self-criticism is part of becoming independent. A few minutes practice each day working with an adult in this way is enormously beneficial and helps correct letter formation and pencil grip before the incorrect habits have become too firmly established.

In the following example, Stephen, when first tested, could write from memory the first letter of eleven words the teacher said (see Figure 12.2). He put dashes for those he couldn't do. On the retest after the eight-week recovery programme, he knew all the letters, and his letter formation had also improved (see Figure 12.3).

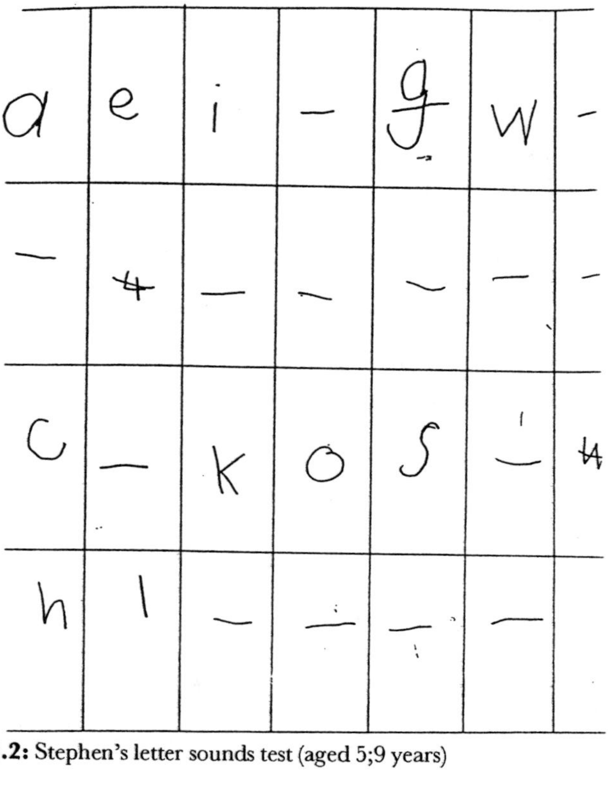

Figure 12.2: Stephen's letter sounds test (aged 5;9 years)

Writing and spelling

Letter-sounds are taught through pictures. Parents note from their children's tests, which letters they need to learn. As they work through the activity books and when the opportunity arises during their reading, their attention is focused aurally, visually and kinaesthetically on initial sounds of words. Parents bring the activity books to each meeting to discuss with the teacher and exchange experiences with other parents. By now they are working with their children daily for up to 30 minutes, and this involves reading and completing one other activity.

Once letter-sounds have been learnt, three-phoneme blending is gradually introduced. Children are encouraged from the start to look at a word with the intention of remembering it, and they always seem delighted when they realize that they can reproduce one, then two and finally three or four letters from memory. At a later stage they are taught how to remember short sentences. By learning to dispense with letter-by-letter copying, the children's confidence increases and becomes evident in classwork. Children who are unable to reach this stage in the eight weeks still benefit from the earlier part of the programme.

In the following example, Lee, when first tested, could write seven words from memory in five minutes but was not fully using his knowledge of letter-sounds. He was beginning to hear first and sometimes last sounds in words (see Figure 12.4).

By the time he was retested he had learned to distinguish medial vowels as well as first and last consonant sounds. This also made him more confident when writing his own words in the written vocabulary test (see Figure 12.5).

Children are also encouraged to write freely, using their own approximate spelling. In doing this they can develop writing strategies more effectively than if they only copy-write or limit themselves to words they can spell correctly. When Lee did the sentence dictation test, he attempted a few words and letters, and put dashes for the rest (see Figure 12.6).

When retested after eight weeks, Lee knew all letter sounds and there was a marked improvement in phoneme segmentation (see Figure 12.7). The teacher noted the auditory confusions of [w] and [r], [f] and [v]. Uncertainty about how to write the sounds of [i] and [e] was also apparent in the three-phoneme retest.

Before he was tested and did the recovery programme, Lee had difficulty attending in class, was easily distracted and generally lacked confidence. His teacher felt he was a slow learner and might need special help, as both reading and writing were poor. However,

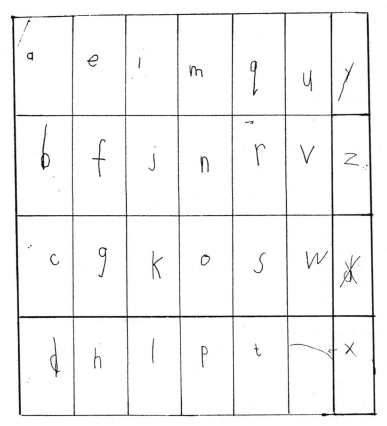

Figure 12.3: Stephen's letter-sound test (retest after 8 weeks)

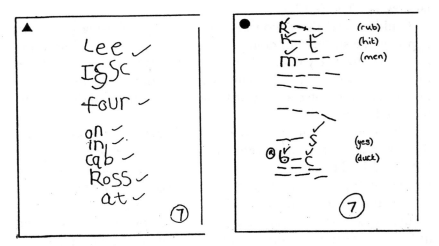

Figure 12.4: a) Lee's written vocabulary tests (aged 6 years)
b) Lee's three-phoneme test

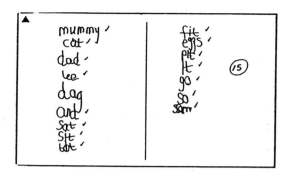

Figure 12.5a: Lee's written vocabulary test (retest)

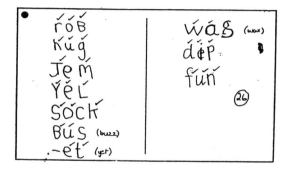

Figure 12.5b: Lee's three phoneme test (retest)

Figure 12.6: Lee's sentence dictation test

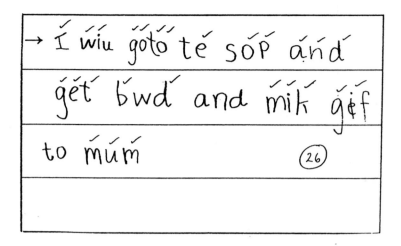

Figure 12.7: Lee's sentence dictation test (retest after 8 weeks)

by the end of the programme, his reading and general confidence had improved considerably and he was working to the class average.

Assessing progress

Before the last meeting the teacher discusses with parents how their children have done on a retest (which they nearly always want to take home to show other members of the family). Their classteacher's assessment of the work is also shown to the parents (see Figure 12.8).

In our study we found that there was always an improvement in children's knowledge of letter sounds and their ability to hear the first and last sounds in words. Many children learn to blend three phonemes and to write sentences using some approximate spelling, which leads to greater confidence and less dependence on the teacher. Attention to formation of individual letters reinforces writing skill. Reading skills always improve. Both reading and writing activities make children more aware of the written language system, so that at the very least they attempt to use context and the first sounds of words. The apparent barrier to success has been removed.

For some this is only a start. The step-by-step progression towards independence needs to be continued as they work through the activity book. In addition, the programme also focuses the classteacher's attention on what the child needs to learn. For others, the boost is sufficient to bring them up to the class average. Most pleasingly, parents and teachers often remark on children's generally enhanced self-esteem and confidence, and more positive attitude to work.

Classteacher's Observations Sheet

During this week please observe the children in your class who have done the Forward Together programme and fill in this sheet for each child.

Child's name: _____   ____ Date _____

Reading

Has there been an improvement in:
- the use of contextual and graphophonic clues?
- self-correcting?
- attitude to reading?

Using the pictures more and blending sounds well. She can now hear when it is not quite right and has a good h/at self-correcting. Attitude to reading is very good

Handwritting

Has there been an improvement in:
- letter formation?
- size?
- control and fluency?

There has been some improvement in formation but not in size. The marks made are harder/darker —ie: has more confidence in her abilities now.

Writing

Has there been an improvement in:
- independence – using *own* spelling?
  - Knowledge of common words (for example 'in', 'to', 'the')?
  - structuring own sentences?
- knowledge of letters sounds and blending?
- spacing words clearly?
- attitude to writing?

A great improvement here. Rachel will now attempt to spell words and will happily write alone. Her spacing is coming but is still not consistent. Confidence has increased.

General

Has there been any general improvement in confidence?

More willing to have a go at things now. Gaining independence which is lovely to see.

Figure 12.8: Classteacher's observations sheet

Reflections on the Programme

Experiences of teachers

We found that to ensure the success of the programme, the atmosphere needs to be as relaxed and cheerful as possible. In fact, as parents get to know one another there is usually a lot of laughter. Leaders have to be patient with anxious or critical parents: as they become more confident about helping their children they nearly always lose these negative feelings.

In a few cases, parents' negative feelings are so deep-rooted that when trying to help their children they only make them anxious. If this is obvious after two or three weeks, the leader considers speaking privately to that parent and suggesting that it would be more appropriate for his or her child to follow the programme at school. In most instances, however, the problems parents experience in getting their children to work are common, temporary and manageable, and when they are aired in the group sessions, other parents often offer helpful suggestions based on similar experiences they have had. They realize that the most effective motivators will be success and praise, and it is largely up to the adults to organize their sessions with the children in such a way that they achieve success and merit praise.

To make sure that everyone would take part, we addressed each parent in turn, before opening the meeting to general discussion, thus avoiding domination by the more extrovert parents. Having had the group leader's full attention while talking about their own child seemed to encourage the more tentative parents to contribute to the subsequent general discussion. Common experiences and problems were shared, for instance how to get your child to work on a sunny afternoon. Parents offered their solutions, ranging from establishing a routine:

> 'every evening after tea - he's come to expect it'

and using certain techniques:

> 'coloured pens revived his interest in the handwriting'

to the consummate success of:

> 'At first James was not too keen but soon overcame that problem as he started to succeed.'

Ways of negotiating with siblings for an uninterrupted half-hour were also discussed.

There were many problems that teachers did not need to try to solve: parents learned from one another. A parent who admitted to impatience opened the floodgates:

> 'There have been times when I have got up-tight so I have packed it away.'

Another, exasperated, confided,

> 'I think he has me on – pretending he doesn't know when he actually does!'

Murmurs of sympathy here and curiosity the following week about the next instalment:

> 'Well I just shut the activity book and said, "We won't bother then - and we won't bother with the story either" ... half an hour later he brought me the books and asked if he could have another try!'

Parents frequently expressed pleasure, not only at their children's progress but also at their own growing awareness of the learning process:

> 'She always tries, when I thought she was just being lazy.'
> 'I understand so much better now how he learns.'

were typical comments.

Finally, the programme has been found more likely to succeed if the children's classteacher is the group leader. Where this is not possible, he or she should attend some of the meetings to be kept informed of what the children are doing from week to week. Teaching points can then be reinforced in class.

Experiences of parents

At the end of the programme, parents are invited to answer five questions. Their answers are summarized below.

1.   a) *How do you feel now about working with your child at home?*
      b) Does it differ in any way from how you felt at the beginning of the programme?

Parents usually admit that at the beginning of the programme they felt anxious about their ability and about finding time to help. They lose this anxiety as they begin to establish a routine and see their children succeeding. They find the guidance they receive at the meetings, and the way the material is structured, very helpful. Many say that as they learn to relax they become more patient, and that both they and their children come to value this special time together.

2.   *Do you think that working with you has benefited your child?*
Parents cite various benefits, ranging from improved skills in reading and writing, to a general improvement in confidence and willingness

to attempt new tasks. They also mention that children have learned to accept a daily work routine.

3.   *Have you learnt anything new about your child or about how he or she learns?*

Parents make many insightful comments:

> 'I have discovered she can't concentrate for long.'
> 'He picks up things quickly.'
> 'Praise is important in developing his self-confidence.'
> 'He likes to be given a lot of time to get his work right and gets frustrated if I attempt to give him the answer before he has worked it out for himself.'

And sometimes they say they did not realize that so much work goes into teaching children to read and write, and that they wish they had known more about how to help their children earlier. They often observe that the experience of working on a one-to-one basis has made them aware of the enormous difficulties teachers must have in satisfying the needs of all the children in a large class.

4.   *Have you had any difficulties doing this project?*

Some parents say they had no difficulties but many complain about the difficulty of finding time, particularly when there are siblings. How to establish a routine and keep younger brothers and sisters engaged for half-an-hour is usually discussed by all parents at the meetings. Although there is no doubt this can be a problem, it does often raise the question of priorities and of how valuable extra attention can be for their children.

5.   *Have you any suggestions to make?*

Parents often say they would like their children's progress to be reviewed some time in the future, particularly if they have not yet finished the programme, and that they would like the programme to become part of school practice, if this is not already the case. Occasionally, however, parents reject the attempt the school has made to involve them in their children's education, and maintain that children's progress is entirely the school's responsibility. In fact this seldom happens because if parents feel this way they generally opt out when first invited to participate.

Thus, during the course of the programme, new insights were gained by parents into their relationship with their children. Tensions were dispelled as understanding of their children's difficulties grew. They appreciated being shown exactly how to help their children, as their previous impatience often stemmed from frustration at not knowing what to do. Their newly-found confidence enabled them to help younger and older siblings where necessary, and to talk to teachers about any concerns regarding their children. The findings of the initial study have been replicated across very different catchment areas.

It is significant how similar our findings have been to those of Wade and Moore (1993) who questioned parents of children in New Zealand who had done the Clay Reading Recovery programme. Although this programme has been designed for use without the help of parents, Wade and Moore found that because some parents were eager to participate, schools invited them to see sessions of Reading Recovery so that they could imitate the methods teachers use. In doing so they found that:

- they changed the kind of support they gave their children at home
- they acknowledged the importance of giving children time to work things out themselves, and of praising their self-corrections and responses to prompts
- although they sometimes had difficulty finding time, they took their role seriously, and persevered
- they had fun helping, and sometimes involved the rest of the family
- their children's improvement extended beyond reading into writing and other areas of language

Experiences of schools

What then are the school's perceptions of this level of parental involvement? Initially, it is common for schools to doubt that parents would be capable of or willing to give this degree of commitment. It is true that there are sometimes intractable difficulties and in those instances the recovery programme is best used at school. However, some of our most successful programmes have been run in what might be described as deprived areas. Many teachers welcome the opportunity the programme gives them of closer contact with parents, and would agree with this teacher's remarks:

> As these children are poor readers, their parents are often those too apprehensive to approach the classteacher. This has helped me meet and get to know mums who may have been difficult to get to know...

Teachers also claim that close contact with parents gives them a clearer insight into their children's problems.

Our experience has been in line with research findings that show that teachers who frequently involve parents in their children's education, rate all parents higher than average in helpfulness and follow-through than do other teachers. Parents who have older children often say they wish they could have had these opportunities earlier, and those with younger children are determined to use their new skills and perceptions to help them. They sometimes offer to help in school, and to speak to parents of subsequent programmes.

Working with families, then raises teachers' expectations and perceptions of parents as partners. They are less likely to make as many stereotypic judgements about poor, less educated or single parents as other teachers.

However, some schools traditionally like to keep sole control of their pupils' learning. This was expressed by one school in the following way:

> The perception of the staff shifted in a subtle way. There was an initial reluctance about involving parents so closely. By allowing all the staff (in turn) to attend one of the meetings, and by involving them in assessing the improvement in the children, the teachers have become enthusiastic about involving parents in the programme.

And a teacher who had recently returned to teaching remarked that the programme had helped her own confidence, with both the parents and the staff. Teachers who before doing the project might view parental involvement as an extra pressure and burden, discover it is a surprisingly refreshing and inspiring experience.

In the case reported above where the staff's initial reluctance changed, the head had gently eroded their misgivings and had chosen teachers to run the programme who were keen to try. It became part of the school policy, accepted and appreciated by both parents and teachers. More problematic, however, are those schools with a fragmented approach. Good management by heads is essential for a whole school approach to liaising with parents.

Schools who use the programme wholeheartedly always report improvements in the children's ability and attitude – even when parents are less than completely supportive. In the case of the most successful projects the change can be remarkable:

> The children enjoyed all the activities and most of them progressed greatly–confirmed by the scores on the reading tests before and after the programme. They have been given extra input at exactly the right time and they are now abreast of the others in the class and are coping better all round in the classroom.

Some schools do not use standardized pre- and post-reading tests, but are satisfied if the children become more confident readers. The benefits have a ripple effect; improved self-confidence and self-esteem often clear up behavioural problems.

What the *Forward Together Recovery Programme* has shown is that, given good management, a school's investment of one hour a week for 8–12 weeks, pays rich dividends in terms of children's progress, enhanced self-esteem of children, parents and teachers, and the development of a strong triangular relationship between parent, child and school.

Epilogue: Current Themes and Future Directions

In this book we have been concerned with children's reading and spelling difficulties. A recurring theme has been that the manifestations of these difficulties are diverse; they may be obvious, they may be hidden; they may be specific to the reading process or found in combination with language or perceptual problems; most importantly, they may be nascent or compensated. However, in all cases, these difficulties, if unattended, can cause significant educational underachievement and untold damage to children's confidence and self-esteem. It is therefore important to reflect here upon four main issues. First, which children are at risk of reading and spelling problems; second, what is the relationship between spoken and written language difficulties; third, what kinds of intervention do these children need; and fourth, who should deliver this intervention.

Which Children are At Risk of Reading and Spelling Problems?

The causal relationships between children's underlying cognitive and linguistic abilities and their reading and spelling skills have been the subject of a great deal of research, much of which has been discussed in the foregoing chapters. It is not our purpose to review the findings here. But what is of particular interest to practitioners is the identification of vulnerability factors, both intrinsic and extrinsic to the child. We have not had much to say about the role of environmental factors in relation to reading failure. It is well recognized that there is a relationship between occupational status and reading skill, and that mother's educational level is a particularly potent factor in explaining between-child differences in reading achievement. Children from disadvantaged families need support with the development of reading, and very often, this encompasses support for their parents too. However, as we have seen, even children who are

234

socially advantaged may be at risk of reading difficulties, and this is particularly so if they have one or more of the following :

- a family history of reading, speech or language problems
- a history of, or persisting, speech difficulties
- spoken language difficulties
- poor phonological awareness for their age

Such children need assessment to identify the nature of any processing difficulties they experience, and also their individual strengths.

What is the Relationship between Spoken and Written Language Difficulties?

The arguments that have been woven throughout this book make clear that the relationship between spoken and written language difficulties is not straightforward. Whereas it is accepted that spoken language skills form a foundation for the acquisition of reading and writing, the mechanisms by which alphabetic reading skills are mapped onto speech and the role of other language factors in this process are not fully understood. We have seen that, at the very least, we must consider spoken language abilities to comprise three sets of subskills. For simplicity, we will refer to these as speech, understanding and expressive language. In the same way, we can consider written language to comprise at least three subskills, namely, reading as a decoding process, reading for meaning and spelling. Arguably, these spoken and written language processes have reciprocal links with one another. In particular, adequate speech seems necessary for the development of decoding and spelling skills, language comprehension feeds reading comprehension and expressive language will be intricately linked with the development of writing ability.

There is no doubt that, when individual children are considered, these relationships can be complex and difficult to decipher. The current manifestation of a reading problem, sometimes referred to as a reading profile, will depend upon the interaction of a number of factors including:

- the age of the child and the developmental stage they have reached
- the precise nature (and locus) of their speech or language difficulty
- the severity of their phonological processing difficulties, including their current levels of phonological awareness

- the extent to which they have been able to compensate using intact skills
- the amount and type of intervention they have received

Thus, in children with reading difficulties, there is considerable heterogeneity, though usually without clear subtypes. It is essential to bear in mind that the ways in which the different language skills combine and inter-relate is not clear-cut, and there can be many modifying factors at the level of individual children. Nonetheless, we offer the model in Figure 13.1 as a working hypothesis of the spectrum of literacy disorders as they relate to spoken language difficulties.

In the model, the x axis represents phonology, and the extent to which it is intact from left (intact) to right (impaired). The y axis, in contrast, represents a dimension of meaning, semantics, from high (intact) to low (impaired). We propose that, a child's position in this two-dimensional space determines the nature of the literacy difficulties they experience. Moving from the left, children have been

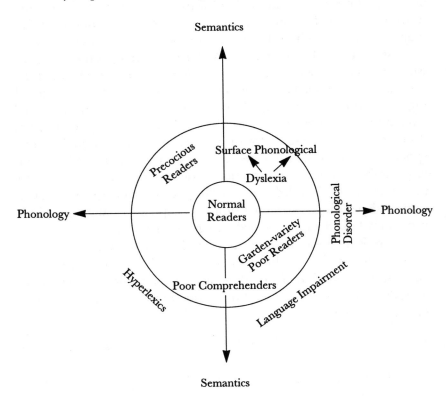

Figure 13.1: Dimensional classification of reading and language abilities

described who have good phonology for their age, and exceptional reading talent; these children have been referred to as precocious readers (Stainthorp and Hughes, 1995). In contrast, children who have good phonology but difficulties with the semantic aspects of language may be *hyperlexic*; commonly this pattern of reading, characterized by very poor comprehension of what is read, is associated with childhood autism and related disorders.

Normal readers occupy the centre portion of our model, with individual variation in normal populations being associated with different levels of phonological and semantic skill. Children who have specific difficulties with reading comprehension occupy the lower portions of this space; their problems are often associated with subtle language difficulties and may often go unnoticed in classroom situations.

On the right of our model are the reading disorders with which this book has been mainly concerned. The core of these problems is poor phonology, albeit obvious, as in children with frank speech disorders, or hidden, as in the dyslexic child. In our view, the phonology dimension is continuous, and the severity of the phonological processing problem will determine whether the child falls at the extreme end (where we expect children with speech difficulties described as phonological disorder or developmental verbal dyspraxia), to the left, as in developmental *phonological dyslexia* or more centrally as in children with the reading profile often described as *surface dyslexia*. Finally, the lower portions of this space are occupied by children with general reading problems (sometimes referred to as garden-variety poor readers). In addition to their phonological processing problems, these children have semantic processing impairments; they experience problems both with decoding and reading comprehension skills.

We must emphasize however, that we are not committed to the view that children show stable patterns of reading impairment. Their position in this two-dimensional classification is prone to change with development, and as a consequence of intervention.

What Kinds of Intervention do these Children Need?

This book has emphasized the powerful influence of training in phonological awareness on subsequent reading achievement. A number of different interventions have been described. The combination of training in phonological awareness with systematic reading instruction is seemingly the most effective. However, what type of intervention works best must of course depend to a large extent on individual difference variables, including once again :

- the age of the child
- their current levels of phonological processing
- whether they have on-going speech and language difficulties
- the integrity of the other skills that contribute to reading, namely visual and semantic skills
- the persistence of spelling and writing difficulties

And to this list we should add a range of psychosocial factors including confidence and self-esteem, behaviour and attention, and parental support.

The research literature cannot yet tell us precisely which of a number of related interventions work best with individual children. Perhaps it is over-optimistic to expect it to do so. However, there are some hints to be found. Hatcher, Hulme and Ellis (1994) reported that, in their intervention study with 7-year-old poor readers, there were different predictors of prognosis in different training conditions. Phonological ability at pretest was the best predictor of progress in an intervention that involved training in reading alone, whereas it was reading ability at pretest that was the best predictor for the group who received phonology alone (neither phonological nor verbal ability being significant) (p. 54).

Similarly, Olson and Wise (1992), who have carried out extensive research on the teaching methods that are effective for dyslexic readers in the Colorado remediation project, have reported an interaction between the severity of children's reading deficit and accompanying phonological impairment, and their response to treatment. Comparing reading interventions that focused on segmentation of written words at different levels, they reported that the most severely disabled readers responded least well to onset-rime feedback during training. In contrast, the least severely retarded responded best to this type of feedback. On the other hand, syllable feedback led to only modest gains in the least severely retarded readers but to the greatest gains in the most severely retarded. Thus, in line with the findings of Hatcher, et al. (1994), it appeared that children with lower phoneme awareness benefited less from the reading instruction than children with higher levels of segmentation ability.

The next step was to design a programme to promote phonological awareness and to use this in conjunction with reading remediation. Wise and Olson (in press) compared two kinds of reading intervention incorporated into computer-reading routines. One group of 9-year-old disabled readers were assigned to a teaching condition in which they were instructed in metacognitive comprehension strategies. They had opportunities to practise these strategies both when reading as a group and individually on the computer. A comparable group of children were assigned to a phonological awareness training condition. These children received training in speech-motor phoneme awareness, based on the *Auditory Discrimination in Depth* method devised by Lindamood and Lindamood (1975). This approach places emphasis on the development of articulatory (speech-motor) representations to distinguish and compare phonemic differences. The next stage of the phonological awareness programme involved printed/spoken nonword matching and spelling with speech feedback.

At the end of training, the group who had received phonological awareness training had made significantly greater gains in phonological awareness and in recognition of the words in the texts they read. The other group, however, had gained more in time-limited word recognition and their reading comprehension was relatively better. It can be concluded that the phonological awareness training was successful in promoting the skills which were necessary prerequisites for the reading programme. The results are generally in line with the findings of reading interventions that are not computer-based, in that combining reading with phonological training is the most effective method for dyslexic readers. Another way of approaching the problem might be to train phonological skills prior to the commencement of reading remediation (see Snowling, 1996, for a fuller discussion of this and other interventions).

Who Should Deliver this Intervention?

It is not coincidental that the contributors to this book cover a range of disciplines: teachers, speech and language therapists, educational and clinical psychologists and researchers. Reference is also made to the work of occupational therapists, physiotherapists, paediatricians, ENT surgeons, audiologists and linguists. All have their role to play alongside parents and carers in the management of children with spoken and written language difficulties. Who is involved depends on the child's age and presenting symptoms. The management team changes over time depending on how the child's difficulties unfold. It is not possible here to go into the detailed contribution of each team member, but inevitably the face-to-face delivery of the intervention programme will fall to the teacher and therapists.

Traditionally, it has been educationists who have been most involved in the management of children with specific learning difficulties. However, the emphasis on the centrality of phonological processing skills to the normal and atypical development of literacy, has led to a redefining of the role of the speech and language therapist with respect to these children. This role will encompass investigating the causes of the child's speech processing difficulties, and in collaboration with the teacher, assessing the impact of the child's psycholinguistic abilities on the development of literacy skills (Stackhouse and Wells, forthcoming). Taken together, a child's ability to access the curriculum will depend on their speech, language and literacy skills. Assessment of communication skills within the classroom is therefore essential.

The role of the speech and language therapist does not include *teaching* reading and spelling which is traditionally and rightly the teacher's domain. Rather, the role is one of identification and promoting the underlying skills that contribute to literacy development. Speech and language therapists are well placed to work on the prerequisite skills for literacy development. Arguably, this is particularly true as they are likely to encounter the future, but yet undiagnosed, dyslexics in their preschool therapy groups. These groups provide an ideal opportunity for early identification and training of the child at risk for later literacy problems.

Traditional speech and language therapy activities designed to improve a child's intelligibility can easily be adapted to target spoken and written language skills simultaneously. Sound-letter matched picture cards such as found in *The Nuffield Dyspraxia Programme* (1992) can be used for a range of activities involving both speech production and phoneme-grapheme matching. The *Metaphon* activities (Howell and Dean 1994) promote phonological awareness in young children and can be linked to more explicit literacy activities. Techniques such as *Cued Articulation* (Passy, 1990a and b), which comprise a gesture to remind the child of how a sound is produced, can be linked with the written letter and has been found useful when training phonological awareness in children with speech difficulties. Other techniques using segmentation blocks, beads, or colour coding have also been incorporated successfully in therapy and teaching programmes (Lindamood and Lindamood, 1975; Stackhouse, 1992b). Clearly, the emphasis in all these approaches is to provide multisensory opportunities for the child to compensate for specific processing weaknesses.

However, not all future dyslexics will be referred to the speech and language therapy service in the preschool years. Subtle speech difficulties may go unnoticed or not be considered severe enough to be a priority for referral. It is these children who might best be identified through nursery schools. The role of the speech and language therapist here is therefore to discuss the at-risk signs to look out for with nursery or playgroup staff. Following screening by these staff, individual children can be selected for further investigation by the speech and language therapist. Working with nursery and playgroup staff on the implementation of routine phonological awareness training programmes for all children is a worthwhile aim of the speech and language therapy preschool service.

Once the child has reached school, he or she is in the hands of the teacher. The role of the speech and language therapist continues to be one of identifying the underlying speech and language processing weaknesses which are interfering with educational progress. The child's spoken and written communication skill (which includes social skills training) is a key part of the speech and language therapist's work and can be linked directly with the aims and objectives of the curriculum. Teaching programmes such as those decribed in this volume (see also Gillon and Dodd, 1995) fit well with speech and language therapy activities.

Clearly, the success of a child's teaching and therapy programme hinges on collaborative working between the individuals in the team and the teacher/speech and language therapist relationship, in particular, has been the subject of investigation (Wright, 1992, 1996). In fact, the increasingly shared focus on literacy problems as a result of the emphasis on phonological awareness training, seems to have brought the two disciplines into a much closer working relationship (Popple and Wellington, 1996).

In summary, the professionals who work with children with literacy problems need to identify children with difficulties, describe their presenting problems, plan intervention programmes and collaborate with others in this endeavour. Each member of the team will have a unique piece to contribute but in general, the team's role may be defined in the following way:

1. *Identify* through a knowledge of developmental norms, children who are at risk for literacy problems.
2. *Describe* a child's speech, language and literacy difficulties, using phonetic and linguistic tools as appropriate.
3. *Explain* a child's speech, language and literacy difficulties if possible in terms of a psycholinguistic processing model.
4. *Understand* a child's difficulties in the context of any medical diagnoses.

5.   *Plan* an effective intervention programme taking account of any speech and language difficulties that are contributing to the child's literacy and educational problems.

6.   *Recommend* to parents and colleagues how the child's difficulties might best be managed.

7.   *Collaborate* with parents and colleagues on the implementation of the child's management programme.

8.   *Research* into the nature, assessment and remediation of speech, language and literacy difficulties, in particular the efficacy of combined teaching and therapy programmes.

This book represents the collaborative work of a range of professionals working with children with speech, language and literacy problems. Over the last ten years, there has grown a greater understanding of the nature of children's written language difficulties. We are closer to identifying children at risk for literacy problems and we have a better idea of what to include in teaching programmes. However, further research is still needed. In particular, the best ways of delivering an appropriate teaching and learning programme for a child in the context of a supportive environment needs to be explored. This research agenda is likely to dominate the next phase of the work focusing on children's spoken and written language difficulties.

References

Adams, M.J. (1990) *Beginning to Read: Learning and Thinking about Print*. Cambridge, MA : MIT press.

Alegria, J., Pignot, E., Morais, J. (1982) Phonetic analysis of speech and memory codes in beginning readers. *Memory and Cognition* **10**: 451–6.

Alston, J. (1995) *Assessing and Promoting Writing Skills*. Stafford: NASEN.

Baddeley, A.D., Gathercole, S.E. (1992) Learning to read: The role of the phonological loop. In Alegria, J., Holender, D., Morais, J.J. and Radeau, M., (Eds) *Analytic Approaches To Human Cognition*. New York: Elsevier Sciences Publishers.

Ball, E. W., Blachman, B.A. (1991) Does phoneme awareness training in kindergarten make a difference in early word recognition and developmental spelling? *Reading Research Quarterly*, **26**: 49–66.

Beck, I.L. Omanson, R.C., McKeown, M.G. (1982) An instructional redesign of reading lessons: Effects on comprehension. *Reading Research Quarterly* **17**: 462–81.

Beck, I.L., Perfetti, C.A., McKeown, M.G. (1982b) The effects of long-term vocabulary instruction on lexical access and reading comprehension. *Journal of Educational Psychology* **74**: 506–21.

Bird, J., Bishop D.V.M., Freeman, N.H. (1995) Phonological awareness and literacy development in children with expressive phonological impairments. *Journal of Speech and Hearing Research* **38**: 446–62.

Bishop, D.V.M. (1985) Spelling ability in congenital dysarthria: Evidence against articulatory coding in translating between phonemes and graphemes. *Cognitive Neuropsychology* **2**: 229–51.

Bishop, D.V. M. (1989) Unstable vergence control and dyslexia: a critique. *British Journal of Ophthalmology* **73**: 223–5.

Bishop, D.V.M., Adams, C. (1990) A prospective study of the relationship between specific language impairment, phonological disorders and reading retardation. *Journal of Child Psychology and Psychiatry* **31**: 1027–50.

Bishop, D.V.M., Edmundson, A. (1986) Is otitis media a major cause of specific developmental language disorders? *British Journal of Disorders of Communication* **21**: 321–38.

Bishop, D.V.M., North, T., Donlan, C. (1995) Genetic basis of specific language impairment: Evidence from a twin study. *Developmental Medicine and Child Neurology* **37**: 56–71.

Blachman, B. (1991) Early intervention for children's reading problems: Clinical applications of the research in phonological awareness. *Topics in Language Disorders* **12**: 51–65.

Boberg, E. (Ed) (1993) *The Neuropsychology of Stuttering*. Alberta. Canada: The University of Alberta Press.

Bond, G.L., Dykstra, R. (1967) The cooperative research programme in first grade reading instruction. *Reading Research Quarterly* **2**: 5–142.

Borkowski, J.G. (1992) Metacognitive theory: A framework for teaching literacy, writing, and math skills. *Journal of Learning Disabilities* **25**: 253–7.

Bradley, L. (1981) The organisation of motor patterns for spelling: an effective remedial strategy for backward readers. *Developmental Medicine and Child Neurology* **23**: 83–91

Bradley, L. (1984) *Assessing Reading Difficulties: A Diagnostic and Remedial Approach* (2nd Ed) London: Macmillan Education.

Bradley, L. (1988) Making connections in learning to read and spell. *Applied Cognitive Psychology* **2**: 3–18.

Bradley, L., Bryant, P. (1978) Independence of reading and spelling in backward and normal readers. *Developmental Medicine and Child Neurology* **21**: 504–14

Bradley, L., Bryant, P. (1983) Categorising sounds and learning to read: a causal connection. *Nature* **301**, 419

Bradley, L., Bryant, P.E. (1985) *Rhyme and Reason in Reading and Spelling.* IARLD Monograph No. 1. Ann Arbor, MI: University of Michigan.

Brady, S., Shankweiler, D., Mann, V. (1983) Speech perception and memory coding in relation to reading ability. *Journal of Experimental Child Psychology* **35**: 345–67.

Brandt, J., Rosen, J. (1980) Auditory-phonemic perception in dyslexia: categorised identification and discrimination of stop consonants. *Brain and Language* **9**: 324–7.

Bridgeman, E., Snowling, M. (1988) The perception of phoneme sequence: a comparison of dyspraxic and normal children. *British Journal of Disorders of Communication* **23**: 245–52.

Brooks, P. (1995) A comparison of the effectiveness of different teaching strategies in teaching spelling to a student with severe specific learning difficulties/dyslexia. In: Frederickson, N., Reason, R. (Eds) Phonological assessment of specific learning difficulties. *Educational and Child Psychology* 12.

Brown, A.L. (1980) Metacognitive development and reading. In Spiro R.J. , Bruce B.C., Brewer W.F. (Eds) *Theoretical Issues in Reading Comprehension.* Hillsdale, NJ: Lawrence Erlbaum Associates.

Brown, B. (1989) The ergonomics of handwriting. Paper presented to Handwriting Interest Group Seminar, Institute of Education, London.

Brown, B., Henderson, S.E. (1989) A sloping desk? Should the wheel turn full circle? Handwriting Review. pp. 55-59. (Available from Handwriting Interest Group, Membership Secretary, Fyfield Road, Ongar, Essex CM5 0AH.)

Bruce, D.J. (1964) The analysis of word sounds by young children. *British Journal of Educational Psychology* **34**: 158–70.

Bruck, M. (1990a) Word-recognition skills of adults with childhood diagnoses of dyslexia. *Developmental Psychology* **26**: 439–54.

Bruck, M. (1990b) Persistence of dyslexics' phonological awareness deficits. *Developmental Psychology* **28**: 874–86.

Bryan, A., Howard, D. (1992) Frozen phonology thawed: the analysis and remediation of a developmental disorder of lexical phonology. *European Journal of Disorders of Communication* **27**: 343–65.

Bryant, P.E., Bradley, L. (1985) *Children's Reading Problems.* Oxford: Blackwell.

Bryant P.E., Impey, L. (1986) The similarities between normal readers and developmental and acquired dyslexics. *Cognition* **24**: 121–37.

Bryant, P.E., MacLean, M., Bradley, L., Crossland, J. (1990) Rhyme and alliteration, phoneme detection, and learning to read. *Developmental Psychology* **26**: 429–38.

Byrne, B., Fielding-Barnsley, R. (1989) Phonemic awareness and letter knowledge in the child's acquisition of the alphabetic principle. *Journal of Educational Psychology* **81**: 313–21.

Castles, A., Coltheart, M. (1992) Varieties of developmental dyslexia. *Cognition* **47**: 149–80

Cataldo, S., Ellis, N. (1988) Interaction in the development of spelling, reading and phonological skills. *Journal of Research in Reading* **11**: 86–109.

Catts, H.W. (1991) Early identification of reading disabilities. *Topics in Language Disorders* **12**: 1–16.

Catts, H.W. (1993) The relationship between speech-language impairments and reading disabilities. *Journal of Speech and Hearing Research* **36**: 948–58.

Catts, H.W., Hu, C-F., Larrivee, L., Swank, L. (1994) Early identification of reading disabilities. In Watkins, R.V., Rice, M. (Eds) *Specific Language Impairments in Children*. Communication and Language Intervention Series 4. London Paul H. Brookes Publishing Co.

Chall, J.S. (1967) *Learning to Read: The Great Debate*. New York: McGraw-Hill.

Clay, M.M. (1985) *The Early Detection of Reading Difficulties* (3rd Ed). Oxford: Heinemann Educational

Coltheart, M., Masterson, J., Byng, S., Prior, M., Riddoch, J. (1983) Surface dyslexia. *Quarterly Journal of Experimental Psychology* **35A**: 469–96.

Constable, A., Stackhouse, J., Wells, B. (1994) The case of the missing handcuffs: Phonological processing and word finding in a boy with language impairment. National Hospital's College of Speech Sciences: *Work in Progress* **4**: 1–27.

Cox, A.R., Hutcheson, L., (1988) Syllable division: A prerequisite to dyslexic's literacy. *Annals Of Dyslexia* **38**: 226–42.

Crary, M. (1984) Neurolinguistic perspective on developmental verbal dyspraxia. *Communicative Disorders* **9**: 33–49

Cunningham, A. E. (1990) Explicit versus implicit instruction in phonemic awareness. *Journal of Experimental Child Psychology* **50**: 429–44.

Darley, F.L. (1964) *Diagnosis and Appraisal of Communication Disorders*. Englewood Cliffs, NJ: Prentice-Hall, Inc.

DeFries, J. (1991) Genetics and dyslexia. In Snowling, M., Thomson, M. (Eds) *Dyslexia: Integrating Theory and Practice*. London: Whurr.

Denkla, M.B., Rudel, R.G. (1976) Rapid automatised naming: Dyslexia differentiated from other learning disabilities. *Neuropsychologia* **14**: 471–9

Department for Education (1994) *Code of Practice on the Identification and Assessment of Special Educational Needs*. London: Central Office of Information.

Dodd, B., Gillon, G., Oerlemans, M., Russell, T., Syrmis, M., Wilson, H. (1995) Phonological disorder and the acquisition of literacy. In Dodd, B. *Differential Diagnosis and Treatment of Children with Speech Disorder*. Whurr Publishers, London.

Dutton, K. (1992) Writing under examination conditions: Establishing a baseline. *Handwriting Review* 80–101. (Available from Handwriting Interest Group, Membership Secretary, Fyfield Road, Ongar, Essex CM5 0AH.)

Ehri, L (1985) Sources of difficulty in learning to spell and read. In Wolraich, M.L., Routh, D (Eds) *Advances in Developmental and Behavioural Paediatrics* (Vol. 7) Greenwich, CT.: Jai Press Inc, 121–95.

Ehri, L. C. (1992). Reconceptualizing the development of sight word reading and its relationship to decoding. In Gough, P. B., Ehri, L. C., Treiman R.(Eds) *Reading Acquisition* Hillsdale: NJ,: Lawrence Erlbaum Associates.

Elkonin, D.B. (1963). The psychology of mastering the elements of reading. In : Simon, B., Simon, J.(Eds) *Educational Psychology in the USSR*. London : Routledge and Kegan Paul.

Frith, U. (1980) Unexpected spelling problems. In Frith, U. (Ed) *Cognitive Processes in Spelling*. London: Academic Press.

Frith, U. (1985) Beneath the surface of developmental dyslexia. In Patterson, K.E., Marshall, J.C., Coltheart, M. (Eds) *Surface Dyslexia* London: Routledge & Kegan Paul, 301–30.

Frith, U. (1995) Dyslexia: can we have a shared theoretical framework? In Frederickson, N., Reason, R. (Eds) Phonological assessment of specific learning difficulties. *Educational And Child Psychology* **12**: 6–17.

Frith, U., Frith C. (1980) Relationships between reading and spelling. In Kavanagh, J.F., Venezky, R.L. (Eds) *Orthography, Reading and Dyslexia*. Baltimore, MD : University Park Press.

Galaburda, A.M. (1993) *Dyslexia and Development–Neurobiological Aspects of Extra-Ordinary Brains*. London. Harvard University Press.

Gallagher, A., Frith, U., Snowling, M. (submitted). Language deficits in children at risk of dyslexia.

Gathercole, S. E. (1993) Word learning in language-impaired children. *Child Language, Teaching and Therapy* **9**: 187–99.

Gathercole, S. E., Baddeley, A. D. (1993) *Working Memory and Language*. Hillsdale, NJ: Lawrence Erlbaum.

Gillingham, A,M., Stillman, B.U. (1956) *Reading, Spelling And Penmanship*, (5th Edn) New York: Sackett and Wilhelms.

Gillon, G., Dodd, B.J. (1994) A prospective study of the relationship between phonological, semantic and syntactic skills and specific reading disability. *Reading and Writing* **6**: 321–45.

Gillon, G., Dodd, B.J. (1995) The effects of training phonological, semantic and syntactic processing skills in spoken language on reading ability. *Language, Speech and Hearing Services in Schools* **26**: 58–68.

Godfrey, J., Syrdal-Lasky, A., Millay, K., Knox, C. (1981) Performance of dyslexic children on speech perception tests. *Journal of Experimental Child Psychology* **32**: 401–24.

Goodman, K.S. (1967) Reading: a psycholinguistic guessing game. *Journal of the Reading Specialist* May. 126–35.

Gopnick K,M., Crago, M.B. (1991) Familial aggregation of a developmental language disorder. *Cognition* **39**: 1–30

Goswami, U. (1994a) The role of analogies in reading development. *Support For Learning* **9**: 22–5.

Goswami, U. (1994b) Towards an interactive analogy model of reading development: Decoding vowel graphemes in beginning reading. *Journal of Experimental Child Psychology* **56**: 443–75

Goswami, U., Bryant, P. E. (1990) *Phonological Skills and Learning to Read*. Hove: Lawrence Erlbaum.

Goswami, U., Bryant, P.E. (1992) Rhyme, analogy and children's reading. In Gough, P.B., Ehri L.C., Treiman R. (Eds) *Reading Acquisition*, Hillsdale, NJ: Erlbaum Assocs.

Gough, P.B., Juel, C. (1991). The first stages of word recognition. In Rieben L., Perfetti C. (Eds) *Learning to Read: Basic Research and its Implications*. Hillsdale, NJ: Lawrence Erlbaum Associates.

Gregory, H.M., Gregory, A.H. (1994) A comparison of the Neale and the BAS reading tests. *Educational Psychology in Practice* **10**: 15–18.

Grievink, E.H., Peters, S.A.F., Van Bon W.H.J., and Schilder, A.G.M. (1993) The effects of early bilateral otitis media with effusion on language ability. A prospective cohort study. *Journal of Speech and Hearing Research* **36**: 1004–12.

Hatcher, P.J., Hulme, C., Ellis, A.W. (1994) Ameliorating early reading failure by intergrating the reaching of reading and phonological skills: The Phonological Linkage hypothesis. *Child Development,* **65**: 41–57.

Hayden, S. (1995) *Speaking and Listening*: Stages 1 and 2. Special Education Support Team (SEST). Hereford and Worcester Education Authority, County Hall, Spetchly Road, Worcester.

Henderson, S.E., Sugden, D.A. (1992) *The Movement Battery for Children*. Sidcup, Kent: The Psychological Corporation.

Hinshelwood, J. (1917) *Congenital Word Blindness*. London: Lewis.

Howell, J., Dean, E. (1994) *Treating Phonological Disorders in Children: Metaphon – Theory to Practice* (2nd Ed) Whurr: London.

Hulme, C., Roodenrys, S. (1995) Verbal working memory development and its disorders. *Journal of Child Psychology and Psychiatry* **36**: 373–98.

Hulme, C., Snowling, M. (1992a) Phonological deficits in dyslexia: A 'sound' reappraisal of the verbal deficit hypothesis. In Singh, N., Beale, I. (Eds) *Current Perspectives in Learning Disabilities*. New York: Springer-Verlag.

Hulme, C., Snowling, M. (1992b) Deficits in output phonology: An explanation of reading failure? *Cognitive Neuropsychology* **9**: 47–72.

Hulme, C., Snowling, M (1994) (Eds) *Reading Development and Dyslexia*: London: Whurr.

Hulme, C., Snowling, M., Quinlan, P. (1991) Connectionism and learning to read: Steps towards a psychologically plausible model. *Reading and Writing* **3**: 159–68.

Hummell L.J., Prizant B.M. (1993) A socio-emotional perspective for understanding social difficulties of school-age children with language disorders. *Language Speech and Hearing Services in Schools* **24**: 216–24

Ingram, D. (1989) *First Language Acquisition: Method, Description and Explanation*. Cambridge: Cambridge University Press.

Iversen, S., Tunmer, W.E. (1993) Phonological processing and the reading recovery program. *Journal of Educational Psychology* **85**: 112–26.

Johnston, R., Rugg, M., Scott, T. (1987) Phonological similarity effects, memory span and developmental reading disorders: The nature of the relationship. *British Journal of Psychology* **78**: 205–11.

Juel, C., Griffith, P.L., Gough, P.B. (1986) Acquisition of literacy : A longitudinal study of children in first and second grade. *Journal of Educational Psychology* **78**: 243–55.

Kameenui, E.J., Carnine, D.W., Freschi, R. (1982). Effects of text construction and instructional procedures for teaching word meanings on comprehension and recall. *Reading Research Quarterly* **17**: 367–88.

Kamhi, A.G., Catts, H.W. (1989) *Reading Disabilities: A Developmental Language Perspective*. Boston MA: Little, Brown and Co.

Katz, R. (1986) Phonological deficiencies in children with reading disability: evidence from an object naming task. *Cognition* **22**: 225–57.

Klein, H. (1985) The assessment and management of some persisting language difficulties in the learning disabled. In Snowling, M.J. (Ed) *Children's Written Language Difficulties*. Windsor: NFER-Nelson.

Lewis, B.A., Ekelman, B.L., Aram, D.M. (1989) A family study of severe phonological disorders. *Journal of Speech and Hearing Research* **32**: 713–24.

Lewis, B.A., and Freebairn, L. (1992) Residual effects of preschool phonology disorders in grade school, adolescence and adulthood. *Journal of Speech and Hearing Research* **35**: 819–31.

Lewis, C., Salway, A. (1989) Are you sitting comfortably? *Handwriting Review*. Crewe: Crewe and Alsager College of Higher Education, CW1 1DU

Liberman, I.Y., Shankweiler, D., Fischer, F.W., Carter, B. (1974) Reading and the awareness of linguistic segments. *Journal of Experimental Child Psychology* **18**: 201–12.

Locke, J. (1980) The inference of speech perception in the phonologically disordered child Part II: Some clinically novel procedures, their use, some findings. *Journal of Speech and Hearing Disorders* **45**: 445–68.

Lovegrove, W.J., Williams, M. (1993) Visual temporal processing deficits in specific reading disability. In Willows, D. M., Kruk, R.S., Corcos, E. (Eds) *Visual Processes in Reading and Reading Disabilities*. Hillsdale, NJ: Lawrence Erlbaum, pp. 287–310

Lundberg, I., Frost, J., Peterson, O. (1988) Effects of an extensive program for stimulating phonological awareness in pre-school children. *Reading Research Quarterly* **23**: 263–84.

McCormick, M. (1995) The relationship between the phonological processes in early speech development and later spelling strategies. In Dodd, B. *Differential Diagnosis and Treatment of Children with Speech Disorder*. London, Whurr.

McDougall, S., Hulme, C., Ellis, A.W., Monk, A. (1994) Learning to read: The role of short-term memory and phonological skills. *Journal of Experimental Child Psychology* **58**: 112–33.

McKeown, M.G., Beck, I.L., Omanson, R.C., Pople, M.T. (1985) Some effects of the nature and frequency of vocabulary instruction on the knowledge and use of words. *Reading Research Quarterly* **20**: 522–35.

MacLean, M., Bryant, P.E., Bradley, L. (1987) Rhymes, nursery rhymes and reading in early childhood. *Merrill-Palmer Quarterly* **33**: 255–81.

Magnusson, E., Naucler, K. (1990) Reading and spelling in language disordered children – linguistic and metalinguistic prerequisites: report on a longitudinal study. *Clinical Linguistics and Phonetics* **4**: 1, 49–61.

Manis, F. R., Custodio, R., Szeszulski, P. A. (1993) Development of phonological and orthographic skill: A 2-year longitudinal study of dyslexic children. *Journal of Experimental Child Psychology* **56**: 64–86.

Marion, M.J., Sussman, H.M., Marquardt, T.P. (1993) The perception and production of rhyme in normal and developmentally apraxic children. *Journal of Communication Disorders* **26**: 129–60.

Masterson, J., Hazan, V., Wijayatilake, L. (1995) Phonemic processing problems in developmental phonological dyslexia. *Cognitive Neuropsychology* **12**: 3, 233–59.

Maughan, B. (1994) Behavioural development and reading disabilities. In Hulme, C., Snowling, M. (Eds) *Reading Development and Dyslexia*, London: Whurr, 128–43.

Maughan, B. (1995) Long term outcomes of developmental reading problems. *Journal of Child Psychology and Psychiatry* **36**: 357–71.

Menyuk, P., Chesnick, M., Liebergott, J.W., Korngold, B., D'Agnostino, R., Belanger, A. (1991) Predicting reading problems in at-risk children. *Journal of Speech and Hearing Research* **34**: 893–903.

Michael, B. (1984) Foundations of writing. *Child Education,* January, p. 10–11.

Michael, B. (1985) Foundations of writing. *Child Education,* May, p. 8–11.

Mitchell, J. (1994) *Enhancing the Teaching of Memory* (2nd Edn - Revised) Surrey:. Communication and Learning Skills Centre.

Morton, J., Frith, U. (1995) Causal modelling: A structural approach to developmental psychopathology. In Cicchetti, D., Cohen, D. J. (Eds) *Manual of Developmental Psychopathology*. New York: Wiley.

Muter, V. (1994) Influence of phonological awareness and letter knowledge on beginning reading and spelling development. In Hulme, C., Snowling, M. (Eds) *Reading Development and Dyslexia*, 45–62. London: Whurr.

Muter, V., Snowling, M., Taylor, S. (1994) Orthographic analogies and phonological awareness: Their role and significance in early reading development. *Journal of Child Psychology and Psychiatry* **35**: 293–310.

Nippold, M.A. (1990) Concomitant speech and language disorders in stuttering children: A critique of the literature. *Journal of Speech and Hearing Disorders* **55**: 51–60.

Nittrouer, S., Studdert-Kennedy, M. (1987) The role of co-articulatory effects in the perception of fricatives by children and adults. *Journal of Speech and Hearing Research* **30**, 319–29.

Noordman, L.G.M., Vonk,W. (1992) Readers' knowledge and the control of inferences in reading. In Oakhill, J., Garnham, A. (Eds) *Discourse Representation and Text Processing.* Hove: Lawrence Earlbaum Associates.

Oakhill, J. (1982) Constructive processes in skilled and less-skilled comprehenders' memory for sentences. *British Journal of Psychology* **73**: 13–20.

Oakhill, J. (1984) Inferential and memory skills in children's comprehension of stories. *British Journal of Educational Psychology* **54**: 31–39.

Oakhill, J. and Garman, A. (1988) *Becoming a Skilled Reader.* Oxford. Blackwell.

Oakhill, J., Yuill, N., Parkin, A. (1986) On the nature of the difference between skilled and less-skilled comprehenders. *Journal of Research in Reading* **9**: 80–91.

Olson, R.K. and Wise, B.W. (1992) Reading on the computer with orthographic and speech feedback. *Reading and Writing* **4**: 107–144.

Olson, R.K., Wise, B., Conners, F., Rack, J., Fulker, D. (1989) Specific deficits in reading and component language skills: Genetic and environmental influences. *Journal of Learning Disabilities* **22**: 339–48.

Orton, S.T. (1937) *Reading, Writing and Speech Problems in Children.* London: Chapman Hall.

Paris, S.G., Cross, D.R., Lipson, M.Y. (1984) Informed strategies for learning: An instructional programme to improve children's reading awareness and comprehension. *Journal of Educational Psychology* **76**: 1239–52.

Paris, S.G., Jacobs, J.E. (1984) The benefits of informed instruction for children's reading awareness and comprehension skills. *Child Development* **55**: 2083–93.

Paul, R., Lynn, T.F., Lohr-Flanders, M. (1993) History of middle ear involvement and speech/language development in late talkers. *Journal of Speech and Hearing Research* **36**: 1055–62.

Pennington, B. F., Van Orden, G. C., Smith, S. D., Green, P. A., Haith, M. M. (1990). Phonological processing skills and deficits in adult dyslexics. *Child Development* **61**: 1753–78.

Perfetti, C.A. (1985) *Reading Ability.* Oxford: Oxford University Press.

Perfetti, C.A., Beck, I., Bell, L., Hughes, C. (1987) Phonemic knowledge and learning to read are reciprocal: A longitudinal study of first grade children. *Merrill-Palmer Quarterly* **33**: 283–319.

Perin, D. (1983) Phonemic segmentation and spelling. *British Journal of Psychology* **74**: 129–44.

Popple, J., Wellington, W. (1996) Collaborative working within a psycholinguistic framework. *Child Language Teaching and Therapy,* **12**, 1: 60–70.

Pringle-Morgan, W. (1896) A case of congenital word blindness. *British Medical Journal* **2**: 1378.

Rack, J.P., Hulme, C., Snowling, M., Wightman, J. (1994) The role of phonology in young children's learning of sight words: The direct mapping hypothesis. *Journal of Experimental Child Psychology* **57**: 42–71.

Rack, J., Snowling, M., Olson, R. (1992). The nonword reading deficit in developmental dyslexia: A review. *Reading Research Quarterly* **27**: 29–53.

Ramsden, M. (1992) *Putting Pen to Paper.* Crediton, Devon: Southgate.

Read, C. (1986) *Children's Creative Spelling.* London: Routledge and Kegan Paul.

Reed, M. (1989) Speech perception and the discrimination of brief auditory cues in reading disabled children. *Journal of Experimental Child Psychology* **48**: 270–92.

Robinson, P., Beresford, R., Dodd, B. (1982) Spelling errors made by phonologically disordered children. *Spelling Progress Bulletin* **22**: 19–20.

Rustin, L., Klein, H. (1991) Language Difficulties in Adolescent Stutterers. *Human Communication* **1**: 15–16.

Rustin, L., Purser, H. (1984) Intensive treatment models for the adolescent stutterer: social skills versus speech techniques. *Proceedings of the XIX Congress of the IALP*, Brussels.

Rutter, M., Tizard, J., Whitmore, K. (Eds) (1970) *Education, Health and Behaviour*. London: Longman & Green.

Rutter, M., Yule, W. (1975) The concept of specific reading retardation. *Journal of Child Psychology and Psychiatry* **16**: 181–97.

Ryder, R. (1991) Word and non-word repetition in normally developing children. Unpublished MSc dissertation, National Hospital's College of Speech Sciences/Institute of Neurology, University of London.

Scarborough, H. (1990) Very early language deficits in dyslexic children. *Child Development* **61**: 1728–43.

Scarborough. H. (1991a) Antecedents to reading disability: Preschool language development and literacy experiences of children from dyslexic families. *Reading and Writing: An Interdisciplinary Journal* **3**:219–33.

Scarborough, H. (1991b) Early syntactic development of dyslexic children. *Annals of Dyslexia* **41**: 207–20.

Schneck, C.M., Henderson, A. (1990) Descriptive analysis of the developmental progression of grip position for pencil and crayon control in nondysfunctional children. *American Journal of Occupational Therapy* **44**: 893–900.

Seidenberg, M.S., McClelland, J.L. (1989) A distributed, developmental model of word recognition and naming. *Psychological Review* **96**: 523–68.

Seymour, P.H.K. (1986) *Cognitive Analysis of Dyslexia*. London: Routledge and Kegan Paul.

Seymour, P.H.K., Elder, L. (1986) Beginning reading without phonology. *Cognitive Neuropsychology* **3**: 1–36.

Shankweiler, D., Crain, S. (1986) Language mechanisms and reading disorder: a modular approach. *Cognition* **24**: 139–64.

Share, D.L., Jorm, A.F., MacLean, R., Matthews, R. (1984) Sources of individual difference in reading acquisition. *Journal of Educational Psychology* **76**: 1309–24.

Sheridan, M.D. (1975) *From Birth to Five Years: Children's Developmental Progress*. Windsor: NFER-Nelson.

Siegel, L., Linder, B. (1984) Short-term memory processes in children with reading and arithmetic disabilities. *Developmental Psychology* **20**: 200–7.

Smith, F. (1971) *Understanding Reading: A Psycholinguistic Analysis of Reading and Learning to Read*. New York: Holt Rinehart and Winston.

Snowling, M.J. (1980) The development of grapheme-phoneme correspondences in normal and dyslexic readers. *Journal of Child Psychology and Psychiatry* **32**: 49–77.

Snowling, M.J. (1981) Phonemic deficits in developmental dyslexia. *Psychological Research* **43**: 219–34.

Snowling, M.J. (1985) Assessing reading and spelling strategies. In Snowling, M.J. (Ed.) *Children's Written Language Difficulties*. Windsor, Berks: NFER Nelson.

Snowling, M.J. (1987) *Dyslexia. A Cognitive Developmental Perspective*. Oxford: Basil Blackwell.

Snowling, M.J. (1996) Contemporary approaches to the teaching of reading. *Journal of Child Psychology and Psychiatry* **37**: 139–48.

Snowling, M.J., Frith, U. (1986) Comprehension in 'hyperlexic' readers. *Journal of Experimental Child Psychology* **42**: 392–415.

Snowling, M.J., Goulandris, N. (in press) Development and variation in developmental dyslexia. In Hulme, C., Joshi, M. (Ed) *Cognitive and Linguistic Bases of Reading, Writing and Spelling*. Hillsdale, NJ: Lawrence Erlbaum.

Snowling, M., Hulme, C. (1994). The development of phonological skills. *Transactions of the Royal Society B* **346**: 21–8.

Snowling, M., Stackhouse, J. (1983) Spelling performance of children with developmental verbal dyspraxia. *Developmental Medicine and Child Neurology* **25**: 430–7.

Snowling, M., Goulandris, N., Defty, N. (submitted) A longitudinal study of reading development in dyslexic children.

Snowling, M., Goulandris, N., Stackhouse, J. (1994) Phonological constraints on learning to read: Evidence from single case studies of reading difficulty. In Hulme, C., Snowling, M. (Eds) *Reading Development and Dyslexia*. London: Whurr.

Snowling, M.J., Stackhouse, J., Rack, J.P. (1986) Phonological dyslexia and dysgraphia: a developmental analysis. *Cognitive Neuropsychology* **3**: 309–39.

Snowling, M., van Wagtendonk, B., Stafford, C. (1988) Object-naming deficits in developmental dyslexia. *Journal of Research in Reading* **11**, 67–85.

Snowling, M.J., Goulandris, N., Bowlby, M., Howell, P. (1986) Segmentation and speech perception in relation to reading skill: A developmental analysis. *Journal of Experimental Child Psychology* **41**: 489–507.

Stackhouse, J. (1982) An investigation of reading and spelling performance in speech disordered children, *British Journal of Disorders of Communication* **17,2**: 53–60.

Stackhouse, J. (1989) Relationship between spoken and written language disorders: Implications in an educational setting. In Mogford, K., Sadler, J. (Eds) *Child Language Disability*. Clevedon: Multilingual Matters Ltd.

Stackhouse, J. (1990) Phonological deficits in developmental reading and spelling disorders. In Grunwell, P. (Ed) *Developmental Speech Disorders*. Edinburgh: Churchill Livingstone.

Stackhouse J. (1992a) Developmental verbal dyspraxia: a longitudinal case study. In Campbell, R. (Ed), *Mental Lives: Case Studies in Cognition*. Oxford: Blackwell.

Stackhouse, J. (1992b) Promoting reading and spelling skills through speech therapy. In Fletcher, P., Hall, D. (Eds) *Specific Speech and Language Disorders in Children*. London: Whurr.

Stackhouse, J. and Snowling, M. (1992a) Barriers to literacy development in two children with developmental dyspraxia. *Cognitive Neuropsychology* **9**: 273–99.

Stackhouse, J. and Snowling, M. (1992b) Developmental verbal dyspraxia II: A developmental perspective on two case studies. *European Journal of Disorders of Communication* **27**: 35–54.

Stackhouse, J. and Wells, B. (1991). Dyslexia: The obvious and hidden speech difficulty. in Snowling, M., Thomson, M. (Eds) *Dyslexia: Integrating Theory and Practice*. London: Whurr.

Stackhouse, J. and Wells, B. (1993) Psycholinguistic assessment of developmental speech disorders. *European Journal of Disorders of Communication* **28**: 331–48.

Stackhouse, J. and Wells, B. (forthcoming) *Psycholinguistic Assessment of Children With Speech and Literacy Difficulties*. London: Whurr.

Stahl, S. (1983) Differential word knowledge and reading comprehension. *Journal of Reading Behaviour* **15**: 33–50.

Stainthorp, R., Hughes, D. (1995) The cognitive characteristics of young early readers. In Raban-Bisby, B., Brookes, G., Wolfendale, S. (Eds) *Developing Language and Literacy*. Stoke-on-Trent: Trentham Books. 99–113.

Stanovich, K.E. (1980) Toward an interactive-compensatory model of individual differences in the development of reading fluency. *Reading Research Quarterly* **16**: 32–71.

Stanovich, K. E. (1986) Cognitive processes and the reading problems of learning disabled children: Evaluating the assumption of specificity. In Torgesen, J. K., Wong, B. Y. L. (Eds) *Psychological and Educational Perspectives on Learning Disabilities*. Orlando, FL: Academic Press.

Stanovich, K.E. (1994) Does dyslexia exist? *Journal of Child Psychology and Psychiatry* **35**: 579–96.

Stanovich, K.E., Cunningham, A.E., Cramer, B.B. (1984) Assessing phonological awareness in kindergarten children: Issues of task comparability. *Journal of Experimental Child Psychology* **38**: 175–181.

Stanovich, K. E., Siegel, L. S. (1994) The phenotypic performance profile of reading-disabled children: A regression-based test of the phonological-core variable-difference model. *Journal of Educational Psychology* **86**: 1–30.

Stein, J. (1991) Vision and language. In Snowling, M., Thomson, M. (Eds) *Dyslexia: Integrating Theory and Practice*. London: Whurr: 31–43

Stothard, S.E. (1992) *Reading Difficulties in Children: Problems of Decoding and Comprehension*. Unpublished PhD. thesis. University of York.

Stothard, S.E. (1994) The nature and treatment of reading comprehension difficulties in children: A review. In Hulme, C., Snowling, M. (Eds) *Reading Development and Dyslexia*. London: Whurr.

Stothard, S.E., Hulme, C. (1991) A note of caution concerning the Neale Analysis of Reading Ability (Revised). *British Journal of Educational Psychology* **61**: 226–9.

Stothard, S.E., Hulme, C. (1992) Reading comprehension difficulties in children: The role of language comprehension and working memory skills. *Reading and Writing* **4**: 245–56.

Stothard, S.E., Hulme, C. (1995) A comparison of phonological skills in children with reading comprehension difficulties and children with decoding difficulties. *Journal of Child Psychology and Psychiatry* **36**: 399–408.

Stuart, M., Coltheart, M. (1988) Does reading develop in a sequence of stages? *Cognition* **30**: 139–181.

Tallal, P. (1980) Auditory temporal perception, phonics and reading disability in children. *Brain and Language* **9**: 182–98.

Tallal, P., Piercy, M. (1973) Developmental aphasia: Impaired rate of non-verbal processing as a function of sensory modality. *Neuropsychologia* **11**: 389–98.

Tallal, P., Stark, R.E., Kallman, C., Mellits, D. (1980) Developmental dysphasia: Relationship between acoustic processing deficits and verbal processing. *Neuropsychologia* **18**: 273–84.

Temple, C., Marshall, J. (1983) A case study of a developmental phonological dyslexia. *British Journal of Psychology* **74**: 517–33.

Thomson, M. (1991) The teaching of spelling using techniques of simultaneous oral spelling and visual inspection. In: Snowling, M., Thomson, M. (Eds) *Dyslexia: Integrating Theory And Practice*. London: Whurr.

Toomey, D. (1993) Parents hearing their children read: A review. Rethinking the lessons of the Haringey Project. *Educational Research* **35**: 223–236.

Torgeson, J., Rashotte, C., Greenstein J., Houck, G., Portes, P. (1988). Academic difficulties of learning disabled children who perform poorly on memory span tasks. In Swanson, H. L. (Ed), *Memory and Learning Disabilities: Advances in Learning and Behavioral Disabilities*. Greenwich, CT: JAI Press.

Treiman, R. (1993) *Beginning to Spell. A Study of First Grade Children*. New York: Oxford University Press.

Treiman, R., Weatherston, S., Berch, D. (1994) The role of letter names in children's learning of phoneme-grapheme relations. *Applied Psycholinguistics* **15**: 97–122.

Tunmer, W. (1994) Phonological processing skills and reading remediation. In Hulme, C.,Snowling, M. (Eds) *Reading Development And Dyslexia*. London: Whurr.

Vance, M, (1994) Phonological processing, verbal comprehension and lexical representation. Proceedings of NAPLIC Conference: *Understanding Comprehension: Perspectives On Children's Difficulties With Interpretation Of Spoken Language*, Birmingham.

Vance, M., Stackhouse,J., Wells, B. (1994) 'Sock the wock the pit pat pock'–Children's responses to measures of rhyming ability, 3–7 years. *Work in Progress* **4**: 171–85. National Hospital's College of Speech Sciences.

Vance, M., Stackhouse,J., Wells, B. (1995) The relationship between naming and word repetition skills in children age 3–7 years. *Work in Progress* **5**: 127–33. Department of Human Communication Science, University College London.

Vellutino, F. (1979) *Dyslexia: Theory and Research*. Cambridge, MA: MIT Press.

Wade, B. and Moore, M (1993) Reading Recovery: Parent's views. *English in Education* Vol 27 Issue No2.

Wagner, R.K., Torgesen,J.K. (1987) The nature of phonological processing and its causal role in the acquisition of reading skills. *Psychological Bulletin* **101**: 192–212.

Wagner, R.K., Torgesen,J.K., Laughon, P., Simmons, K., Rashotte, C.A. (1993) The development of young readers' phonological processing abilities. *Journal of Educational Psychology* **85**: 1–20.

Wagner, R.K., Torgesen,J.K., Rashotte, C.A. (1994) Development of reading-related phonological processing abilities: Evidence of bi-directional causality from a latent variable longitudinal study. *Developmental Psychology* **30**: 73–87.

Webster, P.E. (1994) Linguistic factors in reading disability: A model for assessing children who are without overt language impairment. *Child Language Teaching and Therapy* **10**: 259–77.

Wells, B. (1994) Junction in developmental speech disorder: a case study. *Clinical Linguistics and Phonetics* **8,1**: 1–25.

Wells, B., Stackhouse,J., Vance, M. (1996) A specific deficit in onset-rhyme assembly in a 9-year-old child with speech and language difficulties. In Powell, T.W. (Ed) *Pathology of Speech and Language: Contributions of Clinical Phonetics and Linguistics*. New Orleans, LA: ICPLA.

Whitmarsh, E. (1988) First year secondary school children's attitudes to handwriting. *Handwriting Review*. (Available from Membership Secretary, Fyfield Road, Ongar, Essex CM5 0AH.)

Wiig, E.H. (1995) Assessment and management of adolescents' language disabilities. *Seminars in Speech and Language* **16**: 1–84.

Wiig, E.H., Semel, E.M. (1990) *Language Assessment and Intervention for the Learning Disabled*. Columbus. OH: Charles E. Merrill.

Williams, N., Chiat, S. (1993) Processing deficits in children with phonological disorder and delay: A comparison of responses to a series of output tasks. *Clinical Linguistics and Phonetics* **7**: 145–60.

Williams, S., McGee, R. (1994) Reading attainment and juvenile delinquency. *Journal of Child Psychology and Psychiatry* **35**: 441–60.

Willows, D. M., Kruk, R.S., Corcos, E. (1993) (Eds) *Visual Processes in Reading and Reading Disabilities*. Hillsdale, NJ: Lawrence Erlbaum Associates.

Williams, S. and McGee, R. (1994) Reading attainment and juvenile delinquency. *Journal of Child Psychology and Psychiatry* **35**: 441–60.

Wise, B.W., Olson, R.K. (in press) Computer-based phonological awareness and reading instruction. In Hulme, C., Joshi, M. (Ed) *Cognitive and Linguistic Bases of Reading, Writing and Spelling*. Hillsdale, NJ: Lawrence Erlbaum.

Wolk, B., Conture, E.G., Edwards, M.L. (1990) Comorbidity of stuttering and disordered phonology in young children. *South African Speech and Hearing Association* **37**: 15–20.

Wright, J. (1992) Collaboration between speech and language therapists and teachers. In Fletcher, P., Hall, D. (Eds) *Specific Speech and Language Disorders in Children: Correlates, Characteristics and Outcomes*. London: Whurr.

Wright, J. (1996) Teachers and therapists: The evolution of a partnership. *Child Language Teaching and Therapy* **12,1**: 3–16.

Yopp, H. K. (1988) The validity and reliability of phonemic awareness tests. *Reading Research Quarterly* **23**: 159–77.

Yuill, N., Joscelyne, T. (1988) Effect of organisational cues and strategies on good and poor comprehenders' story understanding. *Journal of Educational Psychology* **2**: 152–8.

Yuill, N., Oakhill, J. (1988) Effects of inference awareness training on poor reading comprehension. *Applied Cognitive Psychology* **2**: 33–45.

Yuill, N., Oakhill, J. (1991) *Children's Problems in Text Comprehension*. Cambridge: Cambridge University Press.

Yuill, N., Oakhill, J., Parkin, A. (1989) Working memory, comprehension ability and the resolution of text anomaly. *British Journal of Psychology* **80**: 351–61.

Zhurova, L.E. (1963) The development of analysis of words into their sounds by preschool children. *Soviet Psychology and Psychiatry* **2**: 17–27.

Resource List of Tests

Achenbach, T.M. (1991) *Child Behaviour Checklist*, Checklist and Allied Services. Burlington, VT: University of Vermont, Department of Psychiatry.

Anthony, A., Bogle, D., Ingram, T.T.S., McIsaac, M.W. (1971) *Edinburgh Articulation Test*. Edinburgh: Churchill Livingstone.

Beery, K.E. (1989) *The VMI-Developmental Test of Visual-Motor Integration*. Cleveland: OH Modern Curricululm Press.

Bishop, D. (1983) *Test for the Reception of Grammar*. Manchester: Department of Psychology, University of Manchester.

Carver, C. (1970) *Word Recognition Test*. London: Hodder & Stoughton.

Coltheart, M. (1980) *Analysing Acquired Disorders of Reading*. Unpublished Clinical Tests. Birkbeck College, London.

Dunn, L.M., Dunn, L.M., Whetton, C., Pintilie, D. (1982) *The British Picture Vocabulary Scale*. Windsor, Berks: NFER–Nelson

Elliott, C.D. (1992) *British Ability Scales Reading Test*, Windsor: NFER–Nelson.

Elliott, C.D., Murray, D.J., Pearson, L. S. (1983) *British Ability Scales*. Windsor: NFER–Nelson.

Gardner, M.F. (1982) *Test of Visual Perceptual Skills (non-motor)*. Burlinghame, CA: Psychological and Educational Publications Inc.

German, D. (1989) *Test of Word Finding*. DLM Teaching Resources. Taskmaster Ltd. Morris Road, Leicester. LE2 6BR.

German, D. (1990) *Test of Adolescent Word Finding*. DLM Teaching Resources. Taskmaster Ltd, Morris Road, Leicester. LE2 6BR.

German, D. (1991) *Test of Word Finding in Discourse*. DLM Teaching Resources, Taskmaster Ltd., Morris Road, Leicester. LE2 6BR.

Goldman, R., Fristoe, M. and Woodcock, R. (1976) *Goldman-Fristoe-Woodcock Auditory Skills Test Battery* Revised Edition. NFER-Nelson.

Goodenough, F.L., Harris, D.B. (1963) *Goodenough-Harris Drawing Test* Sidcup, Kent: The Psychological Corporation. (Also available in the *Aston Index*.)

Hagley, F (1987) *Suffolk Reading Scale*. Windsor, Berks: NFER–Nelson.

Hammill, D.D., Brown,V.L., Larsen,S.C., Wiederholt, J. (1987) *Test of Adolescent Language* - 2. Austin, TX: PRO-ED.

Hannavy, S. (1994) *Middle Infant Screening Test*. NFER-Nelson

Henderson, S.E., Sugden, D.A. (1992) *The Movement Battery for Children*. Sidcup, Kent: The Psychological Corporation.

Jastak, S., Wilkinson, G.S. (1984) *The Wide Range Achievement Test Revised–WRAT-R* Wilmington, DE: Jastak Associates Inc.

Jastak, S. and Wilkinson, G.S. (1993) *The Wide Range Achievement Test 3*. Wilmington, D.E: Jastak Associates Inc.

Kirk, S.A., McCarthy, J.J., Kirk, W. (1968) *Illinois Test of Psycholinguistic Abilities -Revised*. Chicago, IL: University of Illinois.

Klein, H., Constable, A., Goulandris, N., Stackhouse, J., Tarplee C. (1994) *Clinical Evaluation of Language Fundamentals (CELF-R: UK). UK Examiners Manual Supplement*. London: The Psychological Corporation.

McKenna, E., Warrington, E. (1983) *The Graded Naming Test*. Windsor: NFER–Nelson.

Macmillan Test Unit (1985) *Macmillan Graded Word Reading Test*. Basingstoke, Hants: Macmillan Education Ltd.

Morgan-Barry, R. (1988) *The Auditory Discrimination and Attention Test*. Windsor: NFER–Nelson.

Naglieri, J.A. (1987) *Draw-a-Person* Sidcup, Kent: The Psychological Corporation.

Neale, M. (1989) *Neale Analysis of Reading Ability Revised British Edition* Windsor, Berks: NFER–Nelson.

Newton, M., Thomson, M. (1982) *Aston Index*. Wisbech, Cambs: LDA.

Raven, J. C. (1984) *The Coloured Progressive Matrices*. London: H K Lewis and Co Ltd.

Rust, J., Golombok, S., Trickey, G. (1993) *Wechsler Objective Reading Dimensions (WORD)*, London: Psychological Corporation Limited.

Schonell, F.J. (1971) *Graded Word Reading Test* Edinburgh:Oliver and Boyd.

Schonell, F.J., Schonell, F. E. (1956) *Diagnostic and Attainment Testing: Including a Manual of Tests, their Nature, Use, Recording and Interpretation*. London: Oliver and Boyd.

Scottish Council for Research in Education (1974) *Burt (Rearranged) Word Reading Test*. London: Hodder & Stoughton.

Semel, E., Wiig, E.H., Secord, W. (1987) *Clinical Evaluation of Language Fundamentals-Revised*. London. The Psychological Corporation.

Snowling, M., Stothard, S.E., McLean, J. (in press) *The Graded Nonword Reading Test*. Bury St Edmunds: Thames Valley Test Publishers.

Stott, D.H., Moyes, F.A., Henderson, S.E. (1972) *The Test of Motor Impairment*. San Antonio, TX.: The Psychological Corporation.

Thorum, A.R. (1986) *The Fullerton Language Test for Adolescents*. Palo Alto, CA: Consulting Psychologists Press, Inc.

Vernon, P.E. (1977) *Graded Word Spelling Test*. London: Hodder and Stoughton.

Vincent, D. and Clayton, J. (1982) *Diagnostic Spelling Tests*. Windsor, Berks: NFER–Nelson.

Vincent, D., De la Mare, M. (1989) *New Macmillan Reading Analysis* Basingstoke, Hants: Macmillan Education Ltd.

Vincent, D. and De La Mare, M. (1990) *Individual Reading Analysis*. Windsor, Berks: NFER–Nelson.

Wechsler, D. (1967) *Wechsler Preschool and Primary Scale of Intelligence*. Psychological Corporation, New York: Harcourt Brace Jovanovich.

Wechsler, D. (1974) *Wechsler Intelligence Scale for Children-Revised*. New York: Psychological Corporation.

Wechsler, D. (1992) *Wechsler Intelligence Scale for Children. Third UK Edition*. London. The Psychological Corporation.

Wechsler, D. (1993) *Wechsler Objective Reading Dimensions*. New York: Psychological Corporation.

Wepman, J.M., Reynolds, W.M. (1987) *Wepman's Auditory Discrimination Test*. (2nd Ed) Western Psychological Services USA.

Wiig, E.H., Secord, W. (1992) *Test of Word Knowledge*. London: The Psychological Corporation.

Young, D. (1978) *SPAR Spelling and Reading Tests*. London: Hodder and Stoughton.

Young, D. (1983) *The Parallel Spelling Tests A and B*. London: Hodder and Stoughton.

Materials

Alston, J. and Taylor, J. (1990) *Handwriting Helpline*. Manchester: Dextral Books.

Bellamy H. and Dart S. (1995) *Rime time*. Crossbow, Bridgwater Somerset TA67 RN.

Brand, V., (1984) *Spelling Made Easy*. Baldock, Herts: Egon Publishers Ltd.

Deterding, G. and Scheib, B. (1992) *Steps to Literacy*. Hitchin, Herts: Hames Nisbet.

Fernald, G.M. (1943) *Remedial Techniques in Basic School Subjects*. New York: Mcgraw-Hill.

Folens Publishers. Apex Business Centre Dunstable LU54 RL.

Hardwick, A.J. (1994) *Making the Alphabet Work*. Somerset TA21 ORX.

Hatcher, P.J., (1994) Sound Linkage; An *Intergrated Programme for Overcoming Reading Difficulties*. London: Whurr.

Hornsby, B., F. (1976) *Alpha to Omega*. London: Heinemann Educational Books.

Kinloch, R. (1994) *Easy Type*. Baldock, Herts: Egon Publishers.

Miles, E. (19890 The Bangor Dyslexia Teaching System. London: Whurr.

Lindamood, C. and Lindamood, P. (1975) *Auditory Discrimination in Depth*. Columbus: OH: Macmillan/McGraw Hill.

Myers, P.W. (1993) *Movement into Writing*. Bolton, Lancs: Jarvis Print.

New Zealand Department of Education. (1987) *Classified Guide of Complementary Reading Materials–Books for Junior Classes: A Classified Guide for Teachers*. Wellington: Department of Education.

Nuffield Dyspraxia Programme (1992) Nuffield Hearing and Speech Centre, Royal National Throat, Nose and Ear Hospital, Gray's Inn Road, London, WC1 8DA

Passy, J. (1990a) *Cued Articulation*. Ponteland, Northumberland: Stass Publications.

Passy, J. (1990b) *Cued Vowels*. Ponteland, Northumberland: Stass Publications.

Pickard, P. (1986) *Handwriting–A Second Chance*. Wisbech, Cambs: LDA.

Sassoon, R. (1983) *The Practical Guide to Children's Handwriting*. London: Thames and Hudson.

Sassoon, R. (1994) *Helping with Handwriting–Key Stage 2 and 3*. London: John Murray.

Showell, R. (1975) Living Things. Loughborough. Ladybird Books Ltd.

Snowling, M., Stothard, S.E., McLean, J. (inpress) *The Graded Nonword Reading Test*. Thames Valley Test Publishing Co.

Tasker, D. (1995) *Helping with Handwriting – Key Stage 1 and 2*. London: John Murray.

Taylor, J. (1979) *Writing is for Reading Book 1*. Available from Willowbank, Watery Lane, Weymouth, Dorset DT3 DP5

Taylor, J. (1981) *Writing is for Reading Book 2*. Available from Willowbank, Watery Lane, Weymouth, Dorset DT3 DP5

Tiburtius, S. (1994) *Write on Target*. Manchester: Dextral Books.

Wendon, L. (1993) The Letterland Handwriting Programme. Barton, Cambs: Letterland, Ltd.

Wilmington, DE: Jastak Associates, Inc.

Wilson, J. (1993) *Phonological Awareness Training Programme*. London Educational Psychology Publishing.

Index

ABX tasks 50–1, 53
accents 26–7
Achenbach, TM 42
Adams, MJ 33, 151
adolescents 71–6
Alegria, J et al 34
alliteration 132, 134–5, 137, 138, 148
    spelling 175, 190
alphabetic phase 8, 22, 78–9, 80–1, 103
    spelling 171, 172–4, 175, 180–5, 190
Alston, J 206, 207
analogy
    reading 37, 38, 44, 91, 92, 94
    spelling 38, 44, 176
Anthony, A et al 57
Aston Index 48, 195
at-risk children 4, 6, 12–30, 33, 35, 42
    identification 12, 31, 40, 43, 234–5,
        240–2
    phonological awareness 13–17, 30,
        129–31, 133, 140, 235, 237
attention 11, 33, 42, 51, 63
Attention Deficit Hyperactivity Disorder
    (ADHD) 195, 197
auditory discrimination 45, 47–53, 60,
    238
    at–risk children 21, 25, 26, 28
Auditory Discrimination and Attention
    Test (ADAT) 51
Auditory Discrimination in Depth 239
Auditory Synthesis 71
Augur, J and Briggs, S 180

Baddeley, AD and Gathercole, SE 139
Ball, EW and Blachman, BA 147
Beck, IL et al 127
Beery, KE 194

behaviour 5, 32, 42, 43, 152–3
    language difficulties 63, 64, 69–70, 72
Bird, J et al 16
Bishop, DVM 10, 16, 115
    and Adams, C 9, 13, 17, 35
    and Edmundson, A 64
    et al 63, 64
Blachman, B 129–30, 141
blends and blending 12, 22, 71, 148,
    150–1
    assessing reading skills 85, 87, 89, 91,
        93
    help of parents 222–3, 226
    predicting reading 33, 36, 37, 39
    Sound Linkage 154–6, 164, 168
    spelling 176, 181
Boberg, E 72
Bond, GL and Dykstra, R 33
Borkowski, JG 186
Boston Naming Test 6
Bradley, L 129, 147, 148, 183
    and Bryant, P 6, 33, 34, 132–3, 147,
        175
Bradley Test 105
Brady, S et al 7
Brand, V 178, 180
Brandt, J and Rosen, J 6
Bridgeman, E and Snowling, M 50
British Ability Scales 21, 164
    Basic Number Skills 42, 148, 150
    Reading Test 38, 42, 43, 125
    Spelling Test 41
    Word Reading Test 103, 148
British Picture Vocabulary Scales 24,
    65–6, 71, 73
Brooks, P 183, 184
Brown, AL 114

Brown, B 195, 196
Bruce, DJ 33, 149
Bruck, M 3, 83
Bryan, A and Howard, D 59
Bryant, P
      and Bradley, L 139, 157, 172, 184
      and Impey, L 8
      et al 147
Byrne, B and Fielding-Barnsley, R 147

Carver, C 148
Castles, A and Coltheart, M 8
Cataldo, S and Ellis, N 147
Catts, HW 14, 143
      et al 29
cerebral palsy 14, 16, 195
Chall, JS 33
Clay, MM 149, 151, 152, 157, 159, 219,
      231
Clay Reading Recovery Programme 231
cleft lip and palate 14, 15
Child Behaviour Checklist 42
Clinical Evaluation of Language Funda-
      mentals - Revised (CELF-R(UK))
      24, 74–5
clumsiness 18, 192
clusters 21, 27, 36, 105
      spelling 25, 99, 105, 181
Coltheart, M 15,
      et al 8
compensation strategies 3, 4, 30, 32, 236
      dysgraphia 83
      speech 47
      spelling 175
Constable, A et al 28
contextual cues 8, 78, 84, 105, 153
      meaning 18, 20, 29, 94–5
continuous speech 21, 28–9
Cootes, C and Simpson, S 8, 99, 100,
      171–91
Cox, AR and Hutcheson, L 187
critical age hypothesis 17
Cued Articulation 240
Cunningham, AE 147
cursive script 201–4, 211

Darley, FL 76
decoding 83, 89–95
      reading comprehension 108–9, 114,
      116, 124–6
Deeny, K 129–45
DeFries, J 3

Denkla, MB and Rudel, RG 6
diagnosis 4, 33, 43–4, 192
Diagnostic Auditory Discrimination Tests
      51
digit span test 39, 121
digraphs 27, 181–2
dimensional classification of reading 236–7
discrepancy definition of dyslexia 2–3
Dodd, B et al 12, 26
doubling rule 188–9
drawings of a person 197–8
Dunn, LM et al 65
Dunlop Test 10
Dutton, K 207
dysarthric speech 16
Dyscoordination Syndrome (DCS) 192–3
dysgraphia 8, 83
dyslexia 1–11, 12–30, 81–3, 236–7
      alphabetic phase problems 172
      defined 2–3
      family history 63, 64, 172
      handwriting 194–5
      heritability 3–5
      intervention 238–40
      language problems 46, 63, 64
      memory 39–40
      prediction 31, 34–5, 39–40
      preschool 131, 132, 139
      speech processing 46, 55, 57
      spelling 172, 176, 184, 190–1
dyspraxia 14–15, 19, 23, 240
      articulatory 14
      verbal 14–16, 21, 23, 24, 57, 237

Early Word Reading Test 164
Edinburgh Articulation Test 57
Effective Reading Test 126
Ehri, L 5, 79
Elkonin, DB 146
Elliott, CD 103, 126, 164
      et al 148
ergonomics and handwriting 195–7, 205,
      210
expressive language 24, 64, 67, 74–5, 127,
      235
      handwriting 206–8

family history 1, 3–5, 12–13, 17, 33, 235
      dyslexia 63, 64, 172
Fernald, GM 183, 184
Fernald Tracing 183, 184
figurative usage 68

flossy rule 181
formulated sentences 75
Forward Together Recovery Programme
    215–33
free writing
    case study 104–5
    handwriting 204, 205, 206–8
    help of parents 223
    Sound Linkage 157–8, 164, 165–7
    speed 101
    spelling 95, 100–1, 172–3, 174, 179,
    206
Frith, U 5, 8, 22, 78, 80, 83, 138–9, 150,
    171
    and Frith, C 185
Fullerton Language Test for Adolescents
    71, 73

Galaburda, AM 63
Gallagher, A et al 4
garden-variety poor readers 236, 237
Gardner, MF 193
Gathercole, SE 139
    and Baddeley, AD 58
gender 3, 13, 126
German, D 66, 67, 69, 74
Gillingham, AM and Stillman, BU 183
Gillon, G and Dodd, BJ 64, 241
Godfrey, J et al 6
Goldman, Fristoe-Woodcock Auditory
    Skills Test Battery 51
Goodman, KS 84
Gopnick, KM and Crago, MB 63
Goswami, U 5, 129, 176
    and Bryant, PE 36, 37, 38, 129,
    146–7, 175
Gough, PB and Juel, C 150
Goulandris, N K 7, 77–107, 177
Graded Naming Test 74
Graded Nonword Reading Test 42, 90–2
grammar 9, 18, 29, 206
graphemes 142, 171
Gregory, HM and Gregory, AH 125
Grievink, EH et al 64
Group Reading Test 126

Hagley, F 124
Hammill, DD et al 73
handedness (laterality) 18
handwriting 11, 19, 82, 192–214

help of parents 222, 226, 228
    resource list 214
    speed 205–6, 207, 212
Hannavy, S 195, 215–33
Hatcher, P J 11, 133, 146–70, 175
    et al 39, 146, 147, 175, 238
Hayden, S 144
hearing problems 14, 63–4
Henderson, SE and Sugden, DA 193
heritability 1, 3–5, 13
    see also family history
Hinshelwood, J 1
homophones 8, 16, 103, 190
Hornsby, B and Shear, F 180
Howell, J and Dean, E 240
Hulme, C
    and Roodenrys, S 39, 40
    and Snowling, M 2, 5
    et al 79
Hummell, LJ and Prizant, BM 70
hyperlexics 237

identification
    at-risk children 12, 31, 40, 43, 234–5,
    240–2
    preschool phonological problems
    130–2, 143–4
    reading difficulties 31–2, 35, 36, 40,
    43, 44
idioms 62, 71
inferences 62, 70, 71
    reading comprehension 111–13, 116,
    118, 121, 123, 127–8
Ingram, D 22
intelligence 19, 21, 64
    performance 24, 64
    phonological awareness 139, 148
    reading 33, 38, 42, 43, 147, 148
    reading comprehension 115–17, 120
    Sound Linkage 163, 164
    spelling 172
    verbal 24, 64, 115–16, 117, 120
    vocabulary 65
intervention 12, 31, 34, 234, 236, 237–9
    delivered by whom 239–42
    sound links in reading 146–70
intrusive sounds 19, 23
irregular words
    reading 8, 23, 90, 91, 92, 177
    spelling 23, 99, 103, 105, 173, 180,
    183–5

Iversen, S and Tunmer, WE 151

Johnston, R et al 6
Juel, C et al 147

Kameenui, EJ et al 127
Kamhi, AG and Catts, HW 130
Katz, R 6
Kinloch, R 212
Kirk, SA et al 37
Klein, H 26, 62–76, 117
     et al 75

labelling diagrams 211–12, 213
language difficulties 3, 6, 9–14, 17–20,
     24, 234–7, 241–2
     assessment of school-age children
       62–76
     at-risk children 12–14, 17–18, 29–30
     comprehension 115–16, 117, 120
     handwriting 195
     reading 33, 35, 62, 64, 71, 75
     speech 46, 66, 74, 235–7
     tests 65–70
Layton, L and Deeny, K 129–45
letter formation 199–204, 205, 208–11,
     222, 227
letter knowledge 4, 40, 41, 43, 44, 83
letter-names 18, 153
     handwriting 199, 205
     reading 33, 38–9, 41–3, 89, 104
     Sound Linkage 167, 169
letter-sounds
     at-risk children 15, 17, 19, 22
     handwriting 199
     help of parents 216, 223–6
     phonological deficit 11
     preschool phonological awareness
       131, 133
     reading 7, 34–5, 78–81, 85–91, 93–4,
       104–5, 149, 153
     Sound Linkage 154, 159, 168–9
     speech difficulties 15, 22
     spelling 78–81, 99, 104, 105, 172–6,
       180, 184
letter strings
     reading 79, 85, 90
     spelling 79, 172, 183
Lewis, BA et al 13
     and Freebairn, L 26
Lewis, C and Salway, A 196

lexical processing 17, 21–2, 84
     representations 24–6, 30, 48
Liberman, IY et al 33, 34
Lindamood, C and Lindamood, P 239,
     240
Linguistic Concepts 75
listening comprehension 9, 115–16, 117,
     120, 121, 123
Locke, J 52, 53, 57
logographic stage 22, 23, 78, 81, 150,
     171, 185
London Reading Test 126
Lovegrove, WJ and Williams, M 10
Lundberg, I et al 129, 133, 136, 147, 154

McCormick, M 23
McDougall, S et al 40, 42
McKenna, E and Warrington, E 74
McKeown, MG et al 127
MacLean, M et al 33, 134, 137–8
Magnusson, E and Naucler, K 9, 13, 14
Manis, FR et al 6, 8
Marion, MJ et al 53
Masterson, J et al 47
Maughan, B 31
memory 3, 5–6, 9, 137, 139, 193–4
     at-risk children 12
     reading 33, 36, 39–40, 44, 169
     reading comprehension 109–11,
       112–13, 121, 125
     speech 48, 58
     spelling 184, 186, 223, 226
Menyuk, P et al 17
metacognition 113–15, 116, 127–8
     spelling 186–7, 191
metalinguistics 130, 133
Metaphon 240
Michael, B 197, 201
Middle Infant Screening Test 195,
     216–17
Miles, E 180
minimal pairs 48–52
Mitchell, J 76
mnemonics for spelling 184–5
Moore and Wade 231
Morton, J and Frith, U 5
motivation
     reading 32, 35, 215, 221, 228
     spelling 178
morphemes 95
motor skills 10–11, 13–14, 33

handwriting 192–3, 194, 210
speech production 14, 58, 60
Movement Assessment Battery for Children (ABC) 193
multiple contexts 68
Muter, V 11, 31–44, 89, 132
et al 38

Naglieri, JA 197
naming 3–6, 14, 17, 24
language difficulties 66–7, 68–9
reading 35, 39
speech processing 21, 28, 57–8, 59
Neale, M
Analysis of Reading Ability 38, 41, 125, 148, 150
Revised 93, 95, 105, 116, 120, 125, 148
Newton, M and Thomson, M 48, 195
Nippold, MA 72
Nittrouer, S and Studdert-Kennedy, M 5
nonphonetic spelling errors 8, 96–7, 100–2, 104
nonwords 4, 7, 16, 21, 83
auditory discrimination 49–53, 60
predicting reading difficulties 35, 42–3
reading 8–9, 17, 83, 87, 90–3, 103–5, 148–51, 239
repetition 47, 58–60
rhyme 54–5
spelling 16–17, 103, 105
Noordman, LGM and Vonk, W 62
novel (new or unknown) words 5, 153
dyslexia 4, 82
reading 34, 93, 187, 220, 221
speech processing 59–60
spelling 79–80, 176
Nuffield Dyspraxia Programme 240
nursery rhymes 4, 33
phonological awareness 130, 134–5, 137, 138, 141

Oakhill, J 112, 113, 125
and Garman, A 62
et al 110
occupational therapists 63, 194, 210, 239
Olson, RK
and Wise, BW 238
et al 3, 13
onset-rime 129, 156, 157, 238

reading 36–7, 38, 44
spelling 180
onsets 17, 136, 155
reading 36, 81
rhyme production 55
spelling 25, 81, 176
opposites 67
orthographic stage 8, 30, 49, 78–80, 171, 185–6
reading 45, 60
spelling 95, 99–100, 103, 174–5, 185–90, 191
Orton, Samuel 1

parents 31, 43, 140, 234
helping children 215–33
intervention 239, 241
language difficulties 62, 63, 64, 69, 71, 73
Paris, SG
and Jacobs, JE 128
et al 128
parsing 87, 91
Passy, J 240
Paul, R et al 64
Pennington, BF et al 3

Perfetti, CA 108
et al 33
Perin, D 20, 83
Phoneme Manipulation Tasks 33
phonemes 71, 148–9, 150–1, 154–8, 164, 238–40
categorization 7
deletion 36, 37, 40–3, 148, 150–1, 154, 157
help of parents 223–6
predicting reading 33, 34, 36–8, 41
preschool awareness 133, 142
reading 81, 104, 129–30, 132–6, 140, 142–3
segmentation 34, 36–8, 42–3, 148–51, 154–8, 167–9, 225
spelling 81, 97, 104, 171, 176
phonetic spelling errors 8, 23, 96–7, 99–101
phonological awareness 3–9, 146–70
at-risk children 13–17, 30, 129–31, 133, 140, 235, 237
dyslexia 3, 11
heritability 3–4

intervention 146, 159–60, 238–41
predicting reading 33–43
preschool children 129–45
reading 7–9, 81, 104, 129–30, 132–6,
    140, 142–3, 146–70
speech 14, 15, 17
spelling 81, 146–52, 172–7, 185, 187
Phonological Awareness Training
    Programme (PAT) 176
phonological core-variable difference 9
Phonological Deficit Hypothesis 5–7
phonological dyslexia 8–9, 236, 237
Phonological Linkage Hypothesis 39
phonological processing 2, 4–11, 60–1,
    236–8
    at-risk children 13, 14–22, 30
    dyslexia 81–3
    predicting reading 33–4, 36, 39–41
    reading 81, 87
    speech 14–17, 21–2, 23–4, 26–9
    spelling 15–16, 22, 23–4, 25, 81,
        95–9
phonological representations 5–7, 45,
    47–54, 57–8, 60
    predicting reading 39–40
physiotherapists 194, 210, 239
Popple, J and Wellington, W 143, 241
posture 193, 196, 205, 210
prefixes 189–90
preschool development 9, 32–4, 240
    at-risk children 13, 17, 18, 21, 26,
        240
    phonological awareness 129–45
    speech 21, 26, 131, 142–5
Pringle-Morgan, W 1
pronunciation 48, 52, 57–8, 83, 85, 91–2
    at-risk children 17, 28
    spelling 78, 104
psychologists 31–2, 44, 63, 239
    WORD test 126
punctuation 105, 164, 167, 192, 205–6,
    209, 211

Rack, JP et al 5, 8, 34
Ramsden, M 200
Raven, JC
    Progressive Coloured Matrices 139
Read, C 78
reading 2–3, 5–6, 7–11, 22, 83–95,
    159–66, 234–7
    assessing skills 77–107

at-risk children 12–30, 234
case study 103–5
Forward Together 220–1
help of parents 215–33
intervention 146–70, 237–42
language difficulties 33, 35, 62, 64,
    71, 75
novel words 34, 93, 187, 220, 221
phonological awareness 7–9, 81, 104,
    129–30, 132–6, 140, 142–3,
    146–70
practising sound links 146–70
predicting difficulties 31–44
Sound Linkage 154–70
speech 17, 22, 33, 35, 40, 43–5, 47,
    60, 105
spelling 171–2, 175, 176–7, 185, 186
tests 15, 83, 84, 103, 106, 124
text 83, 93–5, 149
see also reading comprehension; read-
    ing errors
Reading Ability Series 126
reading comprehension 9, 62, 108–28,
    151, 235–7
    assessment 83, 93–5, 123–7
    at-risk children 14, 29
    case studies 116–23
    intervention 239
    metacognition 113–15
    Neale Test 148, 150
reading errors 85–8, 91, 152–3, 167, 177
    partial phonological access 86, 87
    regularizations 23, 86, 87
    sound-based 85, 103
    unsuccessul sound attempts 85–6
    visual 87, 88, 103
    visually similar 85, 86
Reed, M 6
remediation 1, 2, 5, 46, 56, 109, 139,
    238–9
    handwriting 192, 210–12
    reading 78
    speech 21, 46, 56, 61
    spelling 78, 99, 103, 172, 174, 176–7,
        186
repetition tasks 47, 58–60, 105
rhymes and rhyming 8, 17, 20, 148
    preschool 129–30, 132, 133–8,
        139–42
    production 54–6, 59, 60
    reading 33, 36–8, 40, 44, 220

Sound Linkage 154, 156, 164, 167
speech 47, 53–6
spelling 175, 190
rhythm 136, 141, 220
rime 36–7, 81, 176
see also onset–rime
Robinson, P et al 16, 23
Rustin, L
and Klein, H 72
and Purser, H 72
Rutter, M
and Yule, W 9
et al 35
Ryder, R 58

Scarborough, H 4, 13, 17, 35, 40
Schneck, CM and Henderson, A 197
Schonell, FJ and Schonell, FE 148
Graded Word Spelling List 148, 150, 167
Spelling Test 38, 42, 43
screening for reading failure 31, 32, 34, 41, 44, 216–17
Seidenberg, MS and McClelland, JL 5, 79
segmentation 7, 216, 238
at-risk children 12, 15, 17–19, 22–3
phonemes 34, 36–8, 42–3, 148–51, 154–8, 167–9, 225
predicting reading 33–4, 36–9, 42–4
speech 15, 17, 21–3, 25, 27, 29, 48, 60
spelling 22–7, 99, 175–6, 187–8
syllables 18, 25, 33–4, 37, 99, 187–8
selective association 150
semantics 29, 236, 237
language difficulties 66, 67, 69
reading comprehension 127
speech processing 45, 49, 56, 60
Semel, E et al 24, 74
semi-phonetic spelling errors 96–7, 99–102
sentence assembly 75
sequencing 19–20, 65, 158
at-risk children 12, 15, 19–20
speech 15, 27–8, 50
spelling 176, 184
Seymour, PHK 8
and Elder, L 150
Shankweiler, D and Crain, S 6
Share, DL et al 33

short-term memory 50–1, 93, 139
dyslexia 39–40
reading comprehension 109–11, 121
verbal 3, 5–6, 110
Showell, R 70
Siegel, L and Linder, B 6
sight vocabulary 7, 157
silent reading test 15
Simpson, S 8, 99, 100, 171–91
Simultaneous Oral Spelling (SOS) 183–4
single-word reading 8, 35, 148
tests 83, 84, 103, 106
Smith, F 84
Snowling, MJ 1–11, 12, 26, 63, 81, 96, 98, 129, 239
and Frith, U 118
and Goulandris, N 8
and Hulme, C 5, 58
and Stackhouse, J 23
et al 6, 7, 10, 34, 42, 47, 82, 90, 92
Sound Blending Tasks 33, 37
sound categorization 33, 34, 148, 150, 151
Sound Discrimination Test 48
Sound Linkage Programme 146, 154–70
Spar Reading Test 123
speech 14–17, 21–3, 26–9, 45–61, 215
at-risk children 12–30, 235
errors 4, 66, 74
input 6–7, 14, 46, 47–54, 59
intervention 239–41
language difficulties 46, 66, 74, 235–7
output 6–7, 12–14, 46, 47, 54–6, 57–60
preschool 21, 26, 131, 142–5
processing problems 1–4, 6–7, 9–10, 11
rate 40, 43, 44
reading 17, 22, 33, 35, 40, 43–5, 47, 60, 105
spelling 15–17, 23–4, 27, 47–8, 57, 60, 105
speech and language therapists 5, 31, 44
at-risk children 12, 20, 26–9
intervention 239–40
language difficulties 64, 72–3, 74, 76
liaison with teachers 63, 70, 76, 143–5, 210, 241
preschool children 131–2, 143–5
reading 105, 146
rhyming 56

tests 68–9
spelling 2, 3, 31–44, 95–103, 234, 235, 238
  assessing skills 77–107
  at-risk children 12–30, 234
  case study 103–5
  development models 78–81
  Forward Together 222–5
  free writing 95, 100–1, 172–3, 174, 179, 206
  help of parents 215–33
  language difficulties 64
  lexical representations 24–6, 30
  nonwords 16–17, 103, 105
  phonological awareness 81, 146–52, 172–7, 185, 187
  preschool children 129–30, 132–3, 136, 140, 142, 143
  reading 171–2, 175–7, 185, 186
  Sound Linkage 167, 169
  speech 15–17, 23–4, 27, 47–8, 57, 60, 105
  suggested teaching order 180–5
  teaching 77–8, 87, 171–91
  tests 97, 98, 104, 107
  visual factors 10–11
spelling errors 95–102, 177
  alphabetic stage 172–4
  case study 104–5
  nonphonetic 8, 96–7, 100–2, 104
  orthographic stage 95, 99–100, 103, 174–5, 185
  phonetic 8, 23, 96–7, 99–101
  phonological 95–9
  semi-phonetic 96–7, 99–102
Spelling by Syllable Length Spelling Test 97, 98
spoonerisms 20, 83
Stackhouse, J 10, 12–30, 48, 57, 82, 93, 131, 143, 240
  and Snowling, M 3, 15, 21, 59
  and Wells, B 4, 25–6, 29, 46, 55, 60, 131, 240
Stainthorp, R and Hughes, D 237
stammering and stuttering 13, 72
Stanovich, KE 9
  and Siegel, LS 2, 9
  et al 36
Stein, J 10
Stothard, S E 14, 62, 83, 93, 108–28
  and Hulme, C 108, 109, 110, 111, 115, 126

Stuart, M and Coltheart, M 85
suffixes 181, 188–9
Suffolk Reading Scheme 124, 126
surface dyslexia 8–9, 236, 237
syllables 19, 71, 154, 164, 238
  preschool phonological awareness 133, 141
  reading 33, 36, 37, 81, 95, 103, 105
  segmentation 18, 25, 33–4, 37, 99, 187–8
  spelling 81, 97, 98, 105, 176, 187–9
syntax 4, 71
  at-risk children 12, 13–14, 17, 18–19
  reading 35, 40–1
  spelling 189–90

Tallal, P 47
  and Piercy, M 7
  et al 47
Taylor, J 11, 101, 192–214
teachers and teaching
  handwriting 192–3, 195, 197–209
  helping parents to help children 215–33
  identification of dyslexia 31–2
  implementing programme 209–12
  intervention 239–42
  language difficulties 62, 63, 68–72, 76
  observations 70, 227
  preschool phonological awareness 130–45
  reading 35, 43–4, 77–8, 87, 146–70
  reading comprehension 125, 127–8
  resource list 214
  Sound Linkage 154–70
  spelling 77–8, 87, 171–91
Temple, C and Marshall, J 8
Test of Adolescent Language 73–4
Test of Adolescent Word-Finding 74
Test of Motor Impairment 193
Test for the Reception of Grammar (TROG) 115, 117, 121
Test of Visual-Perception Skills 193–4
Test of Word-Finding 66, 67
Test of Word Knowledge 67, 73
Thomson, M 176, 184
Thorum, AR 71, 73
tool-hold 193, 196–7, 205
Toomey D 215
Torgeson, J et al 6
Treiman, R 23, 78
  et al 90

Tunmer, W 40, 176, 186

Vance, 24, 26, 45–61
    et al 47, 50, 53, 55, 59
Vellutino, F 2
verbal comprehension 14, 18, 20, 29
Vernon Spelling Test 104
visual reading 7–8, 22, 87, 88, 103, 149, 150
visual factors 1, 10–11, 29, 174, 193–4
VMI-Developmental Test of Visual-Motor Integration 194
vocabulary 4, 6, 22, 137
    at-risk children 17, 18, 22
    British Picture Vocabulary Scales 24, 65–6, 71, 73
    help of parents 223, 224, 225
    language difficulties 65–6, 71
    reading comprehension 116, 117, 120, 124–5, 127–8
    sight 7, 157
    spelling 183, 223, 224, 225
vocation 72–6

Wagner, RK and Torgesen, JK 36
    et al 39, 40, 43
Webster, PE 64
Wechsler D 64
    Intelligence Scale for Children-Revised (WISC-R) 24, 64, 115, 117, 120, 121, 172
    Objective Reading Dimensions (WORD) 125, 126
    Preschool and Primary Scale of Intelligence (PPSI) 38, 42, 43
Wells, B 29
    et al 54, 56

Wepman, J and Reynolds, W 48
Wepman Auditory Discrimination Test 48–9
Whitmarsh, E 209
Wiig, EH 71
    and Secord, W 67, 73
    and Semel, EM 70
Williams, N and Chiat, S 59
Williams, S and McGee, R 70, 72
Willows, DM et al 1
Wilson, J 176
Wise, BW and Olson, RK 238
Wolk, B et al 63, 72
Word Analysis Test 149
word attack 85, 94, 95
word families 178, 186
word-finding 12, 28, 29,
    language difficulties 66, 67, 69, 71, 74
word processing 195, 201, 212
word recognition 83, 84–9, 108–9, 239
    reading comprehension 93–5
    sound links 148, 149, 152
Word Recognition Test 148
Word test 126
Words in Words 183, 184–5
Wright, J 63, 70, 143, 241

Yopp, HK 36, 154
Young, D 123
Yuill, N
    and Joscelyne, T 128
    and Oakhill, J 108, 109, 110, 114, 128
    et al 111, 114

Zhurova, LE 146